DAWN IN INDIA

DAWN IN INDIA

BRITISH PURPOSE AND INDIAN ASPIRATION

BY

SIR FRANCIS YOUNGHUSBAND

K.C.S.I., K.C.I.E.

GYAN

Published by

Gyan Publishing House
5, Ansari Road
Daryaganj, New Delhi-110002
Phone: 011-47034999, 9811692060
E-mail: books@gyanbooks.com

Distribution Network
gyanbooks.com
India, USA, Canada, UK, Australia, France

ISBN : 978-81-212-3295-1 (PB)
First Published, 1931

2nd Impression 2020

Printed at: Gyan Press, Delhi.

Dawn in India
Author: Sir Francis Younghusband

TO

THE MEMORY OF

MY FATHER

THE WISEST FRIEND OF INDIA I HAVE MET

I DEDICATE THIS BOOK

PREFACE TO SECOND EDITION

EVENTS have moved fast since this book went to press in August. The Round Table Conference is now actually sitting. The Delegates came unwillingly and against the remonstrances of their own friends. They expected a chilly reception and stubborn criticism. Instead, they received the warmest welcome, and their views were heard with every consideration. And in characteristic Indian way they eagerly responded. Delegate after Delegate declared himself in favour of maintaining the British connection. But—and this is the chief significance of their utterances—they also earnestly urged their claim for Indian self-government. Indian nationhood is what one and all are striving for—the Princes as well as the spokesmen for British India. May this book help to an understanding of the historical and spiritual background of this passionate desire and show the enduring foundation upon which it rests.

F. E. Y.

December, 1930.

PREFACE TO THE FIRST EDITION

This book had its genesis in an informal "talk" on India at a dinner which the University Club at Montreal were kind enough to give me in February of this year. Here were seventy or eighty men in one part of the Empire anxious to hear the experiences of a man from another part. Particularly keen were they to hear about the present position in India. Sensational telegrams were appearing in the Press reporting that the Indian National Congress had declared for "complete independence." This body had an imposing name, and the reports sounded as if the whole of India in Congress assembled had issued a declaration of independence somewhat after the manner of the American. And the Canadians were disturbed. Naturally, they could not know much about India and Indian politics. They had problems in plenty of their own. And India is far from Canada. But in a general way they were proud of what we had done in India. And they did not like the thought of our "losing" India.

I did my best to allay their misgivings. I told them that this self-styled Indian National Congress did not represent either the seventy million people who were still ruled by their own rulers, or the seventy million Moslems, or, indeed, all the Hindus; though it did represent a very natural desire on the part of the Indians to govern themselves—a desire which we on our part were doing our best to meet.

But so keen were these Canadians, both at Montreal and at other towns where I spoke, and so anxious were Americans also, to know about

India that I thought that a book showing the nature, the history, and the probable future of our political connection with India, and showing also the deep spiritual connection, would be interesting not only to Canadians and Americans, but to Indians as well.

And as I addressed these audiences of our premier Dominion—self-governing yet devoted to the Empire—and as I studied more deeply the history of our connection with India, I became more and more convinced that the one thing necessary at this present moment was to assure the Indian people that, when they had eventually attained that responsible self-government which we have declared to be the goal of our policy, we would also leave them the responsibility of deciding for themselves whether they would remain within the Empire or part from it. In my own mind I have not the slightest doubt which course they would take. But after the way in which they stood by the Empire in the Great War I think it only honourable that we should give them the chance of saying for themselves what they would wish.

The further reasons for my holding this view I have given in the chapter entitled "The Crucial Question." And there I have tried to meet the objections that may be raised to our taking what to most will seem too risky a course, but which to me seems not only the most worthy, but the safest. We must trust India—India as a whole, I mean—or else regard our Army as a garrison, increase it, and rule by force. Havering between the two courses is worse than either.

If time had permitted I would have added to this

book an account of what is vastly more important than our political work in India—namely, the spiritual activities of the British and many other peoples. It was the rise of religious feeling in England and missionary enterprise in India that urged the Government a hundred years ago to take up the question of education and made them regardful of the welfare of the people. And the value of missionary effort—Roman Catholic as well as Protestant; and American, French, Belgian, and German as well as British—has never been enough recognised. My only reason for not adding chapters on it to this book is that I am anxious for it to appear while the political issues are prominently before the world.

In the old days the missionaries used to regard the Indians as heathen, and the English administrator would look upon the missionary as a bigoted busybody arousing unnecessary animosity. Nowadays, a vast change has taken place. The missionary still adheres to his fundamental conviction as to the supreme value of Christianity, but he has more consideration for the convictions of others. At the Jerusalem Meeting in 1928 the International Missionary Council stated their views. They had no desire to bind up the Gospel with fixed ecclesiastical forms or to lord it over the personal or collective faiths of others. They obeyed a God who respected their own wills, and they desired to respect the wills of others. But Christ had said, "I am come that they might have life and have it more abundantly." They desired a world in which Christ's spirit would reign; and they would work to produce a Christ-like character in individuals, societies, and nations. And this being the attitude of missionaries, more good—far—will result from their activities than all Government can do in the way of material and intellectual improvement of India. For no people are more appreciative than the Indians of the value of Christ's life and teaching, or quicker to realise a Christ-like life when they see one. And the immense output of spiritual energy which is being poured into India from the many Western nations will bear its rich result, whatever the political connection between India and Great Britain may happen to be.

I should add that I have no practical experience of administration in a British Province. My experience was wholly in that part of India which is still ruled by its own rulers. But that has given me an opportunity of judging what a self-governing India may be. And this should be of value, because in future the British Provinces will probably approximate more and more to the Indian States, while these latter will emulate the efficiency of the British Provinces. And, perhaps, the Governors of British Provinces will come more to resemble the Residents of the greater Indian States, while the Viceroys will be less and less the strenuous, capable administrators of the Lord Curzon type and become more like those gracious craftsmen in the art of kingship, Queen Victoria, King Edward, and King George, and pay more attention to that ceremonial and social side of Indian life which is so necessary for softening the acerbities of political endeavour.

It is impossible to enumerate all the books and articles to which I am indebted; but there are a few in particular that I must name. I am specially indebted to Ramsay Muir's *The Making of British India* for the chapter on "The Reasons for British Dominion"; to Chirol's *Indian Unrest* and Lajput Rai's *Young India* for the description of Indian Nationalism; to Mazoomdar's *Life of Keshub Chander Sen* and Bawa Chajju's *Life of Dayanand Saraswati* for the chapter on "Indian Spirituality"; to Dr. E. J. Thompson's *Rabindranath Tagore* for the chapter on "Tagore"; to Mr. C. F. Andrew's *Mahatma Gandhi's Ideas* for the chapter on "Gandhi"; to Radhakrishnan's *Hindu View of Life* for the chapter on "Radhakrishnan"; and to Heiler's *The Gospel of Sadhu Sundar Singh* for the chapter on "Sadhu Sundar Singh."

I have also carefully studied Mr. Elihu Root's speeches and State Papers relating to the Philippines, and W. Cameron Forbes' *The Philippine Islands*, because the Americans have much the same problem there as we have in India, and we have much to learn from their way of handling it. President McKinley's *Letter of Instructions* (drawn up by Mr. Elihu Root) to the Commission for the Philippine Islands is a model of the kind of guidance officers placed in such positions of responsibility need. It is after the manner of the instructions Warren Hastings used to issue.

Finally, I would acknowledge the debt I owe to Count Keyserling's *Travel Diary of a Philosopher*. He has almost achieved the impossible. He has nearly understood Hinduism.

F. E. Y.

WESTERHAM,
August, 1930.

CONTENTS

CHAPTER XV

GANDHI

CHAPTER XVI

INDIAN WOMEN

CHAPTER XVII

RADHAKRISHNAN

CHAPTER XVIII

SADHU SUNDAR SINGH

CHAPTER XIX

THE ULTIMATE DESTINY

PART I

POLITICAL

CHAPTER I

COMRADESHIP

INDIA is so great, so complex, so variegated that it must necessarily be approached from many sides if it is to be understood. Politicians will regard it from the political point of view and will devise constitutions. Students will study its philosophical aspects. Tourists will seek the picturesque. Journalists will plunge into the crisis of the moment. To my own point of view I must devote this whole first chapter. And I crave the indulgence of my readers because I hope that my own point of view may be in some degree typical of those who have for long years *served* India, and who are in deadly earnest in striving for her welfare, and must therefore be more directly interested in her than either the statesman or the tourist or the journalist or the student.

And, however deficient we Englishmen who serve India may be in that social consideration which should grace our intercourse with Indians, there are few who do not identify themselves whole-heartedly with the country to which they have devoted the best years of their life. And if at times some of us are more insistent on the preservation of order than on political progress, that attitude is only natural in those who are or who have been more directly and immediately responsible for the maintenance of peace. We, better than any, know at what cost and with what delicacy our forefathers have built up the wonderful fabric. We, better than any, know the fury of the gust which may burst upon it. And we, more than any, are passionately interested in handing it on sure and true to our successors. Possibly, therefore, we may sometimes stress too urgently the need for maintaining order.

Yet in this there is no kind or sort of desire to keep the Indians under. Order has to be maintained even in England. Maintaining order in India does not mean suppressing Indians. It is the very first essential for their progress. We have worked with them. We have known them, and they have known us, in times of stress and strain, as well as in times of tranquillity and peace. In our work together we have had to study each other's character, each other's innate dispositions, each other's fundamental way of looking at things, each other's manners and customs and general mode of living. So when we who have served in India press for the preservation of order this does not mean the preservation of our own dominance. It only means that we have the true good of India at heart. We have in our service striven to do our best by India. And our deepest wish is to see India go ahead, strong and prosperous, and contented. We take a pride in her progress as part of our own handiwork. And the better able she is to fend for herself, the more glorious will be our achievement. Our fathers established order in India where they found chaos. And if we can not only maintain the order which they established, but help India to move forward under her own impetus in a direction of her own choosing we shall have that satisfaction which all men desire of having done good in our time.

This, in general, is the feeling of those who have served India in the Indian Army, or the Indian Civil Service, or in the Police, the Engineering, the Medical, the Education, the Forest, the Agricultural, or other services of India. And, in particular, for myself, I would add these additional words in explanation of the attitude taken up in this book.

I was born in India. The air I first breathed was the air of India. And it was cool, fresh, sweet air, for I was born in the Himalaya. My birthplace was one of those beautiful retreats in the mountains which we British have made in the outlying spurs of the Himalaya. Murree was its name. It had just been cut out of the virgin forests. And through the trees it looked out on the one side over the vast plains of India, and on the other to the glorious mountains of Kashmir.

I came to England before the Suez Canal was built. But of neither the place of my birth nor of the voyage home have I any recollection, for I was only six months old at the time. What I do remember, though, from the very first, was being brought up in an atmosphere of India. While my parents were in India, I lived with two of my father's sisters in the beautiful little Somersetshire village of Freshford. Besides my father, three other of their brothers had served in India. Over the old pew in which I sat on Sundays were tablets to the memory of two of them—Edward and George—who had lost their lives on active service in India. Both had been killed when leading Indian troops in the service of India. And I used to read with awe a rather bombastic description of my uncle George being mortally wounded while charging the enemy in 1857. Then in the drawing-room of the house we lived in were wonderful carved ivory boxes, lacquer boxes, miniatures, and various other treasures—all sent back from India by their brothers to my aunts. Letters used to come to me from India from my parents, and I would have to write to them, though of my father I could remember nothing, and of my mother I had only the dimmest recollection.

When I was eight years old they returned, and so also a year later did my mother's brother, Robert Shaw, the explorer. But two years later they were back in India. And by the time they had come to England for good, the new generation was beginning to go out. First the sons of my uncle General Romer Younghusband, George going to India in the Army, Arthur and Romer in the Indian Civil Service, and Alfred in the Public Works Department. Then followed my brother George going to the Army in India. So the air of India was about me throughout my youth.

And all this time I heard nothing but good of India. My mother, as well as my father, had been through the Indian Mutiny. But it left no traces of ill-will against the people. We children were told many stories of the devotion of old Indian servants. And of some big Indians he had worked with, my father often spoke with deepest feeling.

Of Uttar Singh I have special remembrance. In 1850, my father was sent by Lord Dalhousie to the Punjab frontier. This was just after the severe campaign against the Sikhs, when the old East India Company had been compelled to annex the Punjab. And my father's task was to organise three regiments of the old Sikh army and to raise another regiment. All this he had to do by himself —and he was only twenty-seven. Now Uttar Singh was the commandant of one of these Sikh regiments. And to this day I can remember my father telling me when I first went out to India as a lad of nineteen that I was to try and see this Uttar Singh, and if I met him I was "to treat him as a gentleman." I shall have more to say about these officers of the Sikh army later on, for it was my father's firm conviction that Indians as well as Englishmen should be given commissions as officers in the Indian Army. But I only refer to the case of Uttar Singh as an instance of the warm affection my father had for Indians of this stamp. And clearly both my father and my mother must have had a strong devotion to India, for it was always taken as a matter of course that we three boys, George, Leslie, and myself, should go to India. And when at the age of nineteen my turn came I went out, filled with a kind of awe for these old comrades of my father, whom I was enjoined to look up whenever I had the chance.

In a British Regiment I had little chance of seeing real Indian life. And the Indians who come as servants to a British Regiment are not of the best type. But when I was away from the Regiment exploring in Central Asia and in the Himalaya, I came directly in touch with Indians and formed my first attachment to them.

At the age of twenty-four, I found myself in a Central Asian town with orders to cross the Himalaya by a new route. I had run out of nearly all my money. And I was quite without experience of Himalayan passes. But there were Indian merchants in the town. And being an Englishman, and therefore at least a friend, they immediately took me in hand. They advanced me money. They got together a number of Indians, organised them into a party and equipped and supplied them, and sped me on my way rejoicing. And the party themselves—Baltis from the northern frontier of Kashmir—made it a point of honour to see me over the passes. Together we endured hardships, incurred dangers, and overcame all difficulties. Our meals we ate together and out of the same pot. At night in the open we slept on the ground together. And when we parted, having successfully accomplished our object, we were bound together with ties which have lasted for over forty years.

Two years later I was again in close touch with Indians. I had to undertake another dangerous exploration in the Himalaya. This time six Gurkhas accompanied me as escort. We had to traverse unknown and quite uninhabited country, ascend glaciers, climb passes, suffer severe cold, and run great risks in entering the very stronghold of raiders who had perpetually harried the neighbouring peoples of Central Asia. Again, we had come out successfully. And when we parted, the Gurkha sergeant told me that his native officers had had them up before they started and told them that if anything happened to me not one of them was to come back alive to disgrace the regiment. They had been prepared to suffer great hardship and if necessary to die. But they had been so well looked after they had had no hardships, and they were returning safely. There were tears in the hardy little men's eyes as they said Good-bye. And the ties between me and Indians were drawn tighter.

Ten years passed and the scene was very different. I was far away from the mountains, right out in the plains of India. I was now Political Agent in an ancient Indian State ruled by a Maharaja of the most old-fashioned type. A fearful famine threatened the land. A few inches of rain had fallen at the commencement of the rainy season. Then the monsoon clouds had rolled away. The brazen sun appeared and would for certain scorch down on the earth for months to come. The newly-sown crops withered before ripening. And dire disaster was certain. To the old-fashioned ruler this was a calamity sent by God, and it was not for him to oppose the Almighty's decree. At the most he would build a temple. And he would throw out money to the crowd from the palace windows. But when I explained to him that the Government of India would help and expect him to make an effort to relieve his people, he gratefully changed his attitude. All State officials were ordered to fall in with the schemes which Government suggested. Work was provided for the people by digging embankments for a railway and erecting earthen dams for the storage of water in ordinary years at favourable spots. And grain was imported wherewith to pay for the work done. Those who were too feeble to work were collected together at central points and fed and tended. The famine deepened. Cholera, the invariable concomitant of famine, appeared. The people died in thousands and thousands. All the cattle died. The surviving human beings were as living skeletons. But through our combined efforts some fifty thousand persons were saved who without us would have died. And when after exactly a year the rain fell again, when the new crops had ripened, when in those beautiful months of the early cold weather the whole country was smiling again, and I was driving away after my farewell visit to the Maharaja, I once again felt the pull of the ties that bind Englishmen and Indians together. And for nearly thirty years after, till the time of his death, he never failed to write to me at Christmas, thus showing that he too wished to keep up the relation.

Five years pass. I have just left Lhasa and am riding away to India. The whole of an Indian regiment—the 32nd Pioneers—of their own initiative, turn out of their camp to say Good-bye. Together we had crossed the Himalaya in the very depth of winter. Together we had stood a two months' siege in a farm-house. Together we had gone through all the risks and dangers of the advance to Lhasa. And, very largely owing to their good behaviour in a foreign country, the object with which we had been sent to Lhasa had been secured and we had earned a telegram of approval from the King-Emperor. Success in the common enterprise had sealed our feelings of comradeship. And once again Indians and British were bound together by intangible but irrefragable ties.

And so it came about that when on my return to England from Tibet I was invited by the University of Cambridge to deliver the Rede Lecture, I chose this tie between us as my theme. The lecture would be delivered in the Senate House of the University before the Heads of Colleges and a very distinguished audience. It behoved me, therefore, to take advantage of the occasion to say what I most had it in me to say, and what would be worth their hearing.

I chose for my subject "Our True Relationship with India." I was then in the prime of life. I was fresh from a great enterprise undertaken on behalf of India. And I had then served twenty-three years in the country. I bore in mind Lord Palmerston's saying that if you wanted to be thoroughly misinformed about a country you should go to a man who had lived there for thirty years and spoke the language. Still I thought I might have something to say about our attitude towards India which the distinguished audience might deem worth listening to.

And I urged that it was important that we should have a clear view as to what our true relationship with India should be, because upon that governing idea would depend all our actions. I said that no one in the present day would like our relationship to be that of conqueror to conquered, for we had never conquered India for the sake of conquest. We were there in spite of ourselves, being drawn or driven on by circumstances over which we never had complete control. Moreover, we had always used Indian soldiers in establishing our position in India, and it would be ungenerous to forget the aid they had given.

A more evident wish would be that a paternal relationship should subsist between us—that we should regard ourselves as like a wise, kind-hearted father looking after his children. But however appropriate this relationship might be in the case of young colonies, who really are sons of the fatherland, it was scarcely applicable to the case of India.

Nor did I think that our relationship could be brotherly. The idea of the "Aryan brother" did not appeal to me. Indians might be very distant Aryan cousins. But certainly they were not brothers.

What then should our relationship be? It should not be that of conqueror to conquered. It could be paternal or fraternal. What should it be? I replied that it both could and should be that of manly *comradeship*. I recalled how on many a hard-fought battlefield Indian soldiers had proved themselves true comrades, how civil officials at the end of their career looked back with affection on friendships with Chiefs or great landholders or high Indian officials, how the faithful Indian servants had stood by us in many a difficulty and sympathised with us in many a trouble, how the people of India were unbounded and never failing in their hospitality. I bade my audience remember that the great Chiefs had always stood by us, even in the dark days of the Mutiny, and, in time of trouble, whether in China, or South Africa, or elsewhere, had come forward with generous offers of assistance; and that both Princes and people, in the time of sorrow as in times of joy, had shown a depth of sympathy such as could only come from a people having in them the essence of real comradeship. On the death of Queen Victoria the grief was expressed with an intensity of feeling not surpassed even in England, while on each victory in South Africa telegrams had poured in upon Lord Roberts from every part of the Indian

Empire. Could any other relationship than comradeship subsist between us?

And this idea of comradeship I still think, now, a quarter of a century later, and in spite of the changes which have taken place since I spoke at Cambridge, should be the governing idea in all our dealings with India. Indeed, I think it is now more necessary than ever that we should have towards India the feelings of a comrade.

And I specially use the expression comradeship and not fellowship, or friendship, or brotherhood, because comradeship comes of fighting and working together. We are comrades in arms. And we are comrades in building up a more prosperous India.

And comrades we may always remain even if India got the extreme her extremists now are demanding, a complete severance of the political connection with Great Britain. Even if India were as entirely independent of the British Empire as Japan or Persia, she and England might still be comrades. For we British need not be put off by the violent abuse which has recently been hurled upon us by men not yet accustomed to freedom of speech and the responsibilities that freedom must in the end involve. We say some fairly violent things about our own Governments whether they be Conservative, Liberal, or Labour. Abusive language by political leaders and political followers should not prevent the heart of England beating with the heart of India. We do not forget the warm affection individual Indians have shown to individual Englishmen, or the devotion the people of India have shown to our sovereigns. And even if India had a Government composed of Indians, responsible to a Legislature elected by Indians, and completely independent of the British Empire, British men and women, either as individuals or in voluntary association, might still join as comrades with Indians in working for the welfare of India. The political connection might cease. But a deeper connection might remain—and might deepen.

Then, as now, British merchants would be trading in India and Indian merchants would be trading in Great Britain. Then, as now, Englishmen would be going to India as scientific experts, as organisers, as missionaries, and as students of Indian culture, and Indians would be coming to England to study and to tell us of the treasures of both ancient and modern Indian philosophy, religion, and art. From the sheer, cold, hard, business point of view Englishmen would always be wanting India to be orderly, well-governed, and highly-developed in the material sense. The more contented and prosperous India became the better would it suit the material interests of Great Britain. The richer India became the better market would she be for England. And Englishmen would always be ready to give of their initiative, of their energy, or of their organising power to assist in the material development of that naturally-favoured country whether the supreme Government were in the hands of Indians or British. And we cannot imagine a time when we British would not be wanting to pour into India the wealth of our accumulated scientific knowledge, of our literature, our art, and our religion, and when we would not be eager to learn more of Indian architecture, Indian sculpture, Indian culture of all kinds, and to welcome in England such religious leaders as Keshub Chunder Sen, such poets as Tagore, such philosophers as Radhakrishnan, and such scientists as Sir Jagidis Bose.

So even if the political connection were severed, intercourse between England and India would continue. And with communication yearly becoming easier and more rapid, this intercourse would increase. An independent India would not be an isolated India. India would have to come into the comity of nations. In the comity of nations she might need a comrade. And it is easy to see that the severance of political connection might even deepen the spiritual connection.

It is, therefore, in the spirit of comradeship that I approach this study of India as it stands to-day. It is in the spirit of comradeship inherited from my parents and intensified by both military and civil service in the country—and by service both on the frontier and in the interior, and with the great Princes as well as with the peasants—that I try to look at the dangers and difficulties which British and Indians together will have to face. And it is, I believe, through that spirit alone that together we shall be able to overcome the obstacles before us and that India will in the end achieve that status which is her due.

What then is the position in India?

CHAPTER II

THE CALL FOR SELF-GOVERNMENT

WHAT strikes us most in the India of to-day is her insistent demand for self-government. By persuasion, if possible; by boycotting foreign goods and Government service; if persuasion fails by bombs in the last resort, Indians want to be rid of their alien rulers. Not all are agreed on the method. Not all want the British rule to cease at once. But all want as soon as feasible to be as free to control their own destiny as Japanese, Turks, and Persians are to control theirs. Indians resent their position of subordination. They remember the past glories of their country. They regard themselves as being fully as intelligent as their present rulers. Spiritually they look upon themselves as superior. And they want India to stand among the nations free and proud as Japan.

And with this sentiment few Englishmen would not sympathise. The desire of India to stand erect by herself and to shape her own course all can understand. But when I gave my lecture to Cambridge University twenty-five years ago I did not contemplate the possibility of India ever being fit for self-government. I thought and said that we could not look forward to a time when India could, with advantage to Indians or anyone else, be left to govern herself. I specially referred to the opinions of great Anglo-Indians of an earlier time, like Sir John Malcolm and Sir Mountstuart Elphinstone, who held that we should so train and educate the people of India that they would eventually be able to govern themselves. But I thought that with the increasing pressure of Europe upon Asia, and considering the difficulties the Indians would have in composing the differences which might arise between themselves owing to diversities in religion and race in the interior of India, and the still greater difficulty of warding off attacks by Afghans, frontier tribes, and perhaps European nations, and by sea as well as by land, we could not expect Indians by themselves to hold their own. They would always ultimately be dependent upon us for the defence of their frontier and coast-line.

And when we consider the position that view was at that time not unreasonable. For India is as big as Europe without Russia. It has a population of 320 millions. And these are not of the same religion, as are the Europeans. There are seventy million Moslems, and three times as many Hindus, and Hindus and Moslems are at enmity with one another. In addition there are eleven million Buddhists (in Burma), three and a quarter million Sikhs, ten million of primitive tribal religions, and five million Christians. The Hindus are divided into hundreds of castes. There is no common language for the whole of India. The people are as varied in character as the flowers of a garden are in form and colour. The martial Sikhs of the Punjab or Pathans of the frontier being as different from the cultured Bengali as a Highland gillie is from an Italian poet. Moreover, Indians have no strong natural aptitude for politics or for organisation on a great scale. And it is only for brief periods in some thousands of years that they have ever been united in the semblance of an Empire such as the present Empire of India. And as for sea defence, a real Indian navy capable of defending the entire coast-line of India has never existed in the whole course of her history.

If we then consider what India would have to face if left to herself, it is not surprising that I should have thought she could not stand without us. In the course of her history India has repeatedly been invaded from the North-West. The north-eastern frontier is well guarded by the Himalaya. But on the north-western side is the gate through which many invaders have passed into India. And against such an invasion India must ever be on the guard. And say another invasion from Afghanistan occurred—such an invasion, for instance, as actually did take place as recently as in 1919, when that very same Ammanula whom we and the rest of Europe fêted so generously thought to make himself King of India. Say that this invasion coincided with one of those communal conflicts between Hindus and Moslems which are so frequent in India. Say that the Afghans were supported by the Turks in a great Jehad against the Hindus. Say that the Moslem Moplahs in the South of India joined in the fray as they did a few years ago. And say that the Turks sent a cruiser or two to harry the coasts of India as the *Emden* bombarded Madras during the Great War. Say this series of quite probable events occurred, would an Indian-governed India—an India divided against herself—with no British Army to fall back on to defend her land frontier and to preserve internal tranquillity and order, with no British Navy to defend her coast, and with no British High Command to organise her armies, conduct her warfare, and co-ordinate her activities, be able to hold her own? Is it not much more probable that under the impact India would again break up into hundreds of separate and warring states and be again in the condition in which we found her, and which had for centuries been her normal condition?

Or again, suppose that Russia, driven by that very natural impulse she feels within her, and feels just as much under Soviet as under Tsarist rule, to seek an ice-free port on the oceans of the world, were to press down towards India. Suppose that, foiled as she is in Manchuria, she were to seek a port on the Indian Ocean. Suppose that she were to send an army by land and a fleet by sea to seize Karachi as she seized Port Arthur, would an Indian-governed India, an Indian-commanded army, and an Indian fleet be able to prevent her?

I could not believe it possible, and considerations such as these were in my mind when, a quarter of a century ago, I refused to contemplate an India governing herself and holding her own against every hostile attack. The utmost I had in mind was an India in the government of which Indians would be largely employed, but over which we would always hold the supreme control and direction. We might associate Indians more and more with us in the administration. We might admit more into the Councils and give them a larger say in legislation. We might give commissions in the Army to Indians. But the main responsibility, I imagined, must rest with us. We and not the Indians would have to bear the ultimate responsibility for defending the frontier against invasion by land and the coasts against invasion by sea. We and not the Indians would have to conduct foreign relations. And we, too, would have to bear the main responsibility for preserving internal order. This was how I viewed the position in 1905.

And my own personal view of the future was that while we thus associated Indians with us in the governance of India to the full measure of their capacity, we would, by keeping India free of both internal and external trouble, provide the Indians with the necessary peace and opportunity to develop on the lines most congenial to them. Indians have no great liking for politics, or any aptitude for organisation on a great scale. Politics have never occupied so prominent a part in their lives as they do with us, and organisation they detest. What Indians have cared for most have been things of the spirit—religion and philosophy. And I had envisaged an India in which Indians would develop a higher religion under the ægis of our rule as the Jews had developed Christianity under the Romans. A self-governing India, responsible for its own destiny and wholly independent of our support, was not in my thoughts.

But in the last quarter of a century vast changes have occurred, both in the world as a whole and in India, and my views have changed too. And perhaps the greatest change of all has been in the Indians themselves. At that time the idea of governing themselves had hardly occurred to them.

The most they then claimed was a greater share in the administration, a larger representation on the Legislative Council, and a greater freedom of criticism. Twenty years previously there had come into existence a body called the Indian National Congress which expressed this claim. Political grievances and the advancement of India were discussed at these annual meetings. And very outspoken comments were made upon the Government. But in these early years the demand was merely for redress of specific grievances and for a greater share in the administration of the country. Now, however, a sharp change had come about. Indians claimed to govern themselves. Not an improvement in the administration but a change of rulers was the demand which came to be pressed. Hitherto they had criticised the British Government in India. Now they would supplant it.

What was the cause of this change? The causes were several. The first, in point of time, was the Western education which had for nearly a hundred years been imparted to the Indians. And not only by the British Government, but by missionary bodies. And not only by British missionary bodies, but by Moravian, French, Belgian, and American missionary bodies. From all these sources Indians had been incited to a sturdier, more self-respecting manhood. They themselves in their inmost hearts think themselves vastly superior to any European. I once asked a most courteous and kindly old Brahmin what I might become in another incarnation if I were very good during my present life; and he replied that I might become a Maharaja. And on my further enquiring what I might become if I were very good as a Maharaja, he unabashedly replied: "A Brahmin like myself." Indians, as I say, in their hearts regard Europeans as rough, vigorous peoples just emerging from barbarism—as stout fighters and stern rulers, but spiritually still barbarians. But though these were their secret thoughts, they had had for a century to keep them secret. During the reign of the Moslem Mogul Emperors the Hindus had to take a subordinate place. And after the collapse of the Empire, while Mahrattas were fighting Afghans and then the British, there was everywhere chaos and disorder in India till the British finally established themselves as the paramount power, and there was a general tendency to lie low till the storms were over. But now that there was calm and peace and order, and energetic Western ideas were vigorously jetted into them, they again began to stand erect. They again felt conscious of their high capacities. And as Western education also stimulated freedom of expression they no longer thought it necessary to keep their ideas of superiority to themselves. They openly expressed them. They dared even to think they might oust their alien rulers and govern India themselves. They began to regain confidence in themselves.

And they acquired this self-confidence not only in the Government and missionary schools in India, but also in visits to Europe and America. Moslems are accustomed to travel freely. But Hindus are essentially a stay-at-home people. To cross the ocean—the black water—is to break their caste. It is a sacrilegious act. They must remain in the Motherland and think of her and care for her. Not go abroad. This is the orthodox outlook of Hindus. But time and the ease and frequency of communications between India and Europe effected a change. No longer did Hindus stay at home. They began to cross the ocean in spite of caste prohibitions. They might make due penance when they returned. But go to Europe they must. And in Europe and in America they found much to affect them. Much to cause them repugnance: the haste and rush of life; the ostentation and luxury; the materiality; the coarseness and vulgarity. But much also to attract: the freedom of life and the freedom of expression.

They came back to India with a distaste for the sheer materiality of what they had seen. But also with fresh air in their lungs and with their backbones stiffened. Manhood was once again beginning to course through their veins, and the idea of nationhood was forming in their brains.

And most of these Indians—Moslems as well as Hindus—who visited Europe and America were students. If Western education was desirable then why not have it at its fountain source? Why not go to the universities of England and America? Thousands of students therefore crossed the ocean in pursuit of that learning which would put them on an equal footing with the British. If they had the same learning as the British—if they knew all the British knew—then clearly they could step into the positions now occupied by Englishmen in India. The thing was too obvious to need demonstration. And when they arrived at the universities, they worked strenuously. All their work had to be in a foreign tongue, and their lives had to be led among strangers with strange ways and customs and an odd outlook on life. But they persevered. They courageously faced all difficulties and disabilities. And they returned to India seething with Western ideas. Often with contempt for the religion of their fathers—and, indeed, for all religion. And also with that habit of freely criticising Government, and all else that is or was or ever will be, that is characteristic of Europe, and so utterly different from India, where all is conducted by tradition and convention and precedent, and accepted without question as divinely ordained. But always with resentment against the foreign ruler in their own land.

For years now there had been pouring back into India this stream of returned students ready to criticise all they found in India, and filled with Western notions of freedom. And now came an event of momentous consequence—the defeat of Russia by Japan in 1905—the defeat of a great European by an Asiatic Power—and defeat by sea as well as by land. This stirred all Asia—and India with the rest. If Japan with thirty-five million inhabitants could defeat Russia, what might not India with three hundred million inhabitants do? The vivid Indian imagination flew swiftly to unmeasured heights.

And soon another event occurred which gave some definition to their dreams. The British Government granted self-government to South Africa. "Self-government is better than good government," said the British Prime Minister, Sir Henry Campbell-Bannerman. The Indians quickly caught up the cry, and have been repeating it ever since. "Self-government is better than good government." The government of India by themselves would be better than the government of India by the British, however "good" that government might be. It was a thrilling thought. And the sooner it was translated into action the better.

So from these various causes—from Western education, from the visits of Indians to Europe and America, from the ideas of freedom and criticism which students at British and American universities brought back with them, and especially from the victory of Japan over Russia and the grant of self-government to South Africa, a great change had come over India in the years following 1905. Uninfluenced by the West, Indians would have accepted things as they were, as having been so appointed by God. In an Indian State ruled by an Indian ruler there is—or was—no free Press, no organisation for criticising his government. He was on the throne, therefore he must have been placed there by God. And the people must and did accept him. Complaints indeed might be made—though at great risk—about the tyranny of his Minister. But he himself was sacrosanct. And never was there a suggestion that he should be supplanted by the people and that the people should govern themselves. And similarly, Indians left to themselves might have complained of this or that act of the British Government or of this or that British official. The Government they would have accepted as divinely instituted. But from these various causes the change came over them. And now the idea of self-government had caught hold of them. No longer would they aspire no higher than an increased share in the administration. They aimed at having the government itself in their hands.

And the Great War strengthened this feeling. It deepened it in the hearts of those who already had it. And it spread it among those who had not yet felt it. The war was a fight for right against might. Oppressors were denounced. Peoples struggling to be free were applauded. Self-determination became the watch-word for the nations of the world. The right of each nation to its nationhood—the right of each nation to determine its own destiny—was acclaimed. When the war was over and victory had been achieved subject peoples would achieve their freedom. India would be free. The Great War brought India a Great Hope.

The Russian Revolution also had its effect. Here, close by them, were a people who in actual fact *had* thrown off their oppressors. The Russian people had planned out and carried through a complete revolt against their rulers. The whole Tsarist régime had been overthrown. The revolutionaries were ensconced in the seats of the mighty. The thing could be done. What was more, these same revolutionaries, with all the arts of the most skilful propagandists, were making known to the whole world the methods by which they had achieved success. And, knowing that their success could not be complete or permanent until they had got all others to do likewise, they were busy urging Indians to rise against the British and seize the reins of power. And this was another contributing cause to the India demand for self-government.

So also was the Irish revolt. The Irish had agitated against their British oppressors. The Irish had plotted and fought against the British—even in the midst of the Great War. And the Irish—or half of them, anyhow—had achieved "self-government." Southern Ireland was able to govern herself free of British control. Why should not India do the same?

From all these causes there now is in India a demand for self-government such as was hardly whispered twenty or thirty years ago. And it is a demand not merely for a share in the government, but for government itself. This is the most striking feature of the present-day India.

CHAPTER III

INDIAN NATIONALISM

The rise of the demand for self-government has been described in the last chapter. Here we have to study the rise of the complementary idea of nationalism, and the spreading of the idea "India, a nation." Especially must we know of the nation-*makers*—of those great Indians who with fine public spirit and steady pertinacity, if sometimes with too heated impetuosity, set the foundation of the Indian nation.

But India is not, and never can be, a nation, critics will spring forward to declare. India is a sub-continent, not a country. It is no more a country than Europe is a country. Not so much. The people are not of the same religion, nor of the same race, nor of the same degree of civilisation; and they have no common language. They are of the two main religions, Hinduism and Islam, bitterly and perpetually opposed to each other. They are of races far more different from each other than Scotsmen are from Spaniards. And the main Hindu majority is divided up into hundreds of castes which will not marry or dine with each other or with any outsiders. How can such a people be called a nation? Or ever expect to be a nation?

So some ask. Nevertheless, there is already an underlying unity among Indians, and this unity may be intensified. Any Indian is an Indian and very easily distinguishable from a Chinese or a Japanese, a Russian or an Englishman. He may be Hindu or Moslem, a high-caste Brahmin or an "untouchable." But he is obviously an Indian—not a Siamese, or a Frenchman, or a Hottentot. Some common spirit runs through the whole of India. And this has a distinct outward expression in all Indians. How to describe it I cannot say. But anyone can see it for himself. It comes out on such occasions as the moving of a resolution in the Council drawing attention to the ill-treatment of Indians in the Transvaal. Then Indians of all creeds and castes and classes are joined. They have a common spirit. All alike resent the ill-treatment of Indians, whether those Indians are Hindus or Moslems, high caste or low caste. The same common spirit was seen on the death of Queen Victoria, at the Indian coronation of King George, and at the outbreak of the Great War. All differences then disappeared. On each such occasion one heart beat through India. India spoke with one voice. And each of these occasions makes India more a nation.

India is one in spirit, however different in race and religion. In the words of the Simon Commission Report, "there is an essential unity in diversity in the Indian Peninsula regarded as a whole . . . which has largely been brought about by British rule." There is a single system of administration throughout the whole of India and the same law runs everywhere. India is a single and a firm political unit. And if there is no common language for all India, at any rate English is the common language for the educated classes throughout the country, and in that language all the debates are carried on.

So the makings of a nation are there, even if the nation is not yet made.

And nation-*makers* are there. Some very splendid men have arisen in India during the last thirty years. And they have worked hard with their own countrymen as well as with the British to break down every obstacle which would stand in the way of India being recognised as a nation. First they would inspire Indians with the idea. Then they would prevail upon the British to adopt it.

Perhaps the first publicly and formally to put forward the ideal of self-government for India, as distinguished from the mere Indianisation of the administration, was that grand old man Dadabhai Naoroji, who was also the first Indian to sit in the British Parliament—though of course for an English and not an Indian constituency. He was one of the earliest supporters of the Congress Movement, of which more will be said in a later chapter. And in 1907, in his Presidential Address to the Indian National Congress, he boldly made self-government for India his principal theme. But during long years before that he had been working in the interests of India. A Parsi of a poor though esteemed family, he had been educated at the Elphinstone College and had so impressed Professor Erskine by his character and intelligence that the generous Professor had offered to contribute half the expenses if his parents would send him to England to study. Public service very early attracted him. He was fired by the lives of the pioneers of the Slavery Abolition Movement. And while he was living in England, working in a Parsi business-house, he laboured hard for the redress of Indian grievances. He pressed for the reform of Indian finances and tried to awaken people to the poverty of India. He was largely instrumental in improving the conditions under which Indians could compete for the Indian Civil Service open to Indians. Throughout all his labours his one enduring aim was to get an honourable place for India among the nations of the world. And he believed this could best be done by promoting Indian nationality.

Another of the earliest pioneers, and a typical gentle-mannered, suave, polished, capable, public-spirited Indian, was Ranade, though he was more concerned with social than with political reform. Of the Brahmin caste, he made it his life-work to purify Hinduism of its worst prejudices and customs and bring it more in line with the general movement of the world. And this is a harder task than Western peoples may imagine and needed moral courage of the highest order. For orthodox Hinduism has its roots thousands of years old deep down in the soil of India. And any would-be reformer has to contend against that social pressure which can be such a torture to the soul in Hindu hands. To suffer imprisonment for daring to flout an alien rule is a light thing in Indian eyes. It may even be a cause of congratulation. To face social ostracism is to face hell itself. For nothing bites so deeply into the soul as the censure of caste opinion.

Yet Ranade, and many another courageous Indian like him, have fearlessly faced this horror. With no chance of posing as heroic martyrs in their country's cause, but with every chance of being denounced as destroyers of their faith, they have persevered on their course, determined to purge their religion and their social system of the stains which pollute it.

Mr. Justice Ranade was, as I have said, a Brahmin, and came from the Deccan. He was fully in favour of promoting reform by constitutional methods and, when necessary, of criticising British administration. But he believed that the reform of social institutions was a more important duty, and to this he devoted his energies, and through sheer force of intellect and nobility of character he was able to do much for the education and what is generally called "uplift" of the Hindus.

A disciple of Ranade and coming also from Western India, and also a Brahmin, was Gokhale. He, too, was a man of great moral and intellectual force, and with his keen, refined, cultured face he proved himself a master-mind in any assembly of his countrymen. Educational reform was the absorbing interest in his life. At one time he was a professor at the Ferguson College in Poona. And one of his last acts was, as an elected member of the Imperial Council at Calcutta, to move a resolution in favour of free and compulsory elementary education. But he abandoned his professorship in order to take a larger share in public life. And more than Ranade had ever done, he devoted himself to politics.

That he would like to have seen India rid of the British is quite intelligible. (And on board ship going out to India I did, in fact, hear him express such a wish.) But he was far too wise and level-headed a man to dwell overmuch on such an idea. Sufficient to the day was the evil thereof. "I would have India free of the British to-day if that were possible. How can we be expected to like being under a foreign yoke? But is it possible? Is it not better to endure British rule for the present and get as much as we can from it?"

So he never favoured violence. At the most he favoured boycott as a political weapon for a definitely political purpose. And he so said when he was President of the Indian National Congress held at Benares in 1905. But he protested against "the narrow, exclusive, and intolerant spirit in which advocates of Swadeshi* seek to promote their cause." And when he saw the lawlessness to which the boycott was leading, he was anxious to undo the words he had spoken in favour of it.

He was elected a Member of the Imperial Legislative Council. And from his seat in Council he was an unrelenting—often bitter—critic of the Administration. Yet he gained the respect of his British colleagues, for he was always urbane and moderate: he had the restraint of a man conscious of his power but conscious also of his responsibilities. To the more impetuous of his Indian colleagues this restraint weighed against him. He was a statesman, they said, not a fighter, not a national hero. Nevertheless, if the more irresponsible of his Indian friends thought that he had too little fire, he himself complained that many of his colleagues had not fire enough. They were wanting in enthusiasm, wanting in the spirit of true comradeship. They were unwilling to make great sacrifices in their country's

* The name of the movement for using home-produced goods.

cause. And they led self-sufficient, luxurious lives.

He himself lived wholly for India and in her service gave his all. And he—a distinguished member of the very highest caste—took up the cause of the very lowest—of the "untouchables" —the "depressed castes"—of those unfortunates numbered by millions whom Hinduism had spurned from it for centuries. In so doing he ran counter to the deep prejudices of the bigoted orthodox. And he who does that in India requires a higher degree of heroism than he who hurls abuse at the British Government, and at the worst gets a few years' imprisonment and becomes a "martyr" and a "national hero" for the rest of his life—if not longer. In taking up the unpopular cause of the "depressed classes" instead of assuming the spectacular rôle of the doughty gladiator assaulting the British giant, he was showing himself a true hero. He was doing his country a real service. And incidentally he was making it more possible for the British to withdraw their control.

As a true Indian he believed in self-sacrifice and ascetic simplicity as the best means of advancing the welfare of India. He believed in men renouncing the world and joining together to devote themselves wholly to social service. And on these principles he founded the "Servants of India" Society, whose objects were "to train national missionaries for the service of India and to promote by all constitutional means the true interests of the Indian people." And it is worthy of note—and this also is typically Indian—that its members "frankly accept the British connexion as ordained, in the inscrutable dispensation of Providence, for India's good," and recognise that "self-government within the Empire and a higher life generally for their countrymen" constitute a goal which "cannot be attained without years of earnest and patient effort and sacrifice worthy of the cause."

The ideal of the Society was to be the good of India. They were to be the servants of India, not the servants of God. They were to seek first the kingdom of India, not the Kingdom of God. On entering the Society each member was to take the vow that the country should always be first in his thoughts and that he would serve her with the best that was in him, seek no personal advantage, regard all Indians as brothers, and work for their advancement without distinction of caste or creed. But while they were to put country first, they were to be trained in a religious spirit, and much of their work was to be directed towards building up in the country "a higher type of character and capacity than is generally available at present."

Such a man, who in the evening of his life could form such a society, may justly be called a great nation-builder.

Of a very different stamp was Tilak. He also was a Brahmin and from the Deccan and well educated. But while Gokhale was suave and moderate, Tilak was all passion and vehemence—all for direct and immediate action. About him there was none of the cautious wisdom of high statesmanship. He saw his goal, and he would go straight at it. India was under the British. The British must be smashed. India must be rescued. He himself was a Mahratta. The Mahrattas had contended for the throne of the Moguls. He would revive the glories of the past. He would awaken memories of Shivaji, their hero king. Especially would he stir the young. He would train them physically—make them men who could fight. Urbanity and self-sacrifice and self-control were not for him. He would brook no restraint. He would act. Force was the only argument.

And cultured though he was—having graduated with honours—he raised a storm of passion against Hindu reformers like Ranade and Gokhale. He allied himself with the bigots of orthodoxy. When, in 1890, the Age of Consent Bill, designed to mitigate the evil of Hindu child-marriage, was introduced, he denounced every Hindu who supported the measure as a renegade and a traitor to Hinduism. And by his violence over this measure and over the control of a certain progressive association, he so discouraged Ranade as to make him retire from the forefront of the fray.

Then he appealed to popular superstitions by organising annual festivals in honour of Ganesh, the elephant-headed god known in every village. These festivals were known as Ganpati celebrations, and Ganpati societies were formed in all the chief centres of the Deccan. Each had its choir and its dramatic society. And at the festivals dramas were acted and songs were sung in which the ancient legends were employed to arouse hatred against the foreigner. One of these was a deliberate attack on Lord Curzon, so thinly disguised that everyone in the crowded audience who came to see it knew who and what was meant. Legendary characters were employed. But everyone understood the allegory. A weak Government in England has given the Viceroy a free hand. He has made use of it to insult and humiliate India. The Moderates advocate constitutional measures. The Extremists abide their time till the ineffectiveness of these gentle methods has been proved. Then they adopt violent methods. The tyrant is disposed of without difficulty and his followers massacred. Then, having freed their country, the Extremists are able to defend it against all invaders. Such was the allegory which the crowded audiences could easily see. And they would scowl at the tyrant, scorn the tameness of the Moderates, admire the courage of the Extremists, and hum with satisfaction at the slaughter of the tyrant. The power of the drama was well used by Tilak to impress his standpoint on the people.

To stimulate disaffection with the foreign rulers, Tilak used yet another measure. Shivaji had risen to power, thrust back the Moslems, and created a Mahratta kingdom. He was almost forgotten now. Tilak would revive his memory and turn it into a living force. So a great "national" propaganda was started. Shivaji's birthday was celebrated in many towns of the Deccan. And at the principal commemoration Tilak himself presided.

"Let us be prompt like Shivaji to engage in desperate enterprises. Take up your swords and shields and we shall cut off countless heads of enemies," exclaimed one speaker. And Tilak himself said: "Great men are above the common principles of morality. . . . The Divine Krishna, teaching in Gita, tells us we may kill even our teachers and our kinsmen and no blame attaches if we are not actuated by selfish desires. . . . God has conferred on the foreigner no grant of Hindustan inscribed on imperishable brass. Shivaji strove to drive them forth out of the land of his birth, but he was guilty of the sin of covetousness. Do not circumscribe your vision like frogs in a well. Rise above the Penal Code into the rarefied atmosphere of the Bhagavat Gita and consider the action of great men."

The expected happened. Two years later two Englishmen, Rand and Ayerst, were shot by a young Brahmin who admitted that doctrines expounded in Tilak's newspapers had driven him to the deed. The disciples were sentenced to death. But the master, as invariably seems to happen in such cases, escaped. He was merely sentenced to a short term of imprisonment on account of a seditious article which appeared a few days before the murder. And on his release he was acclaimed as a martyr and hailed as a national hero.

From the Deccan he extended his influence over India as a whole. He became a dominant personality in the National Congress. And if his violence had not frightened the Moderates he might have been its President. As it was, he became the most prominent of the Extremists in India and exerted a mighty influence over the emotional Bengalis in especial. He was a natural leader of men. He had a high social position and a large way with him. The elderly and the cautious might fight shy of him. But the young flew to him as boys to a hero.

And to all he preached that India was happier and better under Hindu rule than it ever was or could be under aliens—whether those aliens were Moslems or British. The British might have served some useful purpose at one time by introducing Western science to India. But they had done this at too great cost. They had drained the wealth of India. And they had undermined the social and religious institutions. The Brahmins had now learned all there was to learn from the British, and if power were once more restored to them the golden age would return. And by ceaseless and violent agitation he believed that the British could be wearied into surrendering to the Brahmin the reality of power while retaining the shadow of sovereignty for themselves.

Great—perhaps excessive—latitude was allowed to Tilak by the British authorities. But eventually he was prosecuted for publishing in his paper inflammatory comments on the murder of two English ladies in Bengal by a bomb. In summing up, the Parsi Judge, Mr. Justice Davar, said: "The articles are seething with sedition; they preach violence; they speak of murders with approval; and the cowardly and atrocious act of committing murders with bombs not only meets with your approval, but you hail the advent of the bomb into India as if something had come to India for its good."

He was sentenced to six years' transportation, and died a few years after his release.

The idea of Swaraj—self-government—was now well implanted in the Indian mind. And from 1905 onward the Nationalist movement grew. Hitherto the Indian National Congress had welcomed the patronage of Government. The new National movement would boycott Government. The old appealed to the British Government and the British nation.

The new appeal was to the Indian people and to God.

The inspirers of the new movement were Bengalis. These quiet-minded and highly sensitive people had been caught, as we have seen, by the personality and deeds and writings of Tilak. And they now, in their own way, expressed the same hatred of foreign rule and displayed the same ardent desire to see India ruled by Indians. Moreover, they were prepared to go to extreme lengths both in words and in deeds to achieve that end. Never have they been a warlike people. But they shrank not from the most violent methods and were ready to make the supreme sacrifice for what they believed to be their country's good.

One of the first and ablest of these fiery Bengalis was Bepin Chandra Pal. In appearance he was mild and gentle and refined. There was nothing strong and masterful in his look. But in the quietest manner and in perfect English he could set flowing from him an uninterrupted succession of the most scathing comments on British rule and the most radical proposals for supplanting it.

"They had been told that the people of India were unfitted to manage their own affairs, and they had believed it to be true. They had been told that the people were weak and the Government strong. They had been told that India stood on a lower plane of humanity and England's mission was to civilise the native. The Nationalists would expose the hollowness of all these pretensions. They would awake the people to a sense of their own strength and an appreciation of their own culture. They would create a passionate love of liberty, a spirit of sacrifice, and a readiness to suffer in the country's cause. And this must be enforced by example and not precept. British goods must be boycotted. Youths must be withdrawn from Government schools and colleges and officialised universities. And instead they must be trained in institutions conducted on national lines, subject to national control and calculated to help the realisation of national destiny. Also there must be national civic volunteering. The people must voluntarily assume much of the civic duties at present discharged by official agencies. Such duties would be those connected with rural sanitation, economic and medical relief, popular education, preventive police duties, regulation of fairs and pilgrim gatherings. There would be a strong civic sentiment created in the people. And the people would be gradually trained for the larger and heavier responsibilities of free citizenship."

These were Bepin Chandra Pal's views, which he enforced with great intellectual power.

Very much akin to Mr. Pal was another impressionable Bengali also inspired by Tilak, Arabinda Ghose—a fascinating and tragic figure. One of the most brilliant young men of his time, he had passed in England the severe examination for the Indian Civil Service, but had failed to pass the test for horsemanship. On return to India he had held a well-paid post in the educational service of the Gaekwar of Baroda, but had given this up to be Principal of the new National College in Bengal on the insignificant stipend of ten pounds a month. And this also he gave up to edit a paper and throw his whole soul into the National movement.

Not only had he high intellectual attainments; he was also intensely religious. He based all his life-work on the teachings of the Bhagavat Gita. And he interpreted those as meaning that he should sacrifice his life for his religion. His religion was Hinduism. Hinduism was threatened by British rule and Western civilisation. Therefore he must free Hinduism from British rule. He never became the leader of a political organisation. Rather was he the originator of *ideas*. But he did strive to impregnate existing organisations with his ideas and to arouse the lethargic masses into vigorous action. And whether he himself meant to remove British rule by violence or not, most certainly those he wrote for did. His followers, as we shall see, on the strength of his teachings, committed deeds of the most desperate violence. And his brother, Barendra, edited a newspaper which preached revolution as a positively religious duty. And in this respect the Bengalis, like all Indians, are in diametrical contrast to the Russians. To the Indians religion is the base of the whole National movement. And the goal of Indians is an India in which religion will again be supreme in the land. For religion Russians had no use whatever. Lenin and his associates absolutely despised it and directly they came to power made deadly war upon religion in all its forms.

In deep religious faith these Bengali revolutionaries wrote. And they wrote from their very hearts and in language which set all Bengal aflame.

"Righteousness is declining and unrighteousness is springing up in India. A handful of alien robbers is ruining the millions of the people of India by robbing the wealth of India. Through the hard grinding of their servitude the ribs of this countless people are being broken to pieces. Endless endeavours are being made in order that the great nation, by losing, as an inevitable result of this subjection, its moral, intellectual, and physical power, its wealth, its self-reliance, and all other qualities, may be turned into the condition of the beast of burden, or be wholly extinguished.

"Why, O Indians, are you losing heart, at the sight of many obstacles in your path, to make a stand against this unrighteousness? Fear not, O Indians. God will not remain inactive at the sight of such unrighteousness in His kingdom. He will keep His word. Placing firm reliance on the promise of God, invoke His power, and He will descend in your midst to destroy unrighteousness. Do not be afraid. 'When the lightning of heaven flashes in their hearts, men will perform impossible deeds.'

"The independent flag of righteousness will be unfurled. The virtues of India will be restored. Plague and famine will be banished. India's industries will be brought to the highest pitch of scientific development. Her armies and fleets will go forth to use the unlimited strength, knowledge, and righteousness of India for the benefit of the whole world."

And the methods by which independence was to be achieved were set forth in a series of articles in the *Yugantar*, a newspaper edited by Arabinda Ghose's brother. First, the educated classes must learn to hate slavery. Then the aspiration for freedom must be converted into a firm resolve. The Bengali's mind must be taken away from thinking how to gain a livelihood and "must be excited and maddened by such an ideal as will present to him a picture of everlasting salvation." Public opinion must be built up by the newspapers, "which must be filled with the discussion of the necessity of independence and revolution," and by soul-stirring songs, and musical and theatrical performances, glorifying the lives of Indian heroes and their great deeds in the cause of freedom. Above all, the materials for "a great sacrifice for liberty" must be prepared. Secretly and silently bands of young men must be organised. Every band must recognise that cultivation of physical strength is a principal means of attaining their object. Each band must be connected with other bands and must be initiated in the mystical Shakti mantra. In the arming of these bands "there need be no considerations of right or wrong, for everything is laid at the feet of the goddess of independence." Bombs can be manufactured in secret places. Guns can be imported from foreign countries or obtained from the native troops, who, "though driven by hunger to accept service under the Government, are men of our own flesh and blood." Money is to be found either by voluntary donations or "by the application of force," which would be quite justifiable, since the money to be taken would be used "for the good of society." True, dacoities and thefts may destroy the sense of social security. But "to destroy it for the highest good is no sin: rather is it a work of religious merit." "The law of the English is established on brute force, and if to liberate ourselves we, too, must use brute force, it is right that we should do so."

"The number of Englishmen in this country is not above a hundred and fifty thousand, and what is the number of English officials in each district? If you are firm in your resolution, you can in a single day bring English rule to an end. Lay down your life, but first take a life. The worship of the goddess will not be consummated if you sacrifice your lives at the shrine of independence without shedding blood."

The paper containing these doctrines had an unprecedented sale. The spirit it sought to arouse quickly flamed up. And the spirit was transformed into action. Dacoities, outrages, and deeds of violence grew in numbers. Four attempts were made upon the Lieutenant-Governor, Sir Andrew Fraser. A bomb intended for a magistrate killed two ladies. The perpetrator of the outrage was hailed as a national hero. A Bengali, who held the position of Public Prosecutor, was shot dead to show the public displeasure at a Bengali holding such a position. And ever since—during the War and after—associations for violent action have existed in Bengal.

And from Bengal the revolutionary movement spread to the Punjab. The people of the Punjab are not so emotional, or so impressionable, or so idealistic as the Bengalis. But they are more martial and of a sounder practical sense. And if the Nationalist movement took root there, something worth while could be done. And Nationalism did grow there. Lajput Rai became the leader. By his early violence he had incurred the censure of his fellow Arya Samajists, and, following some serious riots, he had been deported without trial by the

British authorities in 1907. But his activities were not only political—and when political were not always violent. He was an eager promoter of religious and social reform. He organised numerous branches of the Arya Samaj, and collected funds and delivered lectures for their support. He said: "These Samajes, Colleges, Sabhas, Leagues, Associations, Congresses, and Conferences are all means to one end: they mark the various stages in our outward march to nationhood." And of the Arya Samaj itself he said that it had to remember that the India of to-day is not exclusively Hindu. "Its prosperity and future depend upon the reconciliation of Hinduism with that greater "ism"—Indian nationalism—which alone can secure for India its rightful place in the comity of nations."

In his more outspoken moments he showed himself no lover of British rule. He maintained that India had never before been governed by foreigners from without in the political and economic interests of a nation not living within her territorial limits. He did not desire to do anything which would in any way harm Great Britain as a world Power. He would much rather Indians gained Home Rule by peaceful measures and remained a part of the British Empire than subvert British authority in India by force or seek the assistance of any other foreign Power to gain their end. But if the British continued to trample on their rights and to humiliate and exploit them as they had done in the past there was no knowing what they might not be tempted or forced to do. And, according to him, the number of Indians who were ready to sacrifice their careers, their prospects, their happiness, and their lives at the altar of what they considered their duty to their country was growing larger and larger every day.

And these Nationalists, Lajput Rai said, maintained that the first condition of a life of honoured respect was political freedom. They wished that every man and woman in India should for the present think of nothing else but political freedom. The first thing they had to do was "to get rid of the foreigner." Who would rule India when the foreigner had gone, and how and what shape the government would take, did not trouble them. They believed that as soon as England left India someone would rise, phœnix-like, who would establish some form of national government. The time would produce the man. And the apprehensions of disturbances of the peace did not frighten them. They were sick of peace. And they did not mind India being split up into a number of kingdoms and principalities on the departure of the British. Anything was better than living under a foreign yoke.

This is how the idea of nationality grew up in India. And these are the various types of men who have been building up the Indian nation. Some are gentle and moderate though strong and persistent. Some are for reform by ordinary constitutional means. Some are for immediate and violent action. But probably all in their hearts would be thankful to see the end of British rule in India and to have India governing herself.

CHAPTER IV

THE REASON FOR BRITISH DOMINION

THE Indian Nationalists resent the rule of foreigners. They demand the replacement of British by Indian rule. And the reader will want to know how it came about that the British are found in their paramount position in India. On the face of it, it is a strange thing that the inhabitants of an island in the Atlantic Ocean should be the dominant power in a country with three hundred and twenty million inhabitants five thousand miles away. How did this come about? How is it that the British ever came to exercise dominion over these millions of Indians? Until we know how and why this happened we cannot rightly judge how the Indian Nationalists' claims can be met.

One would naturally suppose that if the British now hold the dominant position they must have acquired it as the result of a definite design deliberately worked out. To accomplish so amazing a feat a plan must have been carefully thought out in the first instance and then worked out for years. The curious fact is that they had no such design. And the still stranger fact is that they tried *not* to have dominion. They went there as traders. Commerce, and not dominion, was their business. And they wanted to stick to their business. Dominion costs money. And they were out to make money and wished to avoid what would dissipate their gains. Hence their repugnance to dominion.

The dream of dominion did indeed flash momentarily through the brain of one or two Englishmen. Flushed with the victory of Plassey, Clive wrote to Pitt in 1759 and urged the sending out of such a force as would enable the East India Company "to embrace the first opportunity of aggrandising themselves." He believed the opportunity would soon offer and that a body of two thousand Europeans would enable the Company to take the sovereignty of Bengal upon themselves. So large a sovereignty might possibly be an object too extensive for a mercantile Company, and without the nation's assistance the Company would not be able "to maintain so wide a dominion." But he submitted to the consideration of Pitt "whether the execution of a design, that may hereafter be still carried to greater length, be worthy of Government's taking into hand." He thought there would be little or no difficulty in obtaining "the absolute possession of rich kingdoms," meaning Bengal and Behar; and he suggested that "it would be worth the nation's while to take the proper measures to secure such an acquisition."

But Pitt did not prove responsive. And some years later, in 1765, Clive himself writes: "If ideas of conquest were to be the rule of our conduct, I foresee that we should, by necessity, be led from acquisition to acquisition, until we had the whole empire (*i.e.*, of the Moghuls) up in arms against us. . . . Nothing, therefore, but extreme necessity ought to induce us to extend our ideas of territorial acquisitions beyond the amount of those ceded by Kasim Ali Khan." And those acquisitions consisted of only three districts of Bengal. Clive might indeed " stand astounded at his own moderation."

And the aversion from dominion was shared by the Government as well as by the East India Company and its great agent, Clive. The Government stated this in the clearest and most definite terms and in the most prominent fashion a century and a half ago. With all the prominence of a clause in an Act of Parliament it was laid down in 1784—rather ungrammatically it must be admitted—that "to pursue schemes of conquest and extension of dominion in India are measures repugnant to the wish, the honour, and policy of this nation."

Thus the British had no deliberate intention of establishing a dominion in India. They deliberately intended not to. How came it about that they did? And first: What brought them to India at all?

It needs no repeating that they came for trade. They came first more than three hundred years ago. As islanders they were dependent on maritime commerce for their prosperity. And as dwellers in the temperate zone they needed the products of the tropics—spices and cotton and so on. So the East India Company was formed in London with a Royal Charter. And they went to trade not in India only but in Southern Asia generally. And not only English but other Europeans, too, went out in ships for the rich trade of the East. Spaniards, Portuguese, Dutch, French also went.

The discovery of the way to the East by the Cape of Good Hope had stirred the adventurous in all these maritime nations to issue forth from Europe and profit by the lucrative trade of Asia. But from the start of our enquiry it should be noted that it was not only love of gain that drove them forth. It was love of adventure as well. They were venturous souls who went out on to the oceans of the world at that time. The prospects of gain were great. But gain alone would never have induced men to brave the hardship and risks of the voyage to India. For these men sailed the Atlantic and Indian Oceans in tiny ships of only seventy or eighty tons burden. With contrary winds they might take a year to reach India. And on the way they had to fear not only the storms of the Atlantic and the monsoons of the Indian Ocean, but attacks by pirates as well. The seas were infested with pirates. Bad food, no food, shortage of water, disease, cold and heat in extreme they had also to face. Not gain alone would have spurred man to traverse ten thousand miles of ocean and suffer all these hardships. Not gain only, but adventure—and adventure more than gain—drove the English to India in the stirring days of Queen Elizabeth.

And these adventurous traders arrived on the shores of India not as single individual merchants and not as mere pedlars. Small as their numbers were at first, they came as a company. They were organised. And they came under authority. They were sent out from the rich capital of England under a Royal Charter from Elizabeth. And they were armed. To defend themselves against the pirates on the way they had to be.

All this is true. Yet, obviously, aggression on India could not have suggested itself to them for a moment. For India then was ruled by the great Akbar. India was a mighty Empire. And their own distant island was not yet united under one Sovereign. Nor had it yet expanded beyond the seas. Aggression, conquest, dominion—such ideas could never have crossed the minds of these English traders of three centuries ago.

What they did want in India were facilities for regular, orderly trade—for exchanging the woollen goods and bullion which they brought out from England for the calicos and muslins and spices from India. And stable, favourable conditions they did find at first. Through the exertions of the English Ambassador at the court of the Great Moghul at Delhi they obtained a decree permitting them to establish a settlement at Surat, near Bombay. They were troubled by the rivalry of the Portuguese and the Dutch; for in those days each nationality tried to establish a monopoly. Where one got in, it tried to keep out all others. But, in the main, throughout the seventeenth century, they traded peacefully with the people of India. There was order in India and trade was possible.

This was only for a time however. For soon now the great fabric of the Moghul Empire was to break up. It was not an indigenous Empire. Under the broad-minded Akbar the Hindus were employed in the highest positions and the ruling family were encouraged to marry Hindus. But the Moghuls were conquerors from Central Asia. And they were Moslem by religion. They were Asiatic, but they were not Indian. And they were not of the religion of the mass of the people. And from now on there arose a Hindu revolt against the foreign Islamic rule. In the wild, hilly country far from the centre of power of the Moghuls the masterful Mahrattas rebelled against the Imperial authority. For that authority was not wielded by the liberal Akbar now, but by the bigoted Aurungzebe, who was fanatically opposed to Hinduism. He put forth his strength to quell this Hindu revolt. But at that distance and in that hilly country his efforts were in vain. And he exhausted the strength of the effort to no purpose. The Mahrattas grew in power while the Imperial authority waned. And on the death of Aurungzebe the Moghul Empire founded by Baber slowly began to break up. Especially on the outskirts did the dissolution become manifest. While the Mahrattas were establishing an independent power in Western India, the great Viceroys of the Empire were establishing themselves as hereditary rulers in the provinces they were ostensibly governing in the name of the Emperor. In Southern India the Viceroy set himself up as the Nizam of Hyderabad—and remains so to this day. On the eastern confines the Viceroy established himself as the Vazir of Oudh. While Bengal came into the hands of an Afghan adventurer. So did the Moghul Empire disintegrate.

And this breaking up of the Empire meant disorder in India generally. The reins of authority were everywhere loosened. There was no stability in the land. Men became a law unto themselves. Bands of raiders came into being. The Mahratta themselves issued from the western highlands and swept over the plains of India in swarms of irresistible horsemen. They surged up to Delhi itself. They even imprisoned the Emperor. They swept still further. They reached Lahore and set up a Mahratta Governor of the Punjab. Yet there was no political stability in their rule. They had it not in them to organise a firm instrument of authority. Their Brahmin Prime Minister—known as Peshwa—had established an hereditary Premiership at Poona and put the titular Mahratta Sovereign into the background. But they had not been able to maintain their authority over the distant generals. These with their mobile hordes of horsemen were practically independent of the central authority. They gradually settled down on the lands they had raided. Over these lands in Central and Western India they set themselves up as hereditary rulers. And so arose the great principalities of Gwalior, Indore, Nagpur, and Baroda, ruled over respectively by chiefs known as Scindia, Holkar, the Raja of Berar, and the Gaekwar of Baroda. But they not only resisted the authority of the Minister at Poona, they quarrelled among themselves and were incessantly attacking one another. And to add to the confusion the King of Afghanistan, as many of his predecessors had done before him, swept down from his mountain country on to the plains of India. He threw out the Mahratta Governor of Lahore, engaged and routed the Mahratta hosts before Delhi, reached the capital, and might have established another Mohammedan dynasty in India if his armies had not made up their minds to return to Afghanistan with their booty. All he had done was to make the confusion in India still greater.

So India became the battleground of warring chieftains. Upstarts were arising and seizing power. Undisciplined armies were sweeping over the land. No ruler was safe on his throne. No dynasty even was secure. And consequently the people had no security for their property or their lives. All India was in turmoil. There was neither stability, nor order, nor peace. The reign of law had ceased. Chaos prevailed.

Now these are not the conditions for trade. The English, the Portuguese, the Dutch, and the French had come to India to trade. But when the whole country round their settlements was in this disorder, when merchandise could not be transported with security, when the traders themselves and their settlements were liable to attack, they had to take the protection of themselves and their property into their own hands. And the Dutch first and then the English and French began to fortify their settlements, to enlist bodies of armed men, and to set up little self-governing and self-defending communities.

This driving of the European traders to form themselves into armed, self-governing communities was one result of the disorder following the break-up of the Moghul Empire. Another was war between these Europeans themselves. There was in India—or at any rate on the coasts of India, where alone the European settlements were placed—no Power strong enough to preserve the French settlement from attack by the English or the English settlement from attack by the French. Nor did any Power in India much care if the Europeans did fight among themselves. Consequently, when England and France were at war in Europe they would carry on their warfare on the soil of India. The English in Madras would attack the French in Pondicherry. And the French in

Pondicherry would attack the English in Madras; indeed, on one occasion they captured Madras, carried off the English Governor and bore him in triumph through the streets of Pondicherry.

All this necessitated the erection of forts, the increase of military strength, a firmer government of the settlement, and a closer attention to political situations. The French and English companies of traders could not devote themselves only to business. They had to engage in politics and take up arms. And their Governments in Europe had to see to it that the sea route to India was kept open to them. Sea power had to be maintained. The French could not permit the English to have dominance at sea, or the French settlements in India would be isolated and they would fall to the English. And for a like reason the English could not allow the French to be supreme on the Indian Ocean.

From the disorder in India and from the rivalry among themselves the French and English were thus driven to become Powers of consequence on the coast of India. The Portuguese remained there, but they were weak in Europe and consequently weak in India, and therefore were no serious rivals. And the Dutch had practically abandoned India and concentrated their energies on the rich islands of Java and the Malay Archipelago. So it came about that the chief rivalry was between the French and the English. And to be on their guard against each other they had to maintain themselves in strength.

This led to another situation in the mighty drama that was being played out—and played out so strangely without the actors in it knowing anything of the plot or possessing the faintest inkling of what the final dénouement would be. As the French or the English possessed some useful armed forces it would occur to some Indian chief struggling in their neighbourhood that the loan of an English or a French force would be helpful to him. He would therefore apply for the loan of a force on payment. And the French or the English Governor would gladly enough lend the force and be spared the expense of maintaining it. Also the French or the English company would hope that advantage might accrue to their trade through their having special influence with a neighbouring ruler.

This was the way in which that great Frenchman Dupleix gained so preponderating an influence for the French company in the first half of the eighteenth century that if the French had supported him better, had established a stronger sea power, and had been better governed at the centre, they might have set up that dominion in India which eventually came to the British.

Dupleix was a man of energy and genius. But commerce he cared not for. Conquest was his aim. Through armed intervention on the side of one of the several rivals for a throne he would build up French ascendancy in India. When the first Nizam of Hyderabad died, he threw himself on the side of one of the competitors for the throne, hoping thereby to secure a preponderating French influence with the new Nizam—the descendant of the Moghul Viceroy of Southern India who had formed a dynasty on the ruins of the Empire. The other competitor applied to the English for their assistance. And the English were obliged to grant it.

But the French succeeded in putting their protégé on the throne at Hyderabad, where the French general, Bussy, organised a complete *corps d'armée* under his own command, and obtained the assignment of four rich districts lying along the eastern coast for their support. Dupleix thus gained a strong position in India and would have liked to rid her altogether of the English.

The British were, however, not easily disposed of. In expectation of an attack by the French the English had commenced to fortify their settlement at Calcutta. This action gave them a serious setback, for they had no authority from the Indian ruler of Bengal to do this. And he took umbrage at the action. Also, he had been advised by his far-seeing predecessor to get rid of Europeans, as they were a danger to India, and to eject the English first, for they were the strongest. After he had turned out the English he could do likewise with the French at Chandernagore close by. He accordingly attacked the English in their fort, captured it, took the English prisoners, and crowded them up into a single room, now known as the Black Hole of Calcutta, from which only twenty-three out of one hundred and forty-six emerged alive. Calcutta was lost and with it all the other settlements in Bengal. The English were for the moment extirpated from at least that part of India. Yet that act of extirpation proved to be the very deed that led up to the foundation of British dominion. For the English in Madras, though they knew that a strong force was shortly leaving France to attack them, immediately sent ships of war and every available man to recapture Calcutta. The land forces were led by Clive, afterwards to become so famous. Calcutta was recaptured. The ruler of Bengal was made to sign a treaty agreeing to pay compensation for losses and to allow the English to build a fort. The English position was established, and established more strongly than ever. And further was to follow.

The ruler of Bengal—Suraj-ud-daula—was no descendant of a long line of kings native to the soil. Nor was he a Hindu. He was a Moslem. Bengal had for centuries been governed by alien rulers. And he was only the adopted son of that Afghan adventurer who had raised himself from a very humble position to become in 1742 the ruler of Bengal by the simple process of murdering his predecessor. Now the officers of Suraj-ud-daula were dissatisfied with their chief and called in the aid of Clive to oust him and put one Jaffir on the throne in his place. And as Suraj-ud-daula showed no signs of carrying out the treaty the English had made with him, Clive responded to the call, and in 1757, with one thousand Englishmen and two thousand Indian soldiers, defeated the forces of Suraj-ud-daula at Plassey and placed Mir Jaffir on the throne.

Clive did not *mean* to lay the foundation of dominion in India. For he told the new ruler that "for our parts we should not any ways interfere in the affairs of the Government, but leave that wholly to the Nawab; that as long as his affairs required it, we were ready to keep the field, after which we should return to Calcutta and attend solely to commerce, which was our proper sphere and our whole aim in these parts." He did not mean dominion. Nevertheless, dominion inevitably followed. The Battle of Plassey is now commonly accepted as the decisive event which led up eventually to British dominion in India.

For once having interfered it was impossible to draw back. It seemed so simple to Mir Jaffir to supplant a rival by means of the English. It seemed so simple to the English to replace an enemy by a friend by granting Mir Jaffir's request. And it seemed so simple to both that, having given that assistance, the English should retire to Calcutta and go on with their business of trading while Mir Jaffir should rule in peace. But human affairs are not so delightfully simple as that. And both Mir Jaffir and the English soon found themselves involved in a mesh of complications and intrigues and conspiracies.

Mir Jaffir had agreed to pay the English for their services and also to pay that money as compensation for the attack on Calcutta which his predecessor had failed to produce. Money for both these purposes he had to provide. Then he had to reckon with possible rivals within his state and attack from outside, so he had to maintain an army. And that army had to be paid. And for this, also, money was needed. But money Mir Jaffir did not easily find. Indian states are not the inexhaustible wells of wealth they are commonly imagined to be. They are often almost empty wells. And Mir Jaffir found his well was among the nearly empty. He was unable to meet his obligations. He could not pay the English in full. And he could not pay his army in full. And both were soon clamouring for payment.

The English on their side were wanting all the money they could find for re-establishing their settlements in Bengal and fortifying them against a possible French attack. And the Madras Governor was importunate for money to meet the expenses in which an attack by the French had involved him. He had most generously, and at great risk, sent the expedition to recover Calcutta. And now he had good right to expect Calcutta to help him in return.

On all sides the English at Calcutta were being pressed for money. They were on the verge of bankruptcy. And as Mir Jaffir would not pay what he owed them they thought they would better matters by removing him and setting up still another on the throne of Bengal. So they replaced him.

But even then they were no better. For more complications ensued. Their protégé was attacked both from the north and the west. And the English had to protect him or see all their work undone and they themselves driven back to the sea. Bengal was attacked by the Nawab of Oudh, who was one of those Viceroys of the Moghul Empire who had set up a dynasty in his province and ruled as a practically independent prince. It was raided, too, by those Mahratta chiefs who were now aspiring for the overlordship of India. And this situation had also to be met.

The position of the English in India was quivering in the balance. If they had failed to rise to the occasion they might never have become any more in India than the Portuguese. But they did not fail. They fought and won the Battle of Buxar,

1764. They utterly defeated the Nawab of Oudh. And this defeat had far-reaching consequences. For the English were now removed to a distance from the sea coast, and were in contact with the central heart of India. They had crossed the Ganges to the great cities of Benares and Allahabad. And the Nawab of Oudh, whom they had defeated, was the greatest of the Moslem rulers of India, and had in his camp, virtually as his prisoner, the Mogul himself. The English had undesignedly and unwillingly entered the very thick of the struggle for the tottering throne of India.

What were they to do now? They might have retired again to the sea coast, and left the ruler of Bengal to settle up as best he could with the Nawab of Oudh. But the former was too incompetent a ruler to stand by himself. And if the menace from Oudh had been averted there was still the menace of the Mahrattas. Complete withdrawal of the English was out of the question. Instead they took the course of securing Bengal from further attack from the direction of Oudh by making an alliance with the Nawab of Oudh, and by making of him a barrier against any other attack by Afghans or others from the north. At the same time, they made use of the opportunity to put their position in Bengal itself on a better footing. These two measures were taken by Clive as a result of the Battle of Buxar.

For Clive himself had again returned to India. Some urged that he should annex Oudh by right of conquest, and even that he should march with the Moghul to Delhi. And he himself saw that this was perfectly possible. At this very time he wrote :

"It is scarcely hyperbole to say that to-morrow the whole Moghul Empire is in our power. The inhabitants of the country have no attachment to any obligation; their forces are neither disciplined, commanded, nor paid as ours are. Can it then be doubted that a large army of Europeans would effectually preserve us as sovereigns, not only holding in awe the attempts of any country prince, but rendering us so truly formidable that no French, Dutch, or other enemy will presume to molest us?" But he decided otherwise. Rather would he maintain and strengthen Oudh as a friendly state. He would make of it a barrier and confine assistance, conquest, and possessions to Bengal, Behar, and Orissa. "To go further," he said, "is a scheme so extravagantly ambitious and absurd that no Governor and Council in their senses can adopt it, unless the whole system of the Company's interest be first entirely new re-modelled."

Clive therefore concluded a treaty with the Nawab of Oudh, by which the English were to assist him if attacked, and he was reciprocally to assist them. Beyond that he did not go.

But in regard to Bengal itself he made a crucial change. He obtained from the Moghul the right—known as the *diwani*—to collect the revenues of Bengal, Behar, and Orissa. In return for this right the Company were to pay the Moghul a sum of £260,000 per annum. The Company then became the Moghul's revenue agent for these provinces. And by Indian tradition this revenue collection carried with it a share of civil jurisdiction. The titular ruler was to remain, and the Company was to pay him a sufficient allowance for supporting the expenses of his household, his servants, and equipment, and for the "maintenance of such horses, sepoys, peons, etc., as may be thought necessary." But whatever remained of the revenue of Bengal after meeting these expenses was to belong to the Company, and they were to make their own arrangements for collecting the revenue.

An important stage on the way to dominion had now been reached. Not yet were the English exercising direct dominion, but they were collecting revenue and were the dominating influence in two great states—still nominally provinces of the nominal Emperor. This position, however, proved to be unsatisfactory. The English were not responsible rulers. They were merely revenue collectors. And not being restrained by any sense of responsibility they were arrogant and oppressive. The province yielded nothing like the revenue they expected. They came to the verge of bankruptcy. And so scandalous had the position become that the British Parliament determined to intervene. A commercial company could no longer be permitted to continue uncontrolled in the exercise of political functions of such moment. An Act of Parliament was accordingly passed, known as North's Regulating Act, by which the Company's affairs were to be regulated and placed under some supervision by Parliament. And Warren Hastings was appointed Governor of Bengal with a Council and a Court of Judicature.

Even so the position was not yet made wholly satisfactory. For both the British Government and the Company still regarded a province of India as something in the nature of a "property" or "estate"—as indeed the Indian rulers themselves did. They looked upon it as a property which brought in a handsome income and was therefore worth holding. And it was laid down by the new Act that the Company were to pay the British Government £400,000 a year. Not yet had men realised the extreme poverty of India. Their eyes —as most still are—were fascinated by the glamour of Indian Princes arrayed in priceless brocades and decked with jewellery of fabulous wealth. And they did not understand that this display was only made by the Princes taking to themselves an inordinately large percentage of the revenues of their states. To this day there is probably not a ruler in India who does not take as much as 7 per cent., while some take as much as 20 per cent., of the revenue for what is called Palace Expenditure. The state is—or was—looked upon rather as the personal property of the ruler, and he took to himself as much as he personally chose of the revenue it produced. At the end of the eighteenth century the British held much the same kind of view in regard to Bengal. And it was only as they found by experience—an experience pointed by the dreadful famine of 1770—that an Indian province was not the source of wealth that they had imagined that the payment to the British Government was dropped and more careful attention was given to the manner in which British dominion should be exercised. But upon this better method of government more will be said in the following chapter. Here it is only necessary to add that in Warren Hastings the British had lighted upon a genius, and that upon the foundations which Clive had laid he built up a system of government in Bengal, secured the province from external attack, established the reign of law, maintained internal peace and security, and did all this as far as possible in accordance with Indian customs and tradition. The succession of incompetent puppet rulers who had come temporarily to the front disappeared from the scene. They never had had any real claim upon the country. They were only the descendants of adventurers—not of any indigenous dynasty. And now their place was taken by British Governors. In Bengal, British dominion was established. The British had definitely become one of the Powers in India. Another step in the direction of supremacy had been taken.

But beyond Bengal the British did not then intend or even desire that their dominion should extend. For in a second and more comprehensive Act of Parliament regulating the affairs of the Company in India there was expressly inserted that clause already quoted that the extension of dominion in India was "repugnant to the wish, the honour, and policy of the nation." This was in 1784. But even then, though the rivalry of the French was not so acute for the moment, there was arising in India itself a danger which was to prove in the end the very stimulus for further dominion. It was the danger of the Mahrattas. The British had no desire to enter into competition with them for the vacant throne of the Moguls. They had expressly renounced that ambition. And they would willingly have left the Mahrattas alone. Indeed, if the Mahrattas had steadily built up a secure and stable government at Delhi, and established peace and order in India, both the Company and the British Government in those days would have been highly content. For then the British traders would have been able to pursue their business under satisfactory conditions. And nothing more did they want. But much as they would have liked to leave the Mahrattas alone, the Mahrattas would not be equally pacific. They were aggressive and dangerous, and they were given to using the French as an aid against the British.

Centrally situated in the heart of India, they could issue out and strike at Bengal, Madras, or Bombay. And through their seaports on the west they were in touch with the French, whose services were readily at their disposal against the British. Moreover, there was about them more of the characteristic of nationality than there was about any of the other Powers with whom the British had to reckon. The British never had to fight a Bengal "nation," or an Oudh "nation," or a Mogul "nation." And even the Mahrattas could hardly be spoken of as a nation. Still they were nearer to one than anyone else in India at that time. Their defect was that they were too loosely organised to be worthy of nationhood. They did not act with one mind and one will. They were a loose confederacy which was constantly breaking to pieces. The great hereditary generals—turned as they were into hereditary rulers also—did not always obey the hereditary Prime Minister of the non-existent Sovereign. Their states were, according to the standards of the times, well-managed by capable Brahmin officials. But they were managed as independent of one another; not as part of one united whole. These were the defects of the Mahrattas.

Yet even so they were most formidable foes to the British.

At Panipat they had received a severe set-back, for they had over-reached themselves in venturing into the Punjab. But when Warren Hastings was Governor of Bengal they were threatening all India south of the Punjab, harrying the lands of all the kingdoms just springing up, spreading terror everywhere, and exacting heavy contributions. Hyderabad and Mysore in the south had suffered from them. Through his alliance with the Nawab of Oudh Hastings was able to keep himself secure on that side. But on the Bombay side an incompetent Governor had tried to replace an ejected Mahratta chief at the head of the Mahratta Government, and had failed. The British had become involved in an intricate and unsatisfactory war with the whole Mahratta Power. And in 1776, when the United States of America had declared their independence and the British were engaged in a war with the Americans, the French sought to take advantage of the situation. They planned an expedition to India in support of the Mahrattas. In 1777, a French envoy arrived in India with proposals for an alliance with the Mahrattas on condition that they ceded to France a port on the west coast. And French officers and military stores were landed on the south coast for Hyder Ali, the adventurer who had usurped the throne of Mysore.

These proceedings roused Warren Hastings to energetic action. He promptly seized all the French settlements in India. But with the Mahrattas, and with Hyder Ali, he had very serious difficulty. They were most formidable enemies. Hyder Ali was incensed at the seizure of a French settlement on a seaport in what he considered his own territory. He came sweeping down almost to Madras itself. And the Mahrattas resisted the attempt to place the ejected chief on the throne, and severely defeated the British on the Bombay side. The Company's financial resources were almost exhausted. And if the Mahratta federation had been more firmly held together, the Mahrattas, in conjunction with the Nizam of Hyderabad and Hyder Ali, supported by the French fleet, which had also appeared upon the scene, might well have driven the British out of India. In the event, however, the British were able to capture Scindia's capital, and, by offering him favourable terms, secure his interest to end the war with the Mahrattas. And a treaty to this effect was concluded in 1782. At the same time the French fleet, which had succeeded in landing two thousand French troops, was driven off by the British fleet. And though Bussy arrived in 1783 with a large reinforcement of French infantry, the French and Tippu, the successor of Hyder Ali, were not able to effect much before France and England had made peace in Europe, and Tippu, finding himself alone, reluctantly also made peace with the British. By sheer toughness of fibre, Warren Hastings had saved British dominion in India at the moment of its greatest peril. Though even his exertion would have availed nothing if the British fleet had not been able to preserve communication by sea against all the maritime nations of the world arrayed against them. Neither the attacks from without, nor the attacks from within India had been able to expel the British. They had only served to arouse them to the more fixed consolidation of their dominion.

Still, the British had no desire to extend their dominion. After these exhausting efforts the Company naturally needed rest. Nothing less could they want than any extension of their responsibilities. And Lord Cornwallis came out in 1786, fully determined to avoid all war and entanglements. Yet even he was drawn into a war with Tippu Sultan of Mysore. Tippu had sent ambassadors to Constantinople, and to Paris, hoping to get French support, and had attacked the state of Travancore, which was under British protection. The British, with the Mahrattas and the Nizam, had in consequence to take up arms against him. And as a result of a year's campaign, half his territory, including the Malabar coast on the west of India, was taken from him. And when Lord Wellesley came to India in 1798, a still further extension of dominion was necessitated by the activities of both the French and the Mahrattas.

It cannot be said that Wellesley came out with the same stolid determination not to be drawn into a war or expansion of dominion that had characterised Cornwallis. Cornwallis was old and ill. Wellesley was young and never reluctant to fight. But it was the French, not the Indians, that he had in mind when he thought of fight. England was fighting for her life with France. This was no time to think of extending British dominion in India. The French had to be fought there and all over the world. The Indians were an altogether secondary consideration.

The first intelligence Wellesley received on his

arrival in India was that Tippu Sultan had formed an alliance with the French at Mauritius for the purpose of attacking the British. In accordance with this plan a body of Frenchmen had landed on the west coast and marched to Tippu's capital. A little later came news that Napoleon had landed with a large army in Egypt, taken possession of the country, and formed the intention of invading India. And the French position in India was strengthened through Bussy having at Hyderabad a corps of about fourteen thousand men trained, disciplined, and commanded by French officers, who held a considerable portion of the Nizam's territories for the payment of their troops, and exerted a dominant influence in the state. Further, Scindia, who had now become head of the Mahratta confederation, also had a force raised, disciplined, and commanded by French officers. And his policy was rather to support Tippu than the British in any struggle between them. Lastly, an invasion of Oudh by the King of Afghanistan was expected and had to be provided against.

At that time the Battle of the Nile had not yet been fought. The star of Napoleon was in the ascendant. The danger was imminent. Until the power of the French in India was broken, the British could have no peace. Wellesley recognised this from the start and instantly took his measures. He negotiated with the Nizam of Hyderabad a treaty by which a British force was to take the place of the French force which was such a danger. And he made such skilful secret concentration of British forces that the change was made without bloodshed, and has been in operation ever since. He then turned his attention to Mysore. He got both the Peshwa and the Nizam to join with the British in a campaign against Tippu. The result was that Tippu was defeated and killed in the assault on his capital. The Mohammedan dynasty which his father had founded was brought to an end. Over the central portion of Mysore, the ancient Hindu dynasty was restored. One portion of the remainder was allotted to the Nizam, and another portion to the British. And the settlement then made in 1799 remains to this day.

The more serious part of the French danger had now been disposed of, though it might recur at any time, for Napoleon was still unconquered, and still held dreams of world-dominion. But over all Southern and Eastern India British ascendancy was now firmly established and a complete command of the sea coast had been won.

In the west, however, was still a danger. The Mahrattas still threatened the security of British dominion. And Wellesley had to take measures to protect himself against the danger. The Mahratta Power was a loose confederation of chiefs frequently at war with one another, but nominally under the leadership of the Peshwa at Poona—the Peshwa being the hereditary Prime Minister of a nominal chief. This confederation Wellesley sought to break up by making separate treaties with each member. The Peshwa at first refused all overtures. But when he was attacked and defeated by Holkar, whose brother he had executed, he had to fly to the British for protection, and he then signed a treaty of general defensive alliance with them, whereby a strong subsidiary force was to be permanently stationed in his territory and paid for by him and his foreign relations were to be left in the hands of the British.

But as this meant the loss of independence for the nominal head of the Mahratta Power, the Mahratta chiefs quickly resented it, and the Chief of Nagpur proceeded to organise a league against the British. He was not fully successful, for Holkar refused to join. And the Gaekwar kept apart. But Scindia and Nagpur marched towards the frontier of Hyderabad. They were asked for an explanation of their intentions. No explanations being forthcoming and it being urgent to act before they had time to induce Holkar to join them, and before the French could aid them, forces under Generals Arthur Wellesley and Lake marched against Scindia. At the Battle of Assaye (1803) General Wellesley (afterwards the Duke of Wellington) gained a decisive victory though Scindia's troops fought fiercely, and the French-led battalions made a resolute stand. Marching on he inflicted a similar defeat on the Raja of Nagpur. And Lake had been equally successful. He captured Agra and Delhi, broke up the last of Scindia's force, and took charge of the person of the Mogul Emperor.

As a result of this war, the dominant position of the British at Poona, the Mahratta capital, was formally recognised, Scindia ceded to the British his northern districts lying on both sides of the Jumna and his seaports and districts on the west coast; he made over the City of Delhi and the custody of the Emperor; he dismissed all his French officers and he accepted the establishment, at his cost, of a large British force to be stationed near his frontier. And the Raja of Nagpur restored Berar to the Nizam, and surrendered the province of Cuttack, on the Bay of Bengal. From all the states in India French officers had now been removed, and in place of foreign drilled battalions there were substituted British-led troops. And now the British were without question the dominant Power in India.

Nevertheless, the Mahratta Power was not even yet finally broken. On the departure of Lord Wellesley a lull ensued. His activities had alarmed the authorities in England. And his successor, Lord Minto, came out with strict injunctions to make no further accessions of territory. And these injunctions he strove to follow, though even so he had to send an expedition to Java against the Dutch, and missions to Afghanistan and Persia. For Napoleon, in 1808, had concluded the Treaty of Tilsit with the Russians, and Lord Minto averred that "the advance of a considerable force of French troops into Persia under the acquiescence of the Turkish, Russian, and Persian Powers cannot be deemed an undertaking beyond the scope of that energy and perseverance which distinguish the present ruler of France."

Lord Hastings, who followed Lord Minto, had disapproved of Lord Wellesley's procedure and thought his measures high handed and his wars unnecessary. He came out to India resolved to maintain the traditional intentions of the British Government and avoid all wars. Yet he also was soon involved in war—first against the Gurkhas of Nepal, who had invaded British territory in the plains below their mountain kingdom; and secondly, with the Mahrattas. And this last was definitely to settle the question of ascendancy in India.

What led to this final war with the Mahrattas was this time not any fear of French interference: the French danger had been disposed of with the Battle of Waterloo. It was, firstly, the raids of swarms of Pindaris who issued from the heart of the Mahratta country; and secondly, the revival of the Mahratta confederacy.

The Pindaris were simply freebooters numbering in all about thirty thousand men. They would move about in bodies of from one to four thousand, carrying nothing but their arms, and living on the country. And being wholly unencumbered by baggage and capable of enduring extraordinary fatigue they would make long and arduous marches. But they were out to plunder, not to fight. They would carry off everything of value. And what they could not take away they would wantonly destroy. And the inhabitants they would treat with atrocious cruelty, so that villagers were known to burn themselves and their village rather than fall into their hands, so great was the terror they inspired.

These wild freebooters came from Mahratta territory, and the Company's Directors in England had issued orders "against adopting any measures against these predatory associations which might embroil us with Sindhia." But the raids had become so serious that action had to be taken. In a raid in 1816 they were eleven days in the Company's territories, and had plundered 339 villages, killed 182 persons, wounded 505, and tortured 3,603. No Government could allow such raids to continue, and Lord Hastings saw that they must be suppressed. He realised that any measures for extirpating the Pindaris would involve the British in hostilities with Scindia and Holkar, who regarded these freebooters as their dependents. But he felt that that risk must be taken. In his own words, "the suppression of a powerful body, professedly banded for the purpose of indiscriminate plunder, and which accompanied its régime with acts of the most atrocious inhumanity, was in itself an enterprise becoming a British Government." He therefore informed Scindia of his intention and Scindia agreed to join in the extirpation, though he hoped that he might be allowed to occupy the lands from which the Pindaris were driven.

Meanwhile, Hastings had obtained "complete proof of the extensive and desperate treachery of the Peshwa." "It appears," he writes, "that he was soliciting Sindhia, Holkar, Amir Khan, the Gaekwar, the Raja of Nagpur, and the Nizam, to join with him and drive the English out of India." Hastings made the Peshwa aware that he knew what was taking place, that troops were being secretly enrolled, and that a considerable number was being assembled. The Peshwa absolutely denied this, but he redoubled his activity in levying troops and putting his fortresses in a state of defence. Thereupon, in April, 1817, British troops were quietly moved from convergent directions to positions within striking distance of Poona, and the Peshwa was given twenty-four hours to decide whether he would deliver up three fortresses as guarantee of his good faith or face war. He allowed this term to elapse. The British appeared before

Poona, and the Peshwa submitted and handed over the fortresses.

This was, however, by no means the end of the Peshwa, or of the Mahratta struggle with the British. While the operations against the Pindaris were in progress the Peshwa attacked the British Residency in Poona, and the Raja of Nagpur attacked the British Residency there. Holkar marched to the assistance of the Peshwa; and Scindia, though he did not actually oppose the British, had agents with Holkar, Amir Khan (the Chief of the Pindaris), the Gaekwar of Baroda, the Raja of Nagpur, and the Nizam of Hyderabad, soliciting them to join with him in opposition to the British. In the event, the attacks on the Residencies were repulsed, Holkar's army was defeated, the Pindaris were dispersed, and the Peshwa himself pursued till he surrendered. So the most serious rivals the British had encountered in India were finally disposed of and the way was now clear for a settlement clearly acknowledging British supremacy.

And this settlement would be not only with the Mahratta Chiefs, but with the Rajputs and others who were anxious for British protection. "The unfortunate Rajput States of Jaipur, Jodhpur, and Udaipur, mercilessly wasted by Sindhia, Holkar, Amir Khan, and the Pindaris, have assailed me with repeated petitions to take them under protection as feudatories to the British Government," wrote Lord Hastings. So in the final settlement which he now made these requests were also taken into consideration.

It was obvious that the existing Peshwa must be deposed. The question was whether one of the family should be placed on the throne in his place, or whether a stranger should be brought in, or whether his territories should be annexed. Lord Hastings decided on annexation. He had "full and most serious proof that no distinctness of obligation will prevent a Peshwa from secretly claiming the allegiances of other Mahratta sovereigns." There must then, he concluded, be no Peshwa. And resort to a stranger would irritate the lower classes and arouse the antipathy of the greater vassals. Whereas the inhabitants were well aware of the comfort and security of British subjects in the adjoining British territory. The Peshwa's territories were accordingly annexed, while he himself was given a pension and a residence near Cawnpore, where his adopted son, known as the Nana Sahib, during the Indian Mutiny of 1857 played such a sinister part.

Scindia, though he had not directly helped the British in extirpating the Pindaris, had not actively opposed them. No change, therefore, was made in regard to him. Holkar having opposed the British, lands were taken from him to defray the cost of the troops it would be necessary to maintain in his territories to ensure that he did not again attack them. As the Raja of Nagpur had also attacked the British, certain districts of his were annexed that the British might "maintain in them an advanced force as a permanent curb" upon him.

The Nawab of Bhopal had supplied the British forces with provisions and contributed eight hundred horses. He was therefore taken under British protection. So also were Kotah, Bundi, and Kerauli, three very ancient Rajput states. And with the chief Rajput states of Udaipur, Jaipur, and Jodhpur treaties were made by which they were accorded protection and undertook to "act in subordinate co-operation with the British Government and acknowledge its supremacy," though each ruler was to remain "absolute ruler of his own country, and the British jurisdiction shall not be introduced into the principality."

The French danger had been definitely disposed of. All Southern India had been settled by Lord Wellesley. And now by this great settlement Lord Hastings had secured all Central India and Rajputana. And both settlements remain to this day. They have endured for a century.

Further north the British had no desire to interfere. In that quarter the country was governed by a strong and wise ruler, who had the sense to keep on good terms with the British. This was Ranjit Singh, one who, in the manner of the times, had risen from obscurity to make himself head of the Sikh community. And with his powerful army of warlike Sikhs he was precisely the kind of neighbour the British liked to have on their frontier. For he made no aggression on them, while he served as a buffer against those incursions from Afghanistan to which India is periodically subject. But on his death, in 1839, there was the usual scramble for the throne and this desirable state of things came to an end. His reputed son was murdered. Mutinies occurred among the fierce soldiery. They were incited to cross the Sutlej River and attack the British. And it was only with extreme difficulty and with considerable loss that the British were eventually able to thrust them back and occupy

Lahore, the capital. Ranjit's infant son, Dhulip Singh, was then placed on the throne, the Sikh army was reduced, certain territory was annexed, and for a few years the country was administered under the general superintendence and protection of the British. But the settlement did not last. In 1848 the Sikhs broke into revolt. Desperate fighting followed—perhaps the severest the British ever had in India. And when, in 1849, the Sikhs were finally defeated it was decided to annex the Punjab to the British Crown.

And with the annexation of the Punjab, British dominion in India was complete; it extended from the sea coast to the Himalaya and the mountains of Afghanistan. The whole of the Indian peninsula was now under the supremacy of the British. And India became a political unit.

My readers will have found it difficult to follow this very complicated story—hard as I have struggled to simplify it. But at least they may have satisfied themselves that the British dominion was not the working out of a set design. A Napoleon may have dreamed of conquering India. But a stolid London trading company never did. And at a time of sailing ships, and when ships had to sail round the Cape, and when Great Britain was at war with America first and then with France, she could never have deliberately meant to achieve supremacy in India.

How then did it come about? It came about from one perfectly simple and intelligible cause. British dominion in India came about from the inherent necessity there is in things to work for order. And because the British stood for security and order they were never opposed by India as a whole. As long as there was an India which could be called a whole there was order and there was no need for the British to set up dominion. It was only when India was no longer a whole, only when it was disrupted into parts, and there was no semblance of order, stability, or security, that the British under the necessity of things stepped in and set up order and brought security. And then, as the British showed themselves able and willing to maintain order and afford security, Indians themselves rallied to them. And it was always with the aid of Indians that the British went forward. The great mass of Indians felt that the British were only doing what they would like to—but for the moment could not—do for themselves and readily worked with the British. Always in the Army and in the civil administration Indians were employed. There are twice as many Indians as British in the Army in India. And except for the higher posts the civil administration is completely manned by them. Besides which a third of India is still governed by Indian rulers. British dominion was established in the main with the assent of the people of India. They, like the British, wanted order, peace, and security.

So what drove the British forward was the need for security. They wanted trade. And they could not have trade unless they had security. And if the Indian Powers could not give them security they must provide it for themselves. And if Indian rulers could not protect them against their European rivals then they must provide their own protection.

And to this day the same need for security is urging them on—and, as before, sorely against their will. No possible material advantage is to be gained from pressing forward into the hilly country on the North-West Frontier bordering Afghanistan. Yet the British are running roads into it and at great cost establishing garrisons. Here as elsewhere, and as always, the need for security presses them forward.

Thus the call for order is the ultimate compelling cause of British dominion. It is in answer to that call that the British had to take the seat of authority. That is why there is a foreign rule in India to-day. And if it had not been British it would have been French or Dutch—whether to the better advantage of India or no it is not for an Englishman to say, though it is permissible for him to suggest that if the Indians had had any strong preference for the French they would have shown it more unmistakably when the French and British were struggling for supremacy.

CHAPTER V

BENEFICIAL GOVERNMENT

How it happened that Indians came under alien rule, and how that alien rule happened to be British, has been shown in the preceding chapter. We have there seen that when the Moghul Empire broke up India was in such disorder, so split up into warring principalities, so at the mercy of upstart adventurers, so overrun by predatory hordes, that from sheer necessity it had to come under the dominion of either the Dutch, the French, or the British. And we have seen that it was directly against their wishes, their intentions, and, as they then saw it, even their interests that the British first undertook dominion. It was only the pressure of necessity—the necessity of gaining security for their trade—and the presence of rivals who would oust them if they did not look after themselves, that forced the English trading company to go outside its legitimate business and concern itself in political and military affairs.

In the present chapter we shall see that the British, though their primary object in intervening in Indian affairs was to establish and maintain order, and thereby provide security for their trade, did from the first feel a keen responsibility for doing something more than the mere preservation of order. They might, after the manner of the Chinese in Turkestan, have just set up garrisons in forts alongside the principal towns and then left the Indians pretty much to their own devices, neither helping nor hindering them. But we shall now see that the British felt it their duty not only to preserve order but to promote good government for the people—not only to garrison and police the country but to interest themselves in the welfare of the Indians, and to further it according to their lights and to the best of their ability.

A trading company and nothing more were the British when the necessities of the situation thrust the duty of government upon them. And being traders the Company's servants in India had no experience in the art of government. They had no traditions to bind them or examples to guide them. And they were not under parliamentary control. Consequently, their first crude efforts at government were full of errors. And their difficulties were all the greater because their powers were uncertain. They had the right—derived from the nominal Moghul Emperor—to collect the revenue of Bengal, but the ordinary administration was in the hands of an Indian ruler. And that ruler was only the incompetent son of an Afghan adventurer who had seized the throne of Bengal on the weakening of the central authority at Delhi.

So it is not surprising that many complaints of the Company's servants were received by the British Government in London. According to the complainants, Rajas and landholders had been unjustly deprived of their lands, jurisdictions, and privileges: and the tribute, rents, and services which they were required to pay or perform had become grievous and oppressive. The British Government thereupon took notice of the position. It recognised that the proceedings of a trading company must be taken under some kind of control. And by Pitt's India Act of 1784, it laid down that "the principle of justice and the honour of this country require that such complaints should be forthwith enquired into and fully investigated, and if founded in truth effectively redressed." The Company were directed "to give orders to the several Governments and Presidencies in India for effectually redressing in such manner as shall be consistent with justice and the laws and customs of the country, all injuries and wrongs which the Rajas, zemindars, and other native landholders may have sustained, and for the settling, upon principles of moderation and justice, according to the laws and constitution of India, the permanent rules by which these tributes, rents, and services shall be in future rendered and paid to the Company."

Thus early was the desire for "good government" shown by the British. And good government was the passion of the first Governor of Bengal—Warren Hastings. And government to be good for India must be on Indian lines he had the wisdom to see.

He had a hard task. For when he took over the government "every region of Hindustan groaned under different degrees of oppression, desolation, and insecurity"—he wrote to the Directors. And while he had to govern well, he had also to remember that he was the servant of a trading company who looked to their dividends. He soon realised that if these two things were to be combined, the existing plan by which the British collected the revenue and the Nawab conducted the administration must come to an end. Even for the sake of increased revenue he must set up a just and efficient system of government. And he gradually took over the whole administration of Bengal and made it his aim to "relieve the ryots (peasant cultivators) from excessive taxes"; and "to introduce a regular system of justice and protection into the country." And to achieve this aim he planned and executed a new settlement of the amount which the cultivators should pay in land revenue; and he planned and established new courts of justice.

The land revenue settlement was the more immediately important. He fixed it for five years. (Presumably it had before then been fixed annually.) He had the amount assessed by careful inspection on the spot. He had the peasant cultivators provided with written contracts so that they knew what they would have to pay and would be protected against excessive demands. At the same time he had the chief revenue officials paid highly, and he forbade them to engage in trade. A start was thus made in the direction of giving the peasant cultivators security against undue exactions and of ensuring that the demand for revenue was reasonable. The principle was recognised that moderation of demand would lead to greater prosperity of the peasants. And a prosperous peasantry would mean better trade. Hastings also aimed at rendering "the access to Justice as easy as possible." He therefore established two superior courts, one for the decision of civil cases and the other for trial of criminal cases. And to "render the distribution of justice equal in every part of the province" he set up similar or inferior courts for each separate district. At this distance of time these measures appear very commonplace. But in the condition India then was, they were regarded as the greatest boon. Especially was this so as Hastings planned all his actions to be in accordance with the customs and traditions of the people. And, with this end in view, he, at his own expense, engaged ten learned Brahmins to prepare a code of Hindu law.

To educate the people was another aim of Hastings, and, again at his own expense, he instituted an academy "for the study of the different branches of the sciences taught in the Mohammedan schools." "This academy," he remarked, "is almost the only complete establishment of the kind now existing in India, although they were once in universal use, and the decayed remains of these schools are yet to be seen in every capital, town, and city of Hindustan and Deccan"—a significant indication of the decadent state into which India had fallen when the British first intervened.

From this time on immense and particular attention has been paid to the assessment of the amount of revenue which the owners or cultivators of the land should pay, and to the methods of payment. Lord Cornwallis, at the end of the eighteenth century, carried out the Permanent Settlement of Bengal. Whereas by custom the landholders were only tenants of the State—farmers for a lease of a certain number of years—he made them rightful owners of the land. He believed that where the landlord had a permanent property in the soil it would be worth his while to improve that property; and that this was the most effectual mode for promoting the general improvement of the country. But these views of Lord Cornwallis have not been held by others. The land in India was always considered to be the property of Government. And it has been found wiser to retain it as such so that the Government—that is the community—should have the advantage of the increased value of the land which has been brought about by the efforts of the community—by the establishment of order, the increase of trade, construction of roads, railways, canals, and other improvements. But in order that the landholder or peasant proprietor should have reasonable security of tenure it was found by successive Governors-General better, while retaining the land as the property of Government, to fix for a definite term of years—fifteen, or twenty, or thirty, according to circumstances—the amount of revenue he should have to pay and to give him the assurance that as long as he paid it he would not be dispossessed. Further, when at the close of the fifteen or twenty years the amount for the next period was to be fixed, he would still be allowed to remain in possession. Disputes would naturally arise between the landholder and the Government as to what was an equitable assessment. But the general principle was to give the landholder confidence and at the same time to secure to the community the advantage accruing from the general improvement which resulted from orderly and efficient administration. The man on the land was to be secured the fruits of his efforts. And the community, through the Government, were to reap the fruits of their own.

To ensure that the various Acts of Parliament

were given due effect to a Select Committee of the House of Commons was appointed from time to time to make enquiry and report. A Committee so appointed in 1812 recorded "the unremitting anxiety of those to whom the Government of our Indian possessions has been composed, to establish a system of administration best calculated to promote the confidence and conciliate the feelings of the native inhabitants." And this was done "not less by a respect for their own institutions, than by the endeavour gradually to engraft upon them such improvements as might shield, under safeguard of equal laws, every class of people from the oppressions of power, and communicate to them that sense of protection and assurance of justice which is the efficient spring of all public prosperity and happiness."

The Committee allowed that there were imperfections in the system of government, but expressed the opinion that "the dominion exercised by the East India Company has on the whole been beneficial to the natives." The latter were secure "as well from foreign depredation as from internal commotion . . . an advantage rarely experienced by the subjects of Asiatic States." And this, "combined with a domestic administration more just in its principles, and exercised with far greater integrity and ability than the native one that preceded it, may sufficiently account for the improvements that have taken place." In the political and military branches of the public service the prospects of the natives were limited by the nature and circumstances of the situation. Even under the Moghul Government "they were foreigners who generally enjoyed the great offices in those departments." But to agriculture and commerce "every encouragement is afforded under a system of laws, the prominent object of which is to protect the weak from oppression, and to secure to every individual the fruits of his industry."

Twenty years later a like Committee of the House of Commons in their report to Parliament had asserted that "it is recognised as an indisputable principle that the interests of the Native Subjects are to be consulted in preference to those of Europeans, whenever the two come in competition: and that therefore the Laws ought to be adapted rather to the feelings and habits of the natives than to those of Europeans." The Committee found that at that time the natives were only employed "in subordinate situations in the Revenue, Judicial, and Military Departments." But they were said to be "sufficiently observant of the practical merits and defects of our system; and to be alive to the grievance of being excluded from a larger share in the Executive Government." "And," the report continued, "it is amply borne out by the evidence that such exclusion is not warranted on the score of incapacity for business, or want of application, or trustworthiness, while it is contended that their admission, under European control, into the higher offices . . . would strengthen their attachment to British dominion; would conduce to a better Administration of Justice; and would be productive of a great saving in the expenses of the Indian Government."

With this report before them, Parliament, by the India Act of 1833, made the exceedingly important enactment that "No Native of the said Territories, nor any natural-born Subject of His Majesty resident therein, shall, by reason only of his religion, place of birth, descent, colour, or any of them, be disabled from holding any Place, Office, or Employment under the said Company." And this is commonly regarded as one of the three great pronouncements which have served as guiding signs in the development of British policy in India.

And all this time the education of the people of India had been receiving attention. At first this was due entirely to the personal initiative and at the personal expense of Warren Hastings, and to the devotion of the great missionary, Carey. But the British Government also soon took the matter up—and long before there was any State education in England itself. As far back as 1813 it was enacted by Parliament that after all military, civil, and commercial establishments had been provided for, "a sum of not less than one lac of rupees (£10,000) in each year shall be set apart and applied to the revival and improvement of literature, and the encouragement of the learned natives of India, and for the introduction and promotion of a knowledge of science among the inhabitants of the British territories in India."

Nowadays this seems but a humble beginning. Still it was a beginning. And attention to education was all the more necessary because, as Mountstuart Elphinstone, the distinguished servant of the Company, afterwards observed, the British had "dried up the fountains of native talent." And from the nature of their conquest not only was "all encouragement to the advancement of knowledge withdrawn," but even the actual learning of the nation was likely to be lost and the productions of former genius to be forgotten."

A beginning had been made. But the progress of education was, according to Lord Dalhousie, "languid and inconsiderable" till an experiment was made in the North-West Province of Agra and a Government school was established in every sub-district in eight districts of that province. And this measure had been attended with such signal success that in 1853 the Government of India recommended that the system of vernacular education should be extended to the whole of the North-West Province, and that similar measures should be adopted in the lower provinces of Bengal and in the Punjab. About the same period the Hindu College and the Madrissa in Calcutta were revised and improved, and a Presidency College open to all classes of the community and furnishing a higher class of education, especially English education, to the youth of Bengal was established.

These proposals from India were whole-heartedly accepted by the Court of Directors in England. The home authorities went even further. In the famous education dispatch of 1854 they formulated a scheme of education for all India "far wider and more comprehensive than the local or the Supreme Governments could ever have ventured to suggest." According to Dalhousie—"It left nothing to be desired." Vernacular schools throughout the districts, Government colleges of a higher grade, and a University in each of the three Presidencies of India were the main features of this great plan. The bestowal of grants-in-aid (conditional on

Governmental inspection) to all educational institutions was also sanctioned. And female education was to be encouraged.

The East India Company, acting under the increasing supervision and control of the British Parliament, had from the first tried to do something more than only preserve order in the territories over which it exercised dominion. It had striven to better the condition of the people, to secure them in their rights, and latterly to educate them. And when Queen Victoria, in 1858, definitely assumed sovereignty over India, she issued a Proclamation in which she stated that it was her will that "so far as may be, Our subjects of whatever race or creed, be freely and impartially admitted to offices in Our service, the duties of which they may be qualified, by their education, ability, and integrity, duly to discharge."

In accordance with this Proclamation and with the Act of 1833, Indians have been more and more associated with the British in the government and administration of India till now they are found in all but the highest positions. The Viceroy is British and the Governors of Provinces are British. But there has already been one Indian Governor of a Province. Out of the seven members of the Viceroy's Executive Council generally three are Indians. Of the Executive Councils of the Governors half the members are Indian. In the Civil Service, which controls the administration, there were on January 1, 1929, 367 Indians to 894 Europeans, and it is calculated that by 1939 half of the service would be Indian and half European. In the Police Service, by 1949, the personnel will be half Indian and half European. In the Indian Irrigation Service there were 240 Indians and 255 Europeans on January 1, 1929; and ten years later it is estimated that there would be 270 Indians and 229 Europeans. And in the Forest Service and the Educational Service the same process of "Indianisation," but at a faster rate, is in progress. And these figures cover only the highest branches of the administration. There are other grades with a far more numerous personnel which are practically entirely Indian. Then in the general administration there are 5,500 Indians and only 630 Europeans. In the Engineering Department there are 7,500 Indians and 500 Europeans. And in the Judiciary from the High Courts down to the lowest grade of judges there are only 230 Europeans out of 2,500.

Indians have always been associated with the British in the administration. And the rate of association has been rapidly increasing and Indians have been rising to higher and higher posts. In the next chapter we shall see how they have at the same time been welcomed to the Legislative Councils that they may have a larger share in making the laws under which they have to live. But before closing the present chapter a few salient features of the India of to-day may be given.

The poverty of India has rightly been stressed lately, both by the Simon Commission and by the Indians themselves. India is a poor country—not the country of fabulous wealth it is commonly imagined to be. The most optimistic estimate available for the Commission put the average income per head at less than £8, while the corresponding figure for Great Britain was £95. And a sadly large proportion of the population live on the brink of starvation, and from year's end to year's end never have a really full and sufficient meal. The poverty of India needs all the emphasis that can be laid on it and the first attention of statesmen. Those who have seen India in a famine will always insist on that.

India is poor. What is not true is that India has become poorer. The lowest estimate of the income per head obtained by the Simon Commission for 1921-22 was £5 11s. But in 1901-2 it was £2. And letting alone these estimates, which at the best cannot be very accurate, there are signs open for anyone to see. The people travel more, and by bus and motor car as well as by train. More of them go on pilgrimages at the great festivals. Even the poorest classes can afford this. A rise in the standard of living is shown in the way they can now afford to smoke cigarettes, drink mineral waters, buy kerosene oil, and indulge in other simple luxuries. There is also an increase in the Savings Banks' deposits and in the membership of co-operative societies. They clothe themselves better, too, and metal cups, plates, and cooking utensils, better and cheaper than in former times, are found in their homes. Slowly, but quite evidently, the material lot of the poorest is improving.

And the population is increasing—another sure sign of material progress. In 1921 it was 318,942,000, of which 247 millions was included in British India and 72 millions in Indian States. And this is an increase of 53·8 millions in fifty years—exclusive of 43·3 millions due to inclusion of new areas. The population of India has increased by 20·1 per cent. in half a century.

India's trade also has steadily increased. Fifty years ago her exports were valued at 60 million rupees. In 1925 they had almost reached 4,000 millions. And her imports in the same time had risen from 40 millions to 3,000 millions. In 1913 India ranked sixth among the trading nations of the world. By 1925 she had risen to the fifth place.

These facts show an upward and not a downward trend in India's material prosperity. India is getting richer, not poorer—at any rate in this world's goods. Whether she has progressed spiritually is another matter and will be considered later.

Of this increased prosperity the main contributing cause is undoubtedly peace. For seventy years there has been unbroken peace in India itself. If India had been for the last twenty years in the state of civil war that China has suffered from, there would have been none of this prosperity. It has been on the foundation of peace that prosperity has been built up and that the other contributory causes have been able to have full play.

Of these perhaps the most important is improved communications—and especially railways. Because of the railways and roads, cultivators have been able to market their surplus produce and in times of famine receive relief. And in railway construction there has been a great development. In 1872 there were only 5,300 miles of railways, whereas in March, 1929, there were 40,940 in operation and 3,225 more under construction. "It is this improvement in communications," says the Linlithgow Report on Agriculture, "that, more than any other factor, has brought about the change from subsistence farming to the growing of money crops such as cotton, jute, and ground nuts." And the Report goes on to show how good communications react upon every aspect of the cultivator's life. "For the closer connection which they create between the villages and towns stimulates the villagers to demand a higher standard of education as part of a higher general standard of living. Villagers are able to travel and broaden their outlook on life."

And lately another factor has come in tending in the same direction. Motor traffic has expanded rapidly. So rapidly, in fact, that the road construction is greatly behind the needs of the times. While there are 41,000 miles of railways in India there are only 59,000 miles of surfaced roads, and it has been necessary to appoint a Road Development Committee to survey the problem.

Irrigation works have also contributed greatly to the welfare of the country. India is blessed by nature with a great reservoir in the snows of the Himalaya. Through their melting in the hot weather at the very time of year when water is most needed in the parched up plains of Hindustan, the opportunity is afforded for irrigation projects on a great scale. In Southern India, which cannot be reached by the rivers from the Himalaya, immense dams are constructed. Altogether no less than 27·5 million acres are under irrigation by Government works. The length of main and branch canals and distributaries amounts to the huge total of 67,000 miles. And the total capital outlay on irrigation and navigation canals amounted at the end of the year 1927-28 to £87,500,000.

One further contributing cause to the growing prosperity of the agricultural population—and 74 per cent. of the population of India is engaged in agriculture—is the help afforded by the Agricultural Department. By demonstration and by propaganda the Department has brought home to the cultivators the value of better seeds and better methods of cultivation and better implements.

All these and other causes have helped to improve the lot of the agriculturist. But the outlook of the peasant himself has still to be improved. And the Agricultural Commission was of opinion that "no substantial improvement in agriculture can be effected unless the cultivator has the will to achieve a better standard of living and the capacity, in terms of mental equipment and of physical health, to take advantage of the opportunities which science, wise laws, and good administration may place at his disposal." This demand for a better life can be stimulated only by a deliberate and concerted effort to improve the general condition of the countryside. And the responsibility of initiating the steps required to effect the improvement, the Commission say, rests with Government, though success on a large scale can be rendered permanent only if the sympathy, the interest, and active support of the general public can be enlisted.

And India is not *only* agricultural. She claims to be regarded as one of the eight states of chief industrial importance in the world. In the jute industry India leads the world, because jute is grown in India alone. The size of her cotton industry is surpassed by only four other countries. She also possesses important steel and iron works, mills and foundries, dockyards, paper-mills, and match factories. At the time of the last census, 1921, nearly sixteen million persons were engaged in industrial pursuits, nearly two million in transport, and over a quarter of a million in mining. And the value of manufactured articles exported from India during the year ending March 31, 1928, was over £60,000,000.

So much for the material progress that has been made. The intellectual progress still has vast vistas before it. Only 18·6 millions are literate and 229 millions remain illiterate in British India. The people are bound by iron tradition and long custom. Distances are great. Communications not yet what they should be. Women teachers, so useful in other civilised countries, are not yet available in India. All these are drawbacks and difficulties. Still there is a growing demand for education. Indian reformers and ministers are ardently desirous for the spread of education. Indians themselves are quickly responsive to good teaching. The educated women are slowly breaking down barriers and prejudices. And headway is being made. In 1917 the total school-going population of British India attending primary classes numbered 6,404,200. In 1927 it had risen to 9,247,617. And the modest contribution of £10,000 a year, ordered by the British Government a century ago, has now risen to £9,400,000.

These are a few of the more significant features in the India of to-day. And these are the grounds on which the British may fairly claim to have given India good government over and above what she has done in first establishing and then maintaining internal peace and order and in securing India from outside invasion.

CHAPTER VI

SELF-GOVERNMENT

THE exploitation of India for the benefit of the British and the detriment of the Indians had never been the intention of the British. They had at least the sense to see that the more prosperous Indians were the better it would be for themselves. In the words of Queen Victoria's great Proclamation : "In their prosperity will be Our strength, in their contentment Our security, and in their gratitude Our best reward." The British from the time of Warren Hastings, the first Governor-General, have always tried to give India at least *good* government. They have not merely garrisoned India as the Chinese merely garrison Turkestan. And they have not merely exploited India as an "estate" out of which they had to get the utmost. They did not go to India for their health. They went there for their benefit. But, having gone there, they did try also to benefit the Indians. And as the government of India came into their hands through the pressure of circumstance and not of their own desire, they strove to govern well. They took a pride in giving India good government and bringing not only order and justice but prosperity and, as they hoped, happiness. "It is Our earnest desire," said Queen Victoria, "to administer its government for the benefit of all Our subjects resident therein."

But within this idea of beneficial government

there gradually arose in the minds of the British the germ of a greater idea. The Indians were not to be kept in permanent subjection to the British, however beneficial the British might deem their rule. And they were not only to be associated more and more with the British in the government of the country. They were to be fitted and helped to govern themselves. This was the further idea, beyond and within beneficial government, which the British formed in their minds. India was to be not only well-governed but self-governed. India was not to be regarded as a province of Great Britain, as Algeria is regarded as a province of France. The Indians were not to be trained and educated to become British, with British ways and customs, as Algerians are trained and educated to become Frenchmen, with French ways and customs. And Indians, when trained and educated to become British, were not to send representatives to the British Parliament in London as French-educated Algerians send representatives to the Chamber of Deputies in Paris. Indians were to receive a Western education, but were to remain Indian and ultimately have their own responsible government and govern themselves.

This was the idea which grew up within the idea of good government for India—the idea of self-government. Whether the French system of centralising government at the capital is better or worse than the British system of allowing latitude to the parts it is not my purpose to discuss. All it is necessary to say is that the French system is in accordance with the French character and habits of mind and the British system in accordance with the British. And, in all probability, the British could not have worked on French lines, nor the French on British. What we have here to concern ourselves with is how the British system was conceived and how it is now, with much pain and travail, coming to birth.

And first we may note that this idea came as much from the British serving in India as from generous-hearted men in England. The first trace of it may be found in a minute by Sir Thomas Munro, Governor of Madras, written as far back as 1824. He therein urged that the British should endeavour to give the people of India "a higher opinion of themselves, by placing more confidence in them, by employing them in important situations, and perhaps by rendering them eligible to almost every office under Government." "Liberal treatment," he said, "has always been found the most effectual way of elevating the character of any people, and we may be sure that it will produce a similar effect on that of the people of India."

Having thus advocated the more extended employment of Indians in the administration of India, he boldly sets forth the great idea of a self-governing India. "We should look upon India," he says, "not as a temporary possession, but as one which is to be maintained permanently until the natives shall in some future age have abandoned most of their prejudices and superstitions, and become sufficiently enlightened to frame a regular government for themselves, and to conduct and preserve it." This was his idea. And whenever the time comes when it can be carried out he thinks "it will probably be best for both countries that the British control over India should be gradually withdrawn." He saw no cause to despair why such a change should not be effected. It had been made in Britain itself. "If we pursue steadily the proper measures, we shall in time so far improve the character of our Indian subjects as to enable them to govern and protect themselves."

Mountstuart Elphinstone, another great servant of the Company, who rose to the position of Governor of Bombay, likewise wrote: "We must not dream of perpetual possession, but must apply ourselves to bring the natives into a state that will admit of their governing themselves in a manner that may be beneficial to our interest as well as their own and that of the rest of the world; and to take glory of the achievement, and the sense of having done our duty, for the chief reward of our exertion."

This was the view of one of the most distinguished of the Company's servants, who had served long years in India. Another of their servants, who had also served many years in India and through the Indian Mutiny, wrote in a similar strain. Sir Herbert Edwardes, writing in 1861, used these words: "God would never have put upon two hundred millions of men the heavy trial of being subject to thirty millions of foreigners merely to have their roads improved, their canals constructed upon more scientific principles . . . nor even to have their internal quarrels stopped and peace restored, and life in many ways ameliorated. . . . This free and sympathising country, which has now a heart for Italy, and shouts across their narrow seas, 'Italy for the Italians!' should lift that voice still higher and shout across the world, 'India for the Indians!' In short, England, taught by both past and present, should set before her the noble policy of *first fitting India for freedom and then setting her free*. It may take years, it may take a century, to fit India for self-government, but it is a thing worth doing and a thing that may be done."

This was the idea of self-government for India which had been forming itself in the minds of the British and from time to time finding expression. And step by step from very small beginnings and over a long period it had been translating itself into action.

But action had to be adapted to circumstances. In India under purely Indian conditions government is carried on by a very different method from that to which the British and other Europeans are accustomed. At the time when the English Company was beginning to take over the Government of India, it was the custom of the Princes of India to unite in their own persons the whole legislative, executive, and judicial powers of the State, and to exercise them according to the dictates of their own discretion. And to the present time this is still the custom in all but the largest states. And when the Company took over the government of Indian provinces, the Governor-General in Council still exercised legislative as well as executive authority. He made the laws as well as performed all executive acts. But if Indians thus had no participation in framing the laws, "abundant security was afforded to them, that the exercise of that authority would always be directed to their happiness and benefit." And authority was given to the judges "to propose such general or local laws as from their intercourse with the natives in the administration of justice might appear to them necessary to promote the public happiness and prosperity." And though the Governor-General in Council exercised legislative authority, yet judicial authority was entirely independent of him. The judges were independent of the Governor. The Governor had the power of making laws or altering at his pleasure the law itself. But he had not the power of immediate interference with the law.

British rule in those early days was not therefore quite so autocratic as the rule of Indian chiefs around them. Insensibly the people did have an influence on these British rulers. The British did not autocratically govern without any regard to the wishes or feelings of the people. "The happiness and prosperity" of the Indians was in the minds of the British as they made the laws and carried on the administration.

Still that influence of the people was only very indirectly exercised at first, and steps had to be taken to enable the Indians to voice their own wishes. And here it must be noted that autocratic as an Indian ruler may appear, yet under the Indian system the people do have the means of making their influence powerfully felt; and a chief cannot, in practice, go very far from the will of the people —unexpressed in actual words though it may be. By Indian custom the ruler sits in what is known as "Durbar"—that is, in the presence of his nobles and people. To this Durbar all have access. Every kind of topic is discussed. And as a rule people can speak their minds fairly freely. It is a kind of informal Council. And it is a means whereby a ruler keeps in touch with his people. However autocratic he may be he finds it hard to go against the sense of these Durbars—even if that sense is only silently expressed.

But the British had not adopted this system. They had introduced the stiffer and more formal method of regular and definite Councils. The Governor-General with his Council of Englishmen made the laws for India. It is true that this Council tried to legislate in accordance with the customs and needs of Indians. But Indians were not directly concerned in making those laws. And in the course of time the British felt that a change had to be made and that Indians must be more directly associated with them in making the laws of India.

So, soon after the Crown took over the government of India, the Council of the Governor-General was for legislative purpose enlarged. It was reinforced by "additional members," not less than six, not more than twelve in number to be nominated—nominated not elected—for two years, of whom not less than half were to be non-official. Indian members were nominated to this body. And the first step was taken towards giving Indians a voice in framing the laws for India. The step forward was only a very short one. For the functions of the new Councils were strictly limited to legislation, and they were expressly forbidden to transact any business except the consideration and enactment of legislative measures. Still it was some advance. And in a direction which, as has subsequently proved, is the direction of self-government. Through the new Council, Government could receive advice and assistance from the Indians; the Indian public had the right to make itself heard, the Government had to defend its legislation, the advantages of full publicity were ensured at every stage of the law-making process; and the laws once made, the executive were as much bound by them as the public. Grievances could not be enquired into, information could not be called for, the conduct of Government could not be impugned. But Indians for the first time did get the opportunity of having their say in the making of the laws, and this was the germ of something a great deal more than only associating them with the British in the administration.

Thirty years later, in 1892, further advance was made. Indians were to *choose* their representatives; and the representatives were to have more power. Government had found the presence of Indians on the Council useful. They desired to have more, and to those more give more of a voice. During Lord Dufferin's Viceroyalty a Committee was set up to enquire into the matter. And they recommended that the Councils should see papers freely and originate advice and suggestions; that debates on such advice or suggestion should be permitted; and that the estimates connected with local finance should be referred to a standing committee and debated if necessary in council. They even suggested that the principle of *election* should be introduced as far as possible though not more than two-fifths should be elected. Lord Dufferin himself was of opinion that it would be wise to give "a still wider share in the administration of public affairs to such Indian gentlemen as, by their influence, their acquirements, and the confidence they inspire in their fellow-countrymen, are marked out as fitted to assist with their counsels the responsible rulers of the country." He thought it out of the question that the Government should divest itself of any portion of Imperial authority. Over a variety of nationalities, most of whom are in a very backward state of civilisation, "it was necessary to maintain the paramountcy of the ruling Power." But they might associate with themselves in council a considerable number of experienced and able natives of India who might enlighten and assist them in the discharge of their difficult duties. The wishes and feelings of the people would be better known. And those wishes and feelings would be expressed not "through self-constituted, self-nominated, and therefore untrustworthy channels, but by the mouths of those who will be the legally constituted representatives of various interests and classes, and who will feel themselves in whatever they do or say responsible to enlightened and increasing sections of their own countrymen." And he advocated the partial introduction of the elective principle.

This cardinal principle of election was not readily accepted by the Home Government. They thought it unwise to introduce a fundamental change of this description without much more positive evidence in its favour than had been forthcoming. But Lord Lansdowne, who had succeeded Lord Dufferin, supported the recommendation. And the Home Government did not absolutely bar the way. They left the door still open. Mr. Curzon—the then Under-Secretary of State for India, and afterwards

Lord Curzon—in introducing the new Council of India Bill in the House of Commons, said that it would be in the power of the Viceroy "to invite representative bodies in India to elect or select or delegate representatives of themselves and their opinions to be nominated to the Council." And Mr. Gladstone, speaking for the Opposition, expressed the hope that the first step towards introducing the elective element into the Government of India "should be of a nature to be genuine and whatever amount of scope they give to the elective principle should be real."

In the regulations drawn up under this Act of 1892 an official majority was provided for, but the majority of the non-official seats were to be filled by "recommendation." The term "election" was, says the Montagu-Chelmsford Report, sedulously eschewed; but inasmuch as the nominations by recommending bodies came to be accepted as a matter of course, the fact of election to an appreciable proportion of the non-official seats was firmly established.

Indians were to have the opportunity of choosing their own representatives. This was the important step forward now made. It was only to a limited extent that they had this power. But the principle had come into operation—and on the firm insistence of the British officials in India. And the powers of these Indian members of the Legislative Council were also to be increased. So far they had only been able to advise in the making of laws. Now they were given the right of asking questions and of discussing, though not of voting on, the Budget.

In the meanwhile, and only ten years previously, a great advance had been made—or rather planned, for the plan was imperfectly executed—towards self-government, and that was in *local* self-government. And this step was due to Lord Ripon—a man not of doctrinaire but of genuinely liberal tendencies springing from a generous heart and warm sympathy with the people of India. In his Resolution of 1882, advocating the extension of local self-government and the adoption of this principle in the management of many branches of local affairs, his main intention was to make it "an instrument of political and popular education." He did not aim at great *efficiency* of administration—at any rate at first. He anticipated failures. But he hoped that the period of failures would be short, and that real and substantial progress would soon be manifest "if the officers of Government only set themselves . . . to foster sedulously the small beginnings of the independent political life, if they accept loyally and as their own the policy of the Government, and if they come to realise that the system really opens to them a fairer field for the exercise of administrative tact and directive energy than the more autocratic system which it supersedes."

Lord Ripon attached little value to the theory that the people of India were indifferent to the principle of self-government, took little interest in public matters, and preferred to have such affairs managed for them by Government officers. He recognised that as education advanced there was rapidly growing up, all over the country, an intelligent class of public-spirited men whom it was not only bad policy, but sheer waste of power, to fail to utilise. So he considered it the only reasonable plan "*to induce the people themselves to undertake, as far as may be, the management of their own affairs.*"

Following on this resolution a network of local self-government institutions was established. The official element in local bodies was reduced to a third. The principle of election was adopted. In all provinces Rural Boards were for the first time brought into existence, and taxpayers were empowered to elect a proportion of the members of such Boards. And in all towns of reasonable size municipalities were set up.

Thirty years after this hopeful start had been made, the hopes had not been fulfilled. Funds were scarce. Interest in local affairs and capacity to handle them were slow in developing. Results had to be shown, and the educative principle was subordinated to the desire for these more immediate results. The Montagu-Chelmsford Report concluded that with the best intentions the presence of an official element had been prolonged beyond the point at which it would merely have afforded the very necessary help, up to a point at which it had impeded the growth of initiative and responsibility. And the Simon Report saw that "the custom of the country, force of habit, apathy, and lack of desire to assume responsibilities among those elected—together with the natural reluctance of an overworked official, desirous of efficiency, to consume much time in getting things done badly which he felt he could himself do well—combined to prevent real and substantial progress being made in political and popular education in the art of self-government."

The hopes entertained at the start had not been realised. Indians had not shown much desire or aptitude for governing themselves in local affairs. Nevertheless, the idea had been planted, and, as we shall see later on, it is now under better conditions slowly developing.

And at this time, when self-government in local affairs was making its start, another movement of great consequence was initiated. This was the Indian National Congress movement. It was not an official movement. It has, indeed, developed into a movement entirely hostile to Government. But it was started by a retired British official and with the encouragement of a Viceroy. Hume, the founder, had held the high post of Secretary to the Government of India in the Home Department. When he retired he lived on at Simla, and devoted himself to this idea. He was a man of great generosity and of liberal ideas. In addressing the graduates of Calcutta University in 1883, he had reminded them that they were "the most important source of all mental, moral, social, and political progress in India." To them India must look for all vital progress. Aliens, like himself, might give time and trouble, money and thought, but they lacked the essential of nationality, and the real work must ever be done by the people of the country themselves. And what was wanted was an association having for its object to promote the mental, moral, social, and political regeneration of the people of India.

Hume himself, in initiating this national movement, was disposed to begin reform propaganda on the social side. But after taking counsel with the

Viceroy, Lord Dufferin, he took up the work of political organisation. Lord Dufferin argued that "as head of the Government he had found the greatest difficulty in ascertaining the real wishes of the people; and that for purposes of administration it would be a public benefit if there existed some responsible organisation through which the Government might be kept informed regarding the best Indian public opinion."

In this way it came about that the Indian National Congress was formed. It has never been an official body, though it was started with the friendliest sympathy of the highest authorities. And though it is called "National" it is by no means fully representative of India. But it is a great power in the land. And it does make for self-government. Both unofficially, therefore, as well as officially there was forty years ago a great movement in the direction of self-government.

To return to the Act of 1892, the working was on the whole favourable. Useful criticism and valuable suggestions were often made. But India was rapidly ripening for a further advance. And Lord Minto when he arrived in India in 1905, fresh from the Governor-Generalship of great self-governing Canada, soon saw that that advance must be quickly made. He found the political atmosphere was full of change. "The growth of education was bearing fruit." "Important classes of the population were learning to realise their own position, to estimate for themselves their own intellectual capacities, and to compare their claims for an equality of citizenship with those of the ruling race." He therefore set about finding means for " recognising the natural aspirations of educated men to share in the government of their country." Lord Morley assured him that this design had the cordial concurrence of His Majesty's Government, and the reforms of 1909, known as the Morley-Minto reforms, were the result.

Lord Morley disclaimed any intention of aiming directly or indirectly at the establishment of a parliamentary system in India. And the intention of Lord Minto seems to have been rather to combine the autocratic system of rule common in the East with the constitutional system of the West. No relaxation of the control exercised by the British electorate was possible, it was thought, until an Indian electorate had arisen to take the burden from its shoulders. And no such Indian electorate was in sight. Nevertheless, these reforms did constitute a decided step in the direction of responsible government. For the elective principle was definitely adopted—not merely countenanced; the official majority in the Provincial Councils was abandoned; the Councils were empowered to discuss the Budget at length before it was finally settled, to propose resolutions on it, and to divide upon them. And on all matters of general public importance resolutions might be proposed and divisions taken. The Councils were also enlarged—the number of " additional members " being sixty in the Indian Legislative Council, and from thirty to fifty in the Provincial Councils. Thus the old conception of the Councils as a mere legislative committee of the Government was abandoned. And the reforms " did much to make them serve the purpose of an inquest into the doings of Government by conceding the very important rights of discussing administrative matters and of cross-examining Government on its replies to questions.''

The Morley-Minto reforms were indeed at first greatly appreciated by the Indians. But soon one clear obstacle appeared. Indians might criticise the Government as much as they liked and move resolutions to their hearts' content, but they could not displace it. It was irremovable. The Indians in the Council had, as a matter of fact, greater influence upon Government than they imagined. But that influence was not outwardly perceptible. It did not take the form of a change of Government as in England and in most democratic countries. In the hands of the Governor-General was preserved the right of veto over any legislation he might think detrimental. The Indian members of Council knew, therefore, that whatever resolution they passed it need have no effect. And they found this position irritating. Also it left them without any sense of responsibility for their criticism and resolutions. They would never have to form a Government themselves and be responsible for carrying out their own resolutions. So there was no check upon their words. And a sense of unreality pervaded the proceedings.

This was the position when war broke out. Then immediately Indians both in and outside the Council Chamber joined in hearty co-operation with the British. Criticism was silenced. Grievances were forgotten. Indians of all classes and of all shades of political opinion spontaneously joined in the great war for right. The Princes offered their armies and their personal services. The Imperial

Council passed a resolution of sympathy with the cause, and voted one hundred million pounds towards the expenses of the War. And the peasantry readily enlisted in the Indian regiments sent to France.

Now all this stirred India as she has never been stirred before. From participating in the War, from sending out Princes and soldiers to the War, she was brought right out of herself into the great world of nations. With Great Britain, and with the great self-governing Dominions of the Empire, she was taking a real part in world-affairs. She became conscious of herself. And she became conscious of herself as an organised whole—as one single individuality. India was joining in the War. India was sending troops to Europe. The voice of India was being heard in the Councils of the nations. All this made Indians take bigger and wider views. All this made Indians think more highly of themselves. And all this made Indians desire to govern themselves. The War was for freedom and right. The statesmen in the allied countries were making speeches, denouncing oppressors, and upholding the right of peoples to determine their own destiny. Self-determination became the catchword of the times. And Indians were no longer content with the hesitating steps of Lord Morley. Self-government and nothing less was now their demand.

And the British Government on their side were most willing to go forward—most anxious indeed. They, too, were caught in the spirit of the times. They felt, in the words of Mr. Montagu and Lord Chelmsford, that "India has proved herself worthy of further trust and of a more liberal form of government." And in recognition of her progress changes should be made in the Constitution. To meet the new aspirations of the people Lord Chelmsford's Government in India proposed in 1917 a gradual progress towards a larger measure of control of India by her own people. This progress would ultimately result in some form of self-government. But that form might differ from the form enjoyed by other parts of the Empire. It would take into account India's past history and the special circumstances and traditions of her component peoples. To assist her towards this goal, greater powers and a more representative character might be conferred upon existing self-governing units such as District (rural) Boards and Municipal Councils; the proportion of Indians in the higher administrative posts might be increased; and the constitutional powers of the Provincial Legislatures might be enlarged by broadening the electorate and increasing the number of elected members.

These proposals, in the opinion of the Home Government, went a certain way but not far enough in the right direction. The Secretary of State, Mr. Austen Chamberlain, thought that more authority and responsibility should be conferred on members of the Legislature. And to make the policy known he proposed that Government should definitely avow an intention "to foster the gradual development of free institutions with a view to self-government." Mr. Montagu, who at this time, 1917, succeeded to Mr. Chamberlain, submitted to the Cabinet a formula of much the same wording. His exact words were: "The gradual development of free institutions with a view to ultimate self-government within the Empire." But there was objection in the Cabinet to the use of the term "self-government." It was contended that this term had come to mean a parliamentary system of government on a democratic basis. And such a system might be quite unsuitable for India. There was no objection to India being governed more and more by Indians. The objection was to tying India down to a particular form of government when she might prefer one, say, on the Japanese model. The formula finally decided on was drafted by Lord Curzon, then a member of the Cabinet. It runs as follows:

The Policy of His Majesty's Government, with which the Government of India are in complete accord, is that of the increasing association of Indians in every branch of the Administration, and the gradual development of self-governing institutions, with a view to the progressive realisation of responsible government in India as an integral part of the British Empire.

An announcement of the policy of Government in the foregoing words was made in the House of Commons on August 20, 1917. It was the most momentous announcement ever made in regard to India. For it meant in the long run the shifting of the responsibility for the government of India from the shoulders of the British to the shoulders of the Indians. Yet it was made, not after prolonged agitation in England, not after heated debate in Parliament, and not by the Sovereign in some great Proclamation or by the Viceroy in some stately Durbar, but by the Secretary of State in answer to a question across the floor of the House of Commons. That these things can be in a democratic country is the best hope for democracy. There are times and occasions when speed and decision are of the essence of good government. And this was one. It was essential that the people of India should know at once that the British did intend in the end to let them govern themselves. There might be delay while they were fitting themselves not only to govern but to defend themselves. But the British did not intend for ever to govern India. Nor did they intend to keep India as a province of Great Britain. Indians were to be responsible for governing themselves.

In making the announcement Mr. Montagu added that progress in this policy could only be achieved by successive stages. He added also that the British Government must be "judges of the time and measure of each advance." And Indians have thought that these words nullified the previous announcement. Yet it is obvious that responsible government could not be given all at once. There had to be stages of development. And as the announcement of policy was made by a Coalition Cabinet with a Liberal, Mr. Lloyd George, as Prime Minister, and as the announcement was originally drafted by a Unionist, Mr. Chamberlain, and edited by a Conservative, Lord Curzon, and has since received the approval of all three parties, Conservative, Liberal, and Labour, it may be taken as the very definite goal which the British people have set themselves.

To bring the new policy into effect Mr. Montagu himself went to India to discuss the matter with the Viceroy, Lord Chelmsford, and to receive with him the suggestions of representative bodies. And these two high functionaries drew up a report embodying their suggestions for the constitutional reforms required by the announcement.

Their conception of the eventual future of India was, in the words of the Montagu-Chelmsford report, "a sisterhood of states, self-governing in all matters of purely local or provincial interest. . . . Over this congeries of states would preside a Central Government, increasingly representative of and responsible to the people of all of them, dealing with matters, both internal and external, of common interest to the whole of India; acting as arbiter in inter-state relations; and representing the interests of all India on equal terms with the self-governing units of the British Empire." And in this picture they saw a place also for the Native States.

The final form of India's Constitution must be evolved out of the conditions of India. The dominating factor in the intermediate process must be the rate at which the *provinces* could move towards responsible government. And change in the provinces would imply change in the Central Government. The proposals therefore began with a great extension of local self-government so as to train the electorate in matters which they would best understand. Simultaneously there would be a substantial measure of self-government in the provinces and far better representation and more criticism in the government of India.

The province being chosen as the unit in which responsible government should be progressively realised, immediate and complete responsibility in local affairs, such as local self-government, education, agriculture, sanitation, was to be granted. The Executive Councils of the Governor of provinces were to include Indian Ministers, who for those subjects would be responsible first to constituencies and then to Legislative Councils. The responsibility of the Government of India to Parliament was not changed—except in so far as the transfer of these subjects to popular control in the provinces *ipso facto* removed them from the purview of the Government of India and Secretary of State. But greater opportunities for criticising and influencing the actions of the Government of India were to be afforded. Also, the new Legislature was to be so formed that it could develop into a machine adapted to the new motive power when the day of full responsibility had at length arrived.

In introducing the Bill in the House of Commons, Mr. Montagu said: "If we hold on to power in India, and stand fast to the policy of subordination, race-friction will continue and ought to continue. If we surrender our trusteeship to the great provinces of India as speedily as they are ready to take it over, then Indians will have something better and more worth doing than fiercely and impotently to criticise those who are at present the agents of Parliament." He described the Bill as "a bridge between government by agents of Parliament and government by representation of the peoples of India." He argued that empire was not justified merely by giving to a country satisfactory law and order, adequate peace, decent institutions, and a certain measure of prosperity. That would be running the country as an estate and not as a country at all. There must be something more than this, and something more than an expansion of local self-government as promised by Lord Ripon. India must be helped on the path to nationality. They were giving India a growing Constitution, and it would have to win for itself that goal which had been announced as the object of British policy. So far as transferred subjects—that is, education, agriculture, local self-government, etc.—were concerned the British would be already parting with their trusteeship and surrendering it to the representatives of the people of India. And there was no better way of promoting community of action and overcoming the acerbities of caste than by setting to the population a common task to do together, to work out the prosperity of their country.

Lord Sinha, in the House of Lords, said that as a result of the War there had been a great advance in the status of India. India had taken part in the Imperial Conference, in the Peace Conference, and was an original member of the League of Nations. "These experiences," he said, "have further quickened the sense of natural unity and development, a sense which has been steadily fostered for many years by common allegiance to the same beloved Sovereign, by being amenable to one code of laws, by being taxed by one authority, by being influenced for weal or woe by one system of administration, and by being urged by like impulses to secure like rights and to be relieved of like burdens."

The result of these debates was the passing of the Government of India Act of 1919. And when this Act would become law, India would enter upon a new era. She would be formally and officially started off on her career towards self-government. The goal was definitely stated and was embodied in the Preamble of the Act. And great steps had already been taken. First, Indians were already being admitted to higher and higher positions in the Government Service. Lord Sinha himself was an example. He had first been made a member of the Viceroy's *Executive* Council, hitherto exclusively preserved for British. Now he was made a Peer of the Realm in England with a seat in the House of Lords and was Under-Secretary of State for India. (Later he was appointed Governor of Bihar and Orissa.) In the Council of all the provinces of India as well as on the Viceroy's Executive Council two or three Indians would now sit. India was from now onward always represented on Imperial Conferences on an equality with representatives of the Dominions. She was represented on the Peace Conference at Versailles. And she was a member of the League of Nations.

With the passing of this Act, not a step but a great stride was being taken towards that goal which, after a hundred years of gestation in their minds, the British had at last clearly envisaged, and firmly set before themselves.

CHAPTER VII

LAUNCHING THE REFORMS

MATUREST deliberation had gone to fixing the goal. The measure to embody the great step towards that goal had been conscientiously elaborated. And now had come the time to put the measure into actual operation in India.

But the times were out of joint. And the difficulties of launching it were great. It was now 1919, and the War was over. In India, as in all countries, there was grave unsettlement. In Russia there had been revolution of the fiercest description. Ireland was in revolt. In England itself there were strikes of the most threatening nature. It was no very favourable moment for Great Britain to be launching a great movement of reform in so distant a land as India. For she had problems enough of her own to dispose of—the settlement of much industrial strife due to the rise in prices and wages, and the sudden return of two million men from the War; the payment of huge debts incurred by her on behalf of her allies; the urgent settlement of affairs in Egypt, in Palestine, in Mesopotamia, in East Africa; the settlement of peace with Turkey; the settlement with Ireland, one-half of which was rebelling against the British connection, and the other half standing as stoutly for it. These were some of the problems, all of the most urgent character, which Great Britain had to settle at this time, and while she herself was weary and war-worn, and was greatly missing the flower of her manhood killed in the War.

And in India itself she had much to think of besides reforms. For the King of Afghanistan, who had stood loyally to his engagement during the War, had been murdered; and his successor, Ammanula, was preparing to invade India with the ambition of making himself King. At the same time the British troops in India at that moment were mostly Territorials, originally enlisted for Home Service only, and, now the War was ended, impatient to return to their businesses and occupations in England.

And the people of India themselves were still upset by the world-upheaval. Prices had gone up. Peace had not yet brought prosperity. And in India, as in other countries, pure anarchists were at work—men who were not only against the British Government, but against government in any form. Even during the War revolutionary attempts had been made both in Bengal and in the Punjab. These anarchical crimes could not be dealt with effectively by the ordinary law. As in England and in other countries, a special law had to be provided for dealing with them. And it was provided by an Act passed on the recommendation of a Commission of Indians and Englishmen presided over by an English judge—Mr. Justice Rowlatt.

Thus it happened that just as the great measure of self-government for India was being worked out and debated in England, the Rowlatt Act for dealing with anarchy had to be passed by the Indian Legislature. It was an unfortunate occurrence. But if a community is to be organised so as to express the clear will of the majority, those few who are against all organisation of the general will have to be suppressed. And a clear distinction has to be drawn between those who are agitating for healthy reforms, and those who would destroy the whole machinery of government. That distinction is, however, not easy to make. And the cry went up that the British, now the War was over, meant to suppress all Indian aspirations.

Gandhi took up this cry. He had hoped so much of Government. Now he was grievously hurt. And Gandhi's biographer, M. Rolland, took the same view. His theory was, that while the War was on and the British needed Indian assistance they promised reforms, but that for the Indians the awakening was terrible. Danger was over, and gone was the memory of services rendered. After the signing of the Armistice Government saw no reason for feigning any longer. Instead of granting the promised liberties it suspended whatever freedom already existed. Such was the view of this distinguished Frenchman, who, in his enthusiasm for Gandhi, could not pause to inform himself of what was taking place in the British Parliament. And such was the view of thousands of Indians. And though the Rowlatt Act was a small and a temporary measure, and applicable only to a minute fraction of the population, and never put into actual operation, attention was concentrated on it; a prodigious grievance was made out of it; and the great measure of reform which really did give Indians the opportunity of building up a self-governing India was deliberately boycotted by Gandhi and others of the chief leaders. Instead of working with Government in these great days of their country's history, they worked against Government. They publicly inculcated disobedience of the laws and sought to bring the Government of the country to a standstill. Though they had the Montagu-Chelmsford Report before them, and though they knew that a Bill was in preparation to bring its recommendations into effect, they lost all sense of proportion, they set up a vehement agitation against the "Rowlatt Bills," and they violently denounced the British Government as intending only to oppress and enslave the Indians.

The people of India, still unsteady from the effects of the War, were quickly inflamed by what even the Simon Commission describe as "gross misrepresentation." Hindus, Sikhs, and Moslems, for different reasons, joined together in common enmity to the Government. Gandhi himself always advocated "non-violence" and "moral persuasion." But when he was perpetually and in unmeasured terms upbraiding the Government and bringing it into contempt the natural result followed. The people rose against the "tyrannical" Government. Violent disorders broke out in the Punjab. Englishmen and Englishwomen were attacked. Some were murdered. The civil authorities lost all hold over the great city of Amritsar. The military had to be called in. General Dyer marched through the city by beat of drum proclaiming it unlawful for the citizens to hold meetings. And when that same day, in spite of this warning, some thousands of them organised a meeting and came to it armed with staves, he fired on them without further warning and killed some hundreds. The incipient revolt was checked. And Government were free to deal with the Afghan invasion, which was at that very time threatening. But, in the words of the Simon Report, "the racial bitterness aroused was great and lasting, and it produced an atmosphere for the inauguration of the Reforms in the following year which could hardly have been worse."

And out of this racial bitterness and political disappointment there arose what was called the "Non-co-operation Movement." The Moslems, who have a fellow-feeling all the world over, were agitated about the peace terms with Turkey. They wanted the Sultan restored to something like his pre-War position. This was a question to be settled by all the Allies in consultation and not by Great Britain alone—still less by the Indian Government alone. But upon the Government of India fell the brunt of Indian Moslem displeasure. An organised agitation—which became known as the Khalifat Movement—was set on foot in India to bring pressure to bear upon the Imperial Government. And Gandhi allied himself with this movement and brought his following with him. Moslems and Hindus were then for the time being joined together in opposition to the Government.

Gandhi became the leader of the whole movement. As usual, and quite sincerely, he advocated non-violence. But he kept to his assertion that the British had impoverished India and destroyed her liberties, that the British rule was "Satanic," and that the only cure was to end it. His adherents were to resign Government titles and honorary offices; to withdraw from Government service; and to boycott schools, law courts, and the legislative bodies. And if these methods did not succeed, they were to refuse to pay Government dues, and organise mass disobedience to the laws and to the orders of the Administration. Government would be brought to a standstill and British rule would come to an end. And all this he advocated at the very time when the Bill containing the Montagu proposals for a great step towards self-government was actually before Parliament.

The British might well have despaired of doing anything for India. Perhaps, after all, the idea of self-government for India was a mistake. The people were not ripe for self-governing institutions. They had always been accustomed to autocratic rule. And they might be better under the masterful though benevolent rule of a Clive or a Warren Hastings than under the democratic institutions which were in contemplation. The British at the last moment might well have paused ere they took the fateful step. And Lord Selborne did indeed, in the debate on the new Bill in the House of Lords, warn the Indians that "they had come nearer than some of them knew to turning a very great body of public opinion in England against their aspirations." But the Bill, after all, was only part of that great long-rolling sweep of progression in which the British, almost as unwittingly as they had been drawn into dominion, were being carried forward. The Government pursued their way undeflected by the turmoil. And Queen Victoria's last surviving son, the Duke of Connaught, was sent to India in 1920 to inaugurate the new Legislative

Council set up under the new Government of India Act.

Neither the passing of the Act nor the presence of a Royal Prince had, however, any effect upon Gandhi and his followers. On the contrary, on the very day that the British Prince was inaugurating the new Council at Delhi, Gandhi also appeared there with the express object of drawing people away from doing honour to the Duke of Connaught. And 80,000 people followed him. Similarly, when two years later the Prince of Wales visited India, as he had already visited Canada and Australia, to acknowledge on behalf of Great Britain the aid that India had given to the Empire in the Great War, Gandhi went to Bombay to proclaim a day of mourning instead of a day of honour—with the result that serious riots broke out, several people were killed, and many assaults on Englishmen were made on the very day that the Prince was landing to thank the people on behalf of the King-Emperor.

This was the hostile atmosphere in which the Reforms had to be started. But not all Indians followed Gandhi. Many highly disapproved of his offering this insult to the Heir to the Throne. Such conduct ran altogether counter to their innate sense of courtesy. And while the "Nationalists" boycotted the new Council and refused to stand for election, there were public-spirited "Moderates" who accepted the principles of the announcement of 1917, setting forth the goal of responsible government within the Empire as governing the conditions of political advance. Many of them thought that the Act did not go far enough. But they were prepared to do everything in their power to make the new Constitution a success and so justify a further advance. And in spite of every effort of the Nationalists to throw contempt on the elections, they put themselves forward and were returned in preponderating numbers both to the Central Legislature and to the Provincial Councils. And the Simon Commission pay a handsome tribute to the public spirit with which they entered upon their duties. "In these hopes and ambitions for the future of India they had much in common with the non-co-operators, who included many of their friends. Bitterness over the Punjab disturbance of 1919, enthusiasm to push on towards full self-government, and admiration for the personality of Mr. Gandhi were shared by all parties. But the Moderates had accepted the principles of the announcement of 1917, and set themselves stoutly to do what they could to make the Act of 1919 a success."

What then was this India Act of 1919? What new powers did it give the Indians? What new governmental machinery did it set up? The problem, as we have seen, was gradually to shift the burden of responsibility from the shoulders of the British to the shoulders of the Indians. The Indians have not been accustomed to bear the heavy weight of Empire. And if that prodigious burden were placed upon them too suddenly they might crumple up under the weight. So the idea of the Act of 1919 was to transfer the burden gradually. Not to put the full weight on all at once lest disaster should follow. But first to put a part on Indian shoulders—just as much as those slender shoulders could bear for the time. Then it was hoped that as they strained their muscles to bear the weight the muscles would harden. And when their muscles were hardened it would be possible to put more and more of the burden on them. This was the general idea of the Act of 1919. And it was designed to transfer first the lighter part to the Indians, while the heavier part of the Imperial burden was still reserved for the British. And the start was to be made in the provinces. The Provincial Governments, rather than the Central Government, were first to have the strain.

And Local Self-Government was the first part of the burden to be transferred—that is, matters relating to the constitution and powers of municipal corporations and district boards. Since Lord Ripon's time efforts had been made—though not very successfully—to train Indians in the management of their own local affairs. So now Local Self-Government was to be placed under the control of Indian Ministers responsible to an Indian electorate. So also were such subjects as Public Health, Education, Public Works (including Roads and Bridges), Agriculture, Excise, and the Development of Industries. While the Police, the Administration of Justice, Irrigation and Canals, Land Revenue Administration, and Famine Relief were still reserved. And the Central Government still maintained its responsibility in Defence, Foreign Affairs, Posts and Telegraphs, Customs, and other subjects.

In this way the provinces would be selected as the domain in which the earlier steps towards the progressive realisation of responsible government would be taken. They would at once be given the largest measure of legislative, administrative and financial independence of the Government of India as was compatible with the due discharge by the latter of its own responsibilities. At the same time the Central Legislature was enlarged and made more representative, and its opportunities of influencing Government were increased. And as these changes took effect the control of the British Parliament over the Government of India and Provincial Governments was to be relaxed. This authority, instead of being concentrated at the Centre, was to be in large measure devolved on the provinces.

In each of the eight major provinces there was to be set up a one-chamber Legislature called a Legislative Council. And these new Councils, instead of being presided over by the Governor as formerly, were now to have a president who, after the first four years, was to be elected by the members themselves. At least 70 per cent. of the members of a Council were to be elected members, and not more than 20 per cent. were to be "official" members. The great majority of members of these Councils were to be chosen by Indians themselves and their proceedings were to be presided over, not by a British Governor, but by a member of their own choosing.

How these members should be elected was a difficulty. In British India there are 229 million illiterates and only 18·6 million literates. But all illiterates are not fools. Runjeet Singh—the great ruler of the Punjab—was an illiterate. And mere illiteracy was not taken as a bar to the franchise. The limitations were "determined rather with reference to practical difficulties than to any a priori considerations as to the degree of education or amount of income which may be held to constitute a qualification.'' Nevertheless, it was only found possible to confer the franchise on about one-tenth of the adult male population, the normal qualification being residence within the constituency, coupled with the payment of a small amount in land revenue, rent, or local rates in rural areas, and of municipal rates in urban areas. Women's suffrage was not established, but the Legislative Councils were empowered by resolution to remove the sex barrier themselves.

As to the powers of these Provincial Legislative Councils it was enacted that Bills passed by them required the assent not only of the Governor, but of the Governor-General. But besides this usual power of veto there was reserved to the Governor the very unusual power of certifying that the passage of a Bill is "essential for the discharge of his responsibility for the subject," and the Bill would then be put in the same position as though it had been actually passed by the Legislature. But—except in emergency—such a Bill would not become an Act until His Majesty's pleasure had been expressed by the King in Council, and it had been laid before both Houses of Parliament for eight days of their session before being presented for His Majesty's assent. And, in any case, this unusual power of the Governor's only related to "reserved" subjects. If an Indian Minister introduced a Bill dealing with a "transferred" subject and the Legislative Council did not pass it, the usual consequences of rejection would follow.

So much as regards the Provincial Legislative Councils. As regards the Provincial Executive Councils the system known as "dyarchy" was introduced for operation during the transitional period. It was not considered safe to transfer the whole burden of provincial government on to Indian shoulders at once. The majority of members of the Provincial Legislative Councils would be, for the first time, chosen by an inexperienced and largely illiterate electorate. And it was not thought possible to hand over the provincial departments of the Police, the Magistracy, and the Revenue to Ministers whose administrative experience would be necessarily small, and whose responsibility would be solely to these newly-created Legislatures and to newly-enfranchised constituents. So in each province the Executive Government was to consist of *two* parts —this was where the plan of "dyarchy" was introduced. One part was to comprise the Governor and his Executive Council. And the other was to consist of Ministers chosen by the Governor from the elected members of the Provincial Legislative Council. The first part (composed in practice of an Indian non-official element, as well as of a British official element) was charged with the administration of the "reserved" subjects—police, magistracy, revenue, etc. To the second part were committed portfolios dealing with the "transferred" subjects—local self-government, public health, education, etc.—and on these subjects the Ministers, together with Governor, formed the Administration.

Thus there were to be *two sides* to the Provincial Governments: the Governor in Council dealing with reserved subjects, and the Governor acting with Ministers dealing with transferred subjects. The members of Council were to be appointed by His Majesty and were not to exceed four. The Ministers were to be appointed by the Governor from among the elected members of the Legislative Council. Nothing was laid down in the Act as to whether the four members of Council should be Indian or British—though in practice the distribution has been equal.

So, as a net result, Indians were to become almost wholly responsible for the administration of such matters as local self-government, public health, agriculture, education, and industrial development, and were to have a considerable say in matters of police and magistracy. On the other hand, in case of accident in the delicate operation of transferring responsibility from British to Indian shoulders, powers were reserved to the Governor in Council, with the previous sanction of the Secretary of State in Council, to revoke or suspend the transfer of any subject; and, thereupon, such subject relapsed for the time being into the position of a reserved subject, to be administered by the Governor in Council.

In the Central Government there was not to be so much change, though even there the majority of members were to be *elected.* And, whereas the Provincial Legislative Councils were to be one-chambered, in the Central Legislature there were to be two chambers—namely, the Council of State and the Legislative Assembly. The former was to have a maximum of 60 members, and the latter a minimum membership of 140. Out of the 60 members of the Council of State, 34 were to be elected. And for the electorate the property qualification was to be high enough to secure the representation of wealthy landowners and merchants. Previous experience in a Central or Provincial Legislature, membership of a university senate, and similar tests of personal standing and experience in affairs, were likewise to qualify for a vote for the Council of State. In actual practice, out of the 145 members of the Legislative Assembly, 105 are elected, while 26 are official members and 14 are nominated non-officials. The 26 officials include most of the members of the Governor-General's Executive Council, and important members of the Government of India's Secretariat, such as the Military Secretary and the Foreign Secretary; the rest are nominated as representatives of the different Provincial Governments.

The franchise for the Legislative Assembly was arranged on the same lines as for the Provincial Councils, but with somewhat higher electoral qualifications. Moslems were to have a separate representation by the creation of constituencies containing none but Moslem voters. Europeans also were to have separate representation. As also the Sikhs.

This Indian Legislature has to have power to make laws for all persons, courts, places, and things within British India, but with this important limitation. The previous sanction of the Governor-General would be required for the introduction of any measure affecting (*a*) the public debt or revenues, (*b*) the religion of any class, (*c*) the discipline or maintenance of the Army, (*d*) foreign relations. And the Governor-General might secure the enactment of a Bill, whose passage, in the form he considered to be necessary, was refused by the Indian Legislature by certifying that the Bill was essential for the safety, tranquillity, or interests of British India. But when this was done the Act had to be laid before both Houses of Parliament, and had no effect until it had subsequently received His Majesty's assent.

Over finance, the Legislature was to have only limited control. Certain items of expenditure, such as debt charges and Army expenditure, were not subject to vote, though Army policy and expenditure might be criticised by moving a reduction in the expenditure proposed to be voted for the secretarial establishment of the Army Department. But taxes would have to be voted annually, and the demand of the Government for supply, in respect of the various services other than those not subject to vote, would have to be presented to the Legislatures annually in the form of motions to be voted upon. In addition, a standing Finance Committee was to be formed to familiarise elected members of the Legislatures with the process of administration, and to make the relations between the Executive and the Legislature more intimate. They were to be purely advisory, but they would have considerable opportunity of influencing the administration.

These were the measures now taken to give the Indians a greater share in the government of their own country. The Morley-Minto reforms were regarded as a great step forward in their time. But these went far further. In all but the essentials of defence and the preservation of internal order Indians were acquiring a steadily increasing control in the management of their own affairs.

CHAPTER VIII

HINDU-MOSLEM TENSION

WITH all the desire in the world on the part of both Indians and British for self-government, there is, however, one main difficulty in the way—the differences between Hindus and Moslems. There are seventy million Moslems in India to two hundred and sixteen million Hindus, and they will never submit to a Central Government elected by an overwhelming Hindu majority unless there are ample safeguards. And what they fear, and what is the cause of the deep-down differences between the followers of these two great religions, we must discover before we proceed further with our inquiry. For it is unfortunately the case that the nearer is the prospect of India achieving responsible self-government the more anxious do the Moslems become and the more acute the tension between the two peoples.

What each fears is, of course, that if the other gains the power, that power will be used to its own exclusive interest. If the British are ready to hand over power to Indians, then either the Hindus, by their numerical majority, will acquire the power, or else the Moslems, by their greater capacity for governing and through the assistance of co-religionists from outside, will gain the upper hand, as they had it in the time of the Moguls. And in either case the one which is in the position of inferiority would suffer—so each fears. And each has reason to fear. I have been in charge of our political relations at one time with a state in which the ruler was Moslem and the majority of his subjects Hindu, and at another time with a state in which the ruler was Hindu and the majority of his subjects were Moslem. The Moslem ruler might employ a Hindu here and there in his service, but in the main all the highest positions were held by Moslems, and I would be continually appealed to by the Hindus to persuade the Moslem ruler to give them more consideration. And where the ruler was Hindu, even though 90 per cent. of his subjects were Moslem, it was with the greatest difficulty that he could be induced to have a Moslem in any high position. And my own experience is but typical. And the Moghul Emperors, though they employed Hindus in high offices, in the main kept the power very much in their own hands. Akbar was liberal. And the Hindu Finance Minister, Toder Mull, rendered great services to the Empire. Still the power was retained mainly in Moslem hands. It was by no means evenly distributed among all classes of Indians, irrespective of whether they were Hindu or Moslem. And if the Mahrattas had gained the sovereignty of India, Moslems would have had little share in the power. Moslems have, therefore, very good grounds for fearing that if the power which is now in British hands were to be transferred to Indians they might get very little of it.

But why should Hindus and Moslems be thus so opposed to each other? What is the root cause of their mutual antagonism? The root cause is that

Islam is an alien religion and civilisation and whole way of life. Islam came to India from outside. And it came through military invasion. Moslems were men of a different race—Asiatics, it is true, but of a different race. And they brought with them a different system of law and different social habits. Above all, they brought a different religion. The Hindus have gods by thousands and worship idols, and they love elaborate ritual and ornate forms of architecture and music and dancing in their temples. All that is rich and luscious and luxuriant like the tropical growth around them they rejoice in. But Moslems are stern Puritans. Their religion arose in the desert. They believe in only one God. Images and idols are anathema. No image or picture of a man or of any living thing is to be found in their mosques. Theirs is a simple and austere faith.

Now it might have been possible for the Hindus to have tolerated Islam if it had come in peaceful guise. For Hinduism is a tolerant absorptive religion. And though in one sense it recognises many gods, yet these are only the myriad aspects of the one Supreme Being. But Islam came in with a conquering race, and Moslems were on fire with their new religion. They came in and ruled—ruled for centuries—and ruled with rigour. And they were flaming zealots. They would convert by the sword. They would smash the graven images in the temples. They would purify India of its sensuous luxuriance. And all this made it hard for the Hindus to be tolerant. Instead, they only strengthened their barriers of caste. Already they had this system to preserve themselves intact from these original inhabitants of India, whose land they had themselves invaded. Now they would use it against these Moslem invaders from the north-west. So they shut themselves tightly within their caste, and to this day they will neither marry nor eat with Moslems.

One further cause of offence to the Hindus is that the Moslems at certain festivals sacrifice animals—and frequently cows. And to the Hindus cows are sacred—so sacred, indeed, that to the present time the crime of cow-killing is punishable with death in certain Hindu states. The Hindus have the tenderest feelings for all animals. Some of them will not kill a fly. And for the cow they have a special reverence. The cow had given them milk and helped them till their fields. And they felt grateful to it. So when the Moslem conquerors freely killed cows for meat, and when they sacrificed cows at their religious festivals, a shudder of horror went through them.

The Moslems, for their part, resent the Hindu exclusiveness. Islam has no caste. Moslems are brothers and equals. That Hindus should refuse to marry and to eat with them, and consider that Moslems polluted them was deep cause of offence.

These are the fundamental causes of the antipathy between Moslems and Hindus, but there are more superficial contributory causes. Moslems are by their religion forbidden to take usury. Consequently, when they want to borrow money they usually go to the Hindu moneylenders. The result is that Moslem peasants are deeply indebted to Hindus. And the Hindu moneylender is not the ordinary moneylender of Europe. He exercises a tremendous power over those in his debt. And he is detested by Moslems "as a moral and social leper."

Then in the actual practice of their religion Hindus and Moslems often offend one another—and sometimes of malice prepense. At one of their festivals the Moslems will lead a garlanded cow through the streets to the place of sacrifice. And the Hindus, seeing the sacred animal being led away to be killed, are driven frantic with wrath. Then on a Hindu festival the Hindus will march a procession past a mosque with blare of trumpets and clashing of cymbals and beating of drums, and make the Moslems, in their silent prayer, boil with indignation.

From one or other of these causes the inevitable clash has occurred. There have been riots and retaliation and the spilling of blood. Each collision has further accentuated the unfortunate division. And the animosities of centuries are always smouldering beneath the surface.

Now, with reforms, this agelong antagonism is becoming more acute. And the reason is this. As the time gets nearer when the British may hand over the reins of government to the Indians, the Moslems realise, as we have seen, that they will be in a permanent minority of three against one, and as the descendants of men who ruled India for centuries they resent being placed in such a position. They remember with pride their ancient glories. They recall the times when conquering hosts of Moslems debouched from the highlands of Afghanistan on to the plains of India. They remember the magnificence of the Great Moghuls.

And they fear " the transference of power from the hands of the British bureaucracy to that of a majority which, in practice, would mean and resolve itself into a narrow and selfish oligarchy, cruel, hostile, tyrannical, arrogant, domineering, proud, haughty, and unsympathetic to the hopes and aspirations of the minorities." So at least says Dr. Suhrawardy, a member of the Legislative Assembly, in the Minority Report to the Indian Central Committee Report presented to Parliament. He fears the subjection of the Moslems to " the despotism, tyranny, and domination of a narrow, selfish oligarchy or an equally selfish majority."

But the Moslems are not likely to accept such a position without a struggle. They more than hint that if the British were to leave India to govern itself they would take their own means to make their influence felt. They would, in fact, contest for power by force of arms. They would, in Dr. Suhrawardy's words, " give the natural laws of the struggle for existence and survival of the fittest a chance to find a lasting and abiding solution." A new Ahmad Abdali might arise, he foresees, and " find sanction for a Holy War in the dominance of polytheism over Islam and fight on the fateful field of Panipat the fourth battle for the throne of Delhi."

Perhaps it was something of this kind Nawab Sir Umar Hayat Khan had in mind when, in giving his evidence before the Commission, he said that he would like " the whole Government " given to India instead of being fettered by law, for then " those who have some power will get anything they want, but not those who clamour."

And the Moslems have always this feeling at the back—that they are connected with other Moslems throughout the world. They felt acutely with the Turks in those recent wars between Greece and Turkey, between Bulgaria and Turkey, between Italy and Turkey in Tripoli, and also in the Great War. And they assume that all Moslems would likewise feel with them if they were reduced, in the words of the Minority Report, "to the status of serfs and dependents of noisy pen drivers."

And the Moslems are confirmed in their convictions by the recent activity of the Hindus. The Hindu Maha Sabha has been started, they affirm, with the avowed object of subverting the political rights of the Moslems. Its two branches, the Shudhi and the Sangathan, aim at converting Moslems to Hinduism by force or fraud, and at preparing young fanatical Hindus by physical culture for the task of fighting the Moslems when riots occur. The Maha Sabha is "actuated by an implacable hatred of the Moslems, who, according to its political creed, must be exterminated." People outside India, the Minority Report says, have no idea of the extent of the communal tension, nor can they form any estimate of "the daily increasing volume of mutual hatred and rancour." It has sundered social ties which before were strong and cordial. Joint political associations have vanished. Moslems no longer repose any confidence in Hindu *bona fides*. The Hindu Press has launched a campaign of persistent vilification of the Moslems, and have not left even the sacred personality of the Prophet immune from insult and defamation. It openly asserts that the Moslem settlers in India must be expelled from it, that the converted Hindus who form the bulk of the Moslem population must be reclaimed to Hinduism, and that India must once again be exclusively Hindu. And while the Hindu leaders are sowing seeds of trouble which are germinating all over India, Hindu students attend gymnasiums to cultivate physical strength so as to be ready for a final life and death struggle with the Moslems.

The Hindu leaders, this Minority Report continues, have made no attempt to create confidence in the minds of the minority community. "Their intransigence, the arrogance with which they treated the legitimate and reasonable demands of the Moslems, their savage attacks on defenceless Moslems on the occasion of riots, show that they are incapable of humane and orderly government."

And all these frank expressions are made by responsible Moslems, in a report—the Report of the Indian Central Committee—presented to Parliament.

The Hindu members of the Committee do not use such strong language about the Moslems. But they do admit that the most distressing feature of the political development of India since 1921 has been the growth of communal jealousy. There runs through Indian society to-day, they write, a series of cleavages—of religion, race, and caste—which constantly threaten its stability. The two communities, Moslem and Hindu, are in a state of perpetual opposition, which blazes periodically into actual hostilities. The rivalry has assumed grievous proportions in recent years. And since the appointment of the Simon Commission the struggle has been intensified and has developed into a race for power.

And the Hindus complain that if the Moslems, who are confessedly a backward community, educationally and economically, are given an undue proportion of political power, they might act as a drag on the political progress of India.

If there were nothing but this hostility and this increasing hostility between Hindus and Moslems, there would be small hope for India. But there are leading men on both sides who see the dangers of this continued antagonism. And their love for India makes them determined to find a way of adjusting the differences.

Mr. C. Vijiaraghavachari, as quoted in Sir Reginald Craddock's *The Dilemma in India*, says that if Indians would but compose their domestic quarrels arising from religion or caste, and adopt the wise course that Canada did, they might also have dominion from sea to sea, and from sea to mountain, and become as free and prosperous and proud as Canada. He draws attention to the melancholy state of affairs in China and Afghanistan. They are both independent countries. And in both political reforms should have been easy of achievement. Yet in both the reformers have been opposed. And India is more apt than Afghanistan or China to produce disturbances. Its innumerable tributary princes, and religious and racial sections, would all be exploited to oppose the national patriots. He therefore urges that India should always remain within the British Empire. She would thereby have the advantage of assistance in defending herself; she would have the advantage of higher financial credit; and she would have the advantage of the co-operation of Englishmen in the services—civil, military, naval, and aerial. Indians, he says, had long ago lost their capacity and disciplined habits for running a free Government, while Englishmen had all the time been developing those habits. "We sadly, but imperatively, need their association with us in maintaining and developing our newly-won free institutions on the soundest principles tested by their long experience."

There are then Hindus who would work for the unity of India and the composing of Hindu-Moslem hostility. And among these the most prominent is Gandhi. He has been accused of turning Moslem grievances against the British to his own account in his campaign against British authority. And this may or may not be true. But he is obviously quite genuinely intent upon a reconciliation. His patriotism demands it, and his fundamental religious beliefs compel it. Moreover, he has been profoundly impressed by the character of the Prophet Mohammed, by the simplicity of the Moslem teaching, and the fervent faith of Moslems. And the story of the suffering without retaliation of the Prophet's son-in-law, Ali, has deeply moved him.

There are also a few Moslems who would work for unity. The Maharaja of Mahmudabad, for instance, and Sir Ali Imam, who was for some time a member of the Government of India, are opposed to those separate electorates for Moslems which most Moslems contend for. These two believe that the separate electorates are not only against the interests of Moslems and fruitful of evil, but are also opposed to the interests of Indian nationality. They would put Indian nationality first. And the younger generation of Moslems are disposed to do likewise—to be Indians first and Moslems second.

And so, too, would the British Government. They would put Indian nationality and Indian unity before Hindu-Moslem differences. It is not to the wish or the advantage of the British that the antagonism between Hindus and Moslems should continue. A divided India is not a British interest. The British interest is Indian unity, prosperity, and contentment.

Mr. Montagu and Lord Chelmsford in their joint report, the one as Secretary of State for India and the other as Viceroy, expressly state that differences between races and creeds are out of harmony with the ideas on which free institutions run. They appeal to Hindus and Moslems "to cultivate a community of interests in the greater welfare of the whole." They urge that the first duty of the leaders of every party in the state is to unteach partisanship. And if the Hindu or the Moslem displays intolerance of the other's religious practices, it is the business of the enlightened leaders of the community to explain to them that they are only retarding a cause that ought to be dearer to them than their own sectional interests.

A Hindu or a Moslem might possibly reply that what Mr. Montagu and Lord Chelmsford regarded as a sectional interest was their religion, and dearer to them than their country. But even so they could not say that the responsible British representatives were trying to "divide and rule." They would have to admit that the British did at least have the intention of uniting the two great Indian communities.

And this intention was shown again by Lord Irwin. In 1927, when the antagonism between Moslems and Hindus had led to bloodshed and scenes of atrocity throughout India, he did not rejoice at these signs of division and think that because of them he would be able to rule all the better. He made an earnest appeal to Indians to rescue the good name of India from the hurt which their present discords were inflicting on it. "In the name of Indian national life, in the name of religion," he exclaimed, "I appeal to all in each of the two communities who hold position . . . boldly to repudiate feelings of hatred and intolerance, actively to condemn acts of violence and aggression, earnestly to strive to exorcise suspicions and misapprehensions, and so create a new atmosphere of trust. And I appeal in the name of national life because communal tension is eating into it as a canker."

And in the Legislative Assembly Lord Irwin made a similar appeal for united effort, for upon it depended "the building of the Indian nation."

That the antagonism between Hindus and Moslems is deep-seated, and that it has been accentuated rather than diminished by the reforms; that certain leaders on both sides deplore this state of things and would wish to stop it; and that the British Government itself wants the great dissension to be ended, should be evident. How this can be done we have now to consider.

Community of interests is the means suggested by the Moslem Dr. Suhrawardy in his Minority

Report. So long as there is a community of interests the Hindus and Moslems work hand in hand together, he says. He contends that the Swaraj Party all over India derives its main strength from the support of its Moslem members. Even to-day the Hindu Pandit Motilal Nehru has a number of Moslem members of the Legislative Assembly as members of his party, and these follow him as faithfully as any Hindu. And when there is conflict between Hindu and Moslem it is often the conflict between those who have and those who have not, the remedy for which lies in the reconciliation of clashing interests rather than in the stifling of the cry of the weak by the strong.

And, terrible as is the strife once hostility has broken out, there does remain the fact that for long periods the antagonism lies dormant. Hindus and Moslems are not perpetually at one another's throats. In the ordinary run of things in towns and villages they live together as neighbours in all outward amity. And it is by no means always the case that Hindu processions play loud music when passing mosques; they will often accede to a polite request to refrain. And there is no reason why well-directed public opinion should not more frequently be brought to bear upon both communities to be more tolerant towards each other in these small matters which have nothing whatever to do with any fundamental principles.

Gandhi, whose patriotism drives him vehemently towards Hindu-Moslem unity, holds that each should remain true to his own religion and yet be true to the other. The unity consists in their having a common purpose, a common goal, and common sorrows. And it is best promoted " by co-operating in order to reach the common goal, by sharing one another's sorrows, and by mutual toleration." And the common goal is to make " this great country of ours greater and self-governing." All the quarrels between the two have arisen from each wanting to force the other to his view. But he says they cannot live in peace if the Hindus will not tolerate the Moslem form of worship of God and Moslem manners and customs, or if Moslems are impatient of Hindu idolatry or cow-worship. It is not necessary to approve what is tolerated. But there must be toleration.

And as regards fundamental principles, there might even be a nearer approach than the more bigoted might suppose. Islam insists that God is One. Hinduism recognises many gods. The two seem irreconcilable. But the Hindu philosopher holds that these myriad gods and godlets are only manifestations of one Supreme Being. And the ordinary Hindu villager just speaks of " God." God has sent the rain. God has withheld the rain. In his simple mind, as in the philosopher's and in the Moslem's, there is one God.

And surely at the highest, among the mystics of both Islam and Hinduism, Moslems and Hindus are not so very far apart. When the Moslem saint Mansur sings :

> Of how the Highest High can condescend,
> And how the lowest low can rise and soar
> Even to Thy Presence, even to Thy Heart,
> O mightiest of the mighty (yet more dear
> Than mighty), ever nearer and more near,
> Until he is, and shall be evermore,
> O mightiest of the mighty, what Thou art,

he cannot be far distant from the Hindu yogis in their moments of highest rapture.

At the summit the tension between Hindus and Moslems must relax and vanish. In the highest heights both are fellow-worshippers of God.

CHAPTER IX

THE WORKING OF THE REFORMS

FROM this consideration of this greatest obstacle which stands in the way of Indian unity we return now to a consideration of the working of the reforms which were instituted ten years ago.

Substantial steps in the direction of the "development of self-governing institutions, with a view to the progressive realisation of responsible government," had been taken. The attempt had been made to transfer some portion of the burden from the shoulders of the British to the shoulders of the Indians. Have the Indians shown themselves capable of bearing the additional burden? Have the methods of transferring the burden proved adequate? Or can they be improved? And can more of the burden now safely be transferred? These are the questions to which we must, with the aid of the Simon Report, now find an answer.

And on the whole the Commissioners did find that the Indians had been able to bear the amount of responsibility which had been put upon them; and they recommended that they should be given more.

It will be remembered that the advance was to be made chiefly in the provinces. And here the Commission found that substantial progress had in fact been made. Everywhere the conduct of business had been carried on with keenness; there had been much good debating, and the Government had been exposed to considerable challenge and comment from its opponents among the elected members. "It is much to the credit of many of India's public men," the Report says, "that they should so readily have adapted themselves to these new methods." They may have shown themselves indifferent to the practical needs of administrative efficiency, but they have also in many instances exerted a useful influence and thrown an informing light upon the proceedings of Government. Except in two provinces, the reformed Provincial Councils have actually worked, and they have worked better, certainly, than many anticipated at their inception. This is the considered opinion of the Simon Commission. And this in spite of the Extremists having first boycotted the Councils and then entered them for the only purpose of wrecking them from within. Orderly conduct of business was the rule everywhere. And the Commission were struck by the good attendance of members in the Chamber, by the high level of courteous speech, and by the respect shown to the Chair. The public galleries were well filled, and the proceedings were obviously followed with much interest.

The average voter and, still more, the average citizen did not as yet pay close attention to the activities of his representative, the Commission thought. The lack of communications, the prevalence of illiteracy, and the dispersal of so much of the population in small villages make the organisation of political activities very difficult and the progress of political education very slow. But interest was growing. It might be very largely a contest of persons, not policies, which was presented to the elector's mind. That, in the present stage of party organisation in India, was inevitable. But there was a relatively high level of voting at elections. And electoral contests did really attract the interests of the general body of voters.

The "pleader" was the most favoured candidate. Other public men, such as honorary magistrates and presidents of municipalities and district boards, were less ready to submit to the anxieties of an election. In the rural districts substantial landowners, moneylenders, medical practitioners, and retired Government servants would be the principal representatives besides pleaders. And in the towns a number of business men were returned. The presence of non-official European members was welcomed by Indians of all communities, and they have been distinguished in the Legislatures by their public spirit, sympathy, and width of outlook.

All this was to the good. But the system of dyarchy was not a success. It was in any case only a temporary measure, and the Commission did not recommend its continuance. It proved impracticable in the eyes of the Legislature, the electorate, and the public to obtain a clear demarcation of responsibility. The theoretical distinction became "blurred" in practice. And "the fundamental conception of the dyarchic system—complete 'responsibility' of Ministers in a certain defined field, and in that field only—has become hopelessly obscured."

The Central Legislature has received more prominence in the Press than the Provincial Legislatures. But it has been found to suffer from one grave defect. The constituencies electing directly to it cover areas and include populations far too great for the representatives to keep in touch with their constituents. The rural constituencies returning a single member are nowhere less than 6,000 square miles in area. The rest range between 7,000 and 62,000 square miles, with populations reaching in individual cases to as much as six millions. Distance is another factor tending to a divorce of the representative from the life of the constituency. A representative from Madras might have to travel for sixty hours to Delhi or seventy-eight hours to Simla. The result has been that once a member has been elected he takes little interest in his constituency until the next election comes around. His sense of responsibility to his constitutents is small. And they on their part take little interest in his proceedings and make no attempt to hold him to account.

The composition of the two Houses in 1928 was:

	Hindus.	*Moslems.*	*Europeans.*	*Others.*	*Total.*
Council of State ...	21	17	16	6	60
Assembly	70	38	25	12	145

The Assembly, as the popular body, receives most notice in the Press and political circles, and a large proportion of the leaders of public opinion in the country are members—though, as we shall presently see, many important leaders remain outside. Its general atmosphere differs greatly from that of the Council of State. "Antagonisms are sharper, debates more acrimonious, and work generally more strenuous," says the Simon Report. The

Council of State, on the other hand, represents the more conservative elements in the country, and, in particular, sections of society which have most to lose by hasty legislation. Naturally, therefore, it takes a different view on many subjects from the progressive Assembly.

One prominent feature of the working of the Central Legislature is that the Governor-General's Council (the chief executive body in India) is entirely independent of a majority in the Legislature and can rarely count on one. A Cabinet which is defeated in the House of Commons has to resign. In India no defeat in the Assembly could drive the Central Executive from office. The Governor-General has statutory powers in reserve sufficient to prevent the Administration being brought to a standstill. Again, the Opposition in the Indian Legislature has no prospect of succeeding to office. It has not therefore to make good its criticisms. And they tend to be irresponsible. But the course of development has not been so unfavourable as might have been expected. "On the one hand, while the attitude of the Assembly has often been strongly influenced by its constitutional irresponsibility, it has co-operated with Government a good deal. On the other hand, the Executive has been far from irresponsive to the criticism and to the suggestions of the Legislature."

This influence of the Legislature on the Executive has been exercised by putting questions to Government and moving resolutions, by using the financial power it possesses over votable items in the Budget, and by standing committees.

And the indirect influence of the Assembly on the Government has been of still greater importance, says the Report. Members of Government are greatly influenced by contact with the elected representatives.

But the Legislatures, Central and Provincial, did not absorb all the political life of India. Outside was the strong non-co-operation movement led by Gandhi to which we have already referred. And he had as his objective the paralysis of Government. He succeeded, in 1920, in securing the support of the National Congress for his campaign. With its help non-co-operation committees were set up in the villages. Government was everywhere vilified. And, in spite of Gandhi's advocacy of "non-violence," disorder broke out in many provinces. And in August, 1921, the Moplahs rose in rebellion. The Moplahs are a sturdy Moslem people living on the west coast. And thinking that Government could no longer enforce its orders, they proceeded to destroy the machinery of government in their area; they killed or drove off all the officials and turned on the Hindu population in an outburst of murder and arson. Besides this, fifty-three persons were killed and four hundred and three wounded in a riot in Bombay. And at Chauri Charua twenty-one police constables were murdered with revolting cruelty. Defiance of authority became widespread, police stations were attacked, Europeans were assaulted, and every kind of intimidation and social pressure was employed to induce the general body of officials to resign. Matters went near to a complete dissolution of law and order. But on the arrest, trial, sentence, and imprisonment of Gandhi in

March, 1922, the movement subsided—at least for the moment.

And things remained quiet till the arrival of the Indian Statutory Commission set all India in commotion again. The whole future of their country was in debate, so no wonder Indians were excited. And they were not only excited, but resentful. They resented that a Commission composed only of British Members of Parliament and with no Indian members should be sent to enquire into the working of the system of government and to report whether responsible government should be extended or restricted. And they were not appeased when they were told that the Commission was sent out by Parliament to report to Parliament and must therefore be composed of Members of Parliament, nor even when a corresponding Committee composed of representatives of India was allowed to sit alongside the Simon Commission and report independently. Attempts were made to boycott the Commission. Gandhi again appeared upon the scene, and at the meeting of the Indian National Congress in December, 1928, demanded that full self-government should be granted within a year. And in December, 1929, the Congress declared for "complete independence." The Viceroy's declaration that the goal of responsible self-government set forth by the British Government implied Dominion Status, and that the British Government after the receipt of the Simon Report would hold a Round Table Conference, to which representatives of both the Indian States and British India would be invited to meet His Majesty's Government, only allayed feeling for a time. Full self-government, and at once, was the demand. Gandhi started a non-co-operation and civil disobedience campaign and tried to imbue the whole country with contempt for the Government. And it was in this atmosphere that the Simon Commission in June, 1930, submitted their Report to the King.

Their principal recommendation was that a real advance in self-government should be made in the provinces. The provinces, not the Central Legislature, should be the scene of advance. Dyarchy should disappear. A Unitary Government should be established in each province. The Governor should choose the members of the Cabinet, and not necessarily from among the elected members of the Legislature. And every member of it should be required and prepared to take responsibility for the whole policy of provincial government. Thus the Commissioners recommended that even the police should be placed under a Minister responsible to the Provincial Legislature. The Commissioners were quite aware of the gravity of transferring police to an Indian Minister. But they argued that, if dyarchy was to be ended, Ministers must have responsibility for law and order as well as for all other subjects. Responsible government in the provinces could not be achieved without this change. So the aim was to give the maximum of provincial autonomy consistent with the common interest of India as a whole. In future each province would be as far as possible mistress in her own house. And the essence of the plan was to afford to Indians the opportunity of judging by experiment in the provincial sphere how far the British system of parliamentary government was fitted to their needs and to the natural genius of the people. The change involved was great and far-reaching. For henceforward in the provincial sphere all branches of the Administration might pass into the hands of Indian Ministers.

The next main recommendation was that the central body should be *federal*. The Commission wished to bring in the Indian States. And it was only in a federal constitution that units differing so widely as the provinces of British India and the Indian States could be brought together while retaining internal autonomy. British India was too large a unit for the application of the principles of Western democracy. The provinces should be the units. So voters, instead of electing a representative on the Central Legislature, would elect a representative for the Provincial Legislature: and the Provincial Legislature would send their representative to the Central Legislature. British India would evolve into a federation of self-governing units—the provinces. And at some future time the Indian States might adhere to an All-India Federation. The constituent units would preserve their identities but look to the Centre to deal with matters common to all.

What is now known as the Legislative Assembly would be called the Federal Assembly. The Council of State would continue with its existing functions. The existing legislative and financial powers of the two Chambers of the Central Legislature would remain as at present. And the Central Executive would continue to be the Governor-General in Council, but the Governor-General—not the Crown—would henceforward be the authority who would select and appoint his Executive Councillors.

In addition, the Commission recommended the immediate setting up of a consultative Council of Greater India, which would discuss matters of common interest to British India and the Indian States.

These were the principal changes recommended. But the need for safeguards was greatly emphasised by the Commission. There must be full provision for the maintenance and efficiency of the fundamentals of government. "However much," they say, "we may subscribe to the doctrine that good government is no substitute for self-government, we must ensure that we do not put forward proposals that will permit of government being replaced by anarchy." Grave dangers had to be provided for. There was the perpetual menace of the wild tribesmen on the North-West Frontier and the possibility of attack from a foreign enemy. "It is an absolute condition for the development of self-government in India that the gateway should be safely held." But to do this the presence of British troops, and British officers serving in Indian regiments, would "for many years" be essential. And this fact gravely complicated the problem of the introduction of an increasing measure of responsibility into the Central Government. Then the possibilities of internal disturbances are not less grave. And "experience has shown in other countries that a period of transition may easily result, not in ordered advance, but in a lapse into civil war and anarchy." (Presumably the reference here is to China.) The Commissioners thoroughly believed in the doctrine that a sense of responsibility can only be taught by making men responsible for the effects of their own actions. But they desired to secure that that experience was not bought too dearly. So they would have in India a power which could step in and save the situation before it was too late. They would give the fullest scope for self-government, but, if there were a breakdown, then an alternative authority must operate unhampered. They therefore recommended that the Governor-General or the Governor, as the case might be, should be armed with full and ample power.

Then the rights of minorities had also to be safeguarded. Members of minority communities had real reason to fear that their rights might be disregarded. And the Commission considered that "the only practical means of protecting the weaker or less numerous elements in the population is by the retention of an impartial power, residing in the Governor-General and the Governors of provinces, to be exercised for this purpose."

The Commission, therefore, recommended that in certain eventualities and for certain purposes the Governor should have in reserve the power to overrule the joint advice of his Ministers. The powers at present reserved for the Governor-General would be retained.

The Commission have been criticised for their recommendations. It has been said that what they would give with one hand they would take back with the other. As long as Governors have these overriding powers in reserve the Ministers would have no real responsibility. But facts have to be faced. Even since the Great War India has been invaded from outside and has been the scene of grave disorders within. And in the two countries which immediately adjoin her—China on the east and Afghanistan on the west—there has been grave civil war. The Commission had good grounds for combining caution with their boldness.

Another important criticism is that the Central Executive would continue as before to be responsible to the British Parliament and not to the Indian Legislature, and that there is no indication as to how fresh advance in transferring the responsibility from the British to the Indians is to be made. The Commission merely say that an attempt to devise now a detailed and formal Constitution for the Centre would be to ignore the fact that its ultimate form must depend on the action of its constituent parts. And this may be true. But it does not help us forward. What we want to know is how the transfer of responsibility is to be effected—by what steps that transfer is to proceed. The Central Executive remains, as before, completely irremovable. This, we have seen, was the cause of much heartburning among Indians after the Morley Reforms. The Simon Report shows the same objections after the Montagu Reforms. And still the Commissioners propose no change. Presumably this cannot be the permanent and irrevocable condition of government. And some indication is wanted as to how the new Federal Assembly may be gradually led to take over the responsibility of government.

And Indians must have a scheme which they themselves are willing to work. The irreconcilables may determine to work no scheme. But there are numbers of capable men who are prepared to work out a reform scheme. And what is needed is not what may be ideally perfect from the British point of view, but what is reasonably workable and which appeals to them so that they are willing to work it. The will to work the new scheme must exist or the scheme is bound to fail. We cannot brook the Indians rejecting in a pet any and every scheme that is put before them. But we must have regard to their own wishes, and evolve out of the Simon Report some scheme that the Indians themselves would be ready and willing to work. And this will be the task of the Round Table Conference and, after that, of Parliament.

We have, however, in every scheme to bear in mind one grave deficiency which the Report has brought to light. A self-governing India can only hope to function with reasonable prospect of success if it can command military forces of its own, the Commission say. But they also say that, "at least for a very long time to come, it will be impossible for the army entrusted with the task of defending India to dispense with a very considerable British element, including in that term British troops of all arms, a considerable portion of the regimental officers of the Indian Army, and the British personnel in the higher command." And yet as long as there is in the Army in India this British element (which at present amounts to about 60,000 British troops of all kinds and some thousands of British officers) it is impossible to relinquish control over the Army to Ministers responsible to any elected Legislature. "Such a transfer could only take place where no part of the Army in India consists of British officers or troops recruited by the

Imperial Government." And at the present moment no Indian holding the King's Commission is of higher Army rank than a captain—and even of these there are only thirty-nine.

This exceedingly serious deficiency will be considered in the next chapter more fully. Here it is only necessary to add that the Simon Commission recommended that the protection of the frontiers of India, at any rate for a long time to come, should not be regarded as a function of an Indian Government in relation with an Indian Legislative, but as a matter of supreme concern to the whole Empire. So they suggest that the Army in India should no longer be under the control of the Government of India, but should be under an Imperial authority, which would naturally be the Viceroy, acting in concert with the Commander-in-Chief. The Imperial authorities would undertake the obligations of Indian defence in return for the continued provision of definite facilities as to recruitment, arms, transport, and other matters—while the Indian Government would provide from their revenues an annual total sum subject to revision at intervals.

So the sum of the matter is that the Simon Commission would recommend a very decided advance in the provinces, but little or no change at the centre, because India is not in a position to undertake her own defence. The presence of a British Army and British officers is still required, and ultimate responsibility must therefore still remain with the British Parliament.

And here let us pause and notice one significant fact. The steps already taken and the further advances recommended are all in the direction of a *democratic* form of government. And they may not be what Indians themselves would most like or be what is most suited to their genius. They want to govern themselves. They want to be recognised as "equal" to the British, or the Canadians, or the Australians. But parliamentary institutions, assemblies, elections, and the whole paraphernalia of Western democracy may not be according to their taste. They may prefer an autocratic rule of the Indian type—still, maybe, under the British Crown and with Governors, Indians or British, appointed by the British Crown—but with the administration of a character such as may be seen in the Indian-governed part of India to-day, and which will be described in a subsequent chapter.

But however this may be, what is sufficiently clear from the course of events so far described is that the British have made steady progress over a long period of years towards enabling Indians to take over more and more of the government of their own country, and are at this moment satisfied that a still further advance may be made. This does not satisfy the Indians. They are impatient to get control of their destiny and would hurry the slow-moving British. But the British, knowing the risks, think it better to go too slow than too fast. And about that question of pace there will always be difference of opinion. For the moment it is the "unchanging East" that is hustling the West.

CHAPTER X

INDIAN STATES

THAT one-third of India in area and nearly a quarter of the population is under the rule of Indian rulers is a factor in the problem which has now to be considered. The total area of India is about 1,800,000 square miles, and of this about 700,000 square miles lie within the boundaries of the Indian States which are not British territory at all, though their rulers are under the suzerainty of the British Crown. The total population of India is 318,942,000, and of these 71,900,000 were classed as in the Indian States.

These states are 562 in number, but vary enormously in size and importance. The largest, Hyderabad, has an area of 82,700 square miles and a population of 12,500,000. The smallest are little estates of a few square miles. Only 108 of them are of sufficient importance for the rulers of them to be members of the Chamber of Princes in their own right. One hundred and twenty-seven others are represented in the Chamber by twelve members of their order elected by themselves. And 327 are not of sufficient importance to be represented at all. They are merely estates. Among the more important are the historic State of Mysore, with an area of 30,000 square miles and a population of 6,000,000; Baroda, with a population of 2,000,000; Kashmir, with an area of over 80,000 square miles and a population of 3,500,000; and Travancore, with a population of 4,000,000.

Each of these states manages its own internal affairs by making and administering its own laws, and imposing, collecting, and spending its own taxes. The government of all of them is of an autocratic type. Some thirty of them have, indeed, instituted a form of Legislative Council, but this is invariably of a consultative nature. Forty have established High Courts, more or less based on the European model. And thirty-four claim to have separated executive from judicial function—the word "claim" is that used in the Simon Report.

The relations between these states and the British Government are conducted through the agency of a Resident or Political Agent—a Resident in the case of the larger states, a Political Agent in the case of the lesser. All these states are under the protection of the British Government, and their relations with one another or with any Power outside India must be conducted through that British Government. Kashmir, for instance, though it touches Afghan and Chinese territory, cannot have direct relations with either Afghanistan or China. On the other hand, it is protected against aggression from those countries—and from Afghanistan there has been very serious aggression in former times. The internal affairs of an Indian State are managed by the state itself. But the British Government does exercise the right as Paramount Power to intervene in the internal affairs of the state in cases of gross misgovernment, or in cases when such intervention is called for, having regard to the duty of the Crown as Paramount Power to preserve the dynasty, to be answerable for the integrity of the state, and to maintain peace in India.

The Indian States are included with the British Provinces in forming one unit on the League of Nations. That is to say, the India that has a seat on the League is the whole of India and not only British India. And the Indian delegation at Geneva always includes a ruler of an Indian State.

Formerly, it was the custom to discourage, if not actually to forbid, consultation and combination between one Indian State and another. But now a Chamber of Princes has been established for deliberative, consultative, and advisory—though not executive—purposes. And a Standing Committee of this Chamber advises the Viceroy on questions referred to it by him, and proposes for his consideration questions affecting Indian States generally or British India and the states together.

In practice, the extent to which a Resident intervenes in the internal affairs of an Indian State varies considerably. If the state is well-governed he leaves it to itself. But if, as sometimes happens among so large a number of states, the Chief is dissolute or thoroughly incompetent, the Resident has, in the interests of the people, to intervene. In such cases the Government of India would require the Chief to accept the advice of the Resident, or perhaps certain powers would be taken from the Chief, and the annual Budget would have to be placed before the Resident for sanction. Or, again, the Chief might be required to employ an officer from the Government service to put his finances in order, or to reorganise the land revenue system—as was done by Sir Walter Lawrence in Kashmir. But these would be only temporary measures, and as soon as the improvement had been effected the intervention would be withdrawn.

The Chiefs, as is natural, resent such intervention. And I dare say other ex-Residents besides myself are conscious of sometimes having acted not over considerately or tactfully towards a Chief. When things are going all wrong about you, when you are being begged by the people to intervene and you are conscious of having the power to set things right, it is not particularly easy to keep your eyes and ears and mouth shut. But in the main it is the policy of Government to leave the Chiefs to govern their own states. Whether for good or ill, the British have not acted on the same lines as the French in Tunis or Morocco, where the Resident has a whole staff of French officials under him acting alongside the officials of the country throughout the whole administration and intervening most actively (and most beneficially as far as that goes) in the affairs of the state, and designedly striving to bring the administration up to the French standard. There is never such permanent intervention as this in an Indian State. The Chiefs are left to govern their states themselves, and their interests are sympathetically regarded by the Viceroy. And this attitude towards the Chief is, I am convinced, very largely due to the personal influence of British Sovereigns. From the time that the government of India came directly under the Crown a much more sympathetic attitude towards the Chiefs was observable; and Queen Victoria would often say a decisive word on the side of a Chief. Perhaps if Great Britain had been a Republic the Indian States would have been in a very different position to-day. They might be better governed, but they might not be governed by their Chiefs. They might be governed by British officials, with the Chiefs mere puppets in the background.

Perhaps the reader will the better understand the variety of these states and the nature of their peoples and rulers if I describe those with which I have myself been personally connected. The first of the rulers with whom I had to conduct relations was the Mir of Hunza. Hunza is a remote mountain state at the extreme north of India touching the furthest limits of the Chinese Empire. It then owned a very shadowy allegiance to both Kashmir and China. The ruler had come to the throne a few years previously by poisoning his father and throwing his two brothers over a precipice. He had an extremely capable Minister, who transacted all the business of the state. He was a man of fine address and great eloquence. But neither he nor his Chief, nor any of the "nobles," could read or write. There were no laws—only customs. And the Chief considered his people were his own absolute property, like sheep or goats. When he asked that my Gurkha escort should have shots at a man on the opposite side of the valley and I objected, he merely replied, "Why not? The man is my own." The people obeyed him unquestioningly. He would order them off on distant raids across lofty Himalayan passes and through barren, uninhabited country and they would hate going, but they would have to obey, for if they refused, or if they did not bring back sufficient booty, he would have them kept in cold glacier water till they nearly perished. He would levy blackmail—called tribute—from distant villages in Turkestan or from Kirghiz encampments on the Pamirs. And he would frequently be attacking villages of neighbouring states. Similarly, his villages would be attacked by them. There was constant petty warfare. Not much loss of life was the result. But everyone was kept on the *qui vive*. In 1891, as the Chief was defying the British and intriguing with the Russians, who had in that year advanced on to and annexed the Pamirs, he was driven from his throne, and his one surviving brother was put on it in his place. That brother has remained there ever since, and has thus had a reign of unparalleled length in Hunza history. Raids on distant trade routes have ceased. Attack and counter-attack on and by neighbouring villages no longer takes place. No son or other relative dares try to supplant him as his brother supplanted his father. The peace of British paramountcy has descended upon that distant mountain state. The population is growing past the ability of the country to support it. Education is being introduced—and European clothes. And the ruler is now a Knight Commander of the Most Eminent Order of the Indian Empire.

The next ruler with whom I had to do was the Mehtar of Chitral. This was in 1893. Chitral is another mountain state in the extreme north of India. It adjoins Afghan territory, and is so close to Russian territory that in 1891 I came across an armed party of Russians who prided themselves upon having crossed into Chitral territory by one pass and crossed out of it by another. With the support of the British the Mehtar had just been able to place himself on the throne. When his father died the seventeen sons had scrambled for the throne, but after a fortnight only four were left. Of these the eldest had fled to us for support, and it was with that support that he was able to ascend the throne. We gave that support because, with the Russians close at hand, we could not risk the chance of their supporting either him or some other claimant. And with an escort of fifty Sikhs I was in Chitral for nearly two years.

The same autocratic rule as I had observed in Hunza I saw here. The Chief would have liked to murder his remaining brothers. He was in constant expectancy of being murdered, and always had a bodyguard round him. And he was continually murdering nobles whom he thought might cause him trouble. Here, again, as in Hunza, there were no fixed laws—only customs. And the state business was conducted by word of mouth in daily open Durbar. The Chief was never without a following round him, and the business flowed along with the following. Nobles and their retainers would form part of the following, and would be expected to come in turns from distant parts of the state to pay their respects to the Chief and transact any business. Anyone with a grievance would watch his opportunity for presenting his case, and would present it with remarkable eloquence. If he could succeed in enlisting the sympathy of someone of influence or of the Chief himself, he might gain redress ; if not he was shovelled out of the assembly. Anyhow, he had had his say and taken his chance and therein so far was happy. There were no written records, for hardly a dozen men in the whole state could read or write. But the memory of illiterate men is deep. And in the memory of that everchanging but everlasting assembly all essential facts were recorded.

The people of Chitral, as of Hunza, belonged to the Chief. He would take away a wife from one man and give her to another. But though he could do arbitrary acts of this nature, he could not depart by one hair's breadth from the accepted customs of the country. Much as he would have liked to, he could not wear a European hat.

During the time that I was in Chitral life was full of movement. There was the perpetual question whether the Chief could retain his hold over the remoter valleys or whether the Governors of these outlying districts would not set up independently on their own. He would be claiming authority over villages on the fringes of Chitral, and neighbouring Chiefs would be claiming the same villages as belonging to them. And every now and then there would be a scare of invasion, and levies from the interior would be hastily called up. And they would be hurried to the frontier—though where the frontier exactly was no one knew, for it was a line as variable as the tide line by the shore.

After two exciting years the Chief was murdered by his brother. This brother was removed by the British. Other claimants appeared from Afghanistan. The British were attacked. A relief force was sent up. A third brother was put on the throne and has remained there ever since. Excitement has ceased. Order has been established. A

British-Indian force is retained in the country. The frontiers are demarcated. The Chief has no fear of rivals or of attack, and he may not attack anyone himself. All is peaceful and serene—if rather drab and dull compared with former times. Thirty years ago a life insurance company would not have dared to set up an office on this frontier. To-day one would do a roaring business. Of the Chief's eleven sons the eldest will come comfortably to the throne, and the remainder will have to acquiesce—and anyhow be sure of their lives.

I give this account of two frontier states as they were in their own natural condition before the blessings and the dulness of British ascendancy had befallen them because they afford us an example of what most of India must have been like before the advent of the British. For, in addition to the general histories of India, I have often had to examine the detailed history of the various states to which I have been appointed as Political Agent or Resident, and always I have found the record of perpetual strife between neighbouring states, and of struggles between brothers, cousins, and uncles for the throne. And we may presume that before the *pax Britannica* had spread over India, as in Hunza and Chitral thirty years ago so in most of the innumerable little states into which India was then divided there would have been the same struggle for the throne, the same risk of the occupant being supplanted by some rival, the same vagueness of frontiers, the same precarious hold over outlying villages and districts, the same insecurity of life and property, the same obedience to custom, the same absolute autocracy, the same touch between prince and people through the Durbar, the same semi-independence of nobles, and the same alternating gloom over the people when things went wrong and light-hearted gaiety when all went well.

My next experience was very different. I was away now from the frontier and in the heart of India, where for nearly a century there had been no breath of strife between state and state. But this experience was enlightening also because here I saw a fossil state. A state exactly as it had been a hundred years ago and for hundreds of years before that, but now petrified. As Bundi was when I saw it in 1898, so must it have been in 1798 and 1598; though now, when there was neither the necessity to defend itself, nor the ambition to settle some feud with its neighbours, it was, if not petrified, at any rate in a state of suspended animation. The Chief was the scion of a family which had been on the throne for eight hundred years. The Chief Minister was hereditary. The poet laureate was hereditary. Most of the chief posts in the state were occupied by members of the Chief Minister's family. And neither the Chief, nor his Minister, nor anyone else had much need to think, for no preparations for attack from outside had to be made, and all within was governed by custom, tradition, precedent. To the question, "What should be done?" the answer was, "What was done last time?"

But if there was not much life there was lots of colour about Bundi. The Chief was a noble figure in his ancient Rajput dress. He was the personification of dignity and courtesy. And his astute and clever Brahmin Minister, though he ruled ruler and people with the persistent purpose and in the masterful manner of his dominant caste, was as suave in manner as he was immaculate in dress. The proud nobles had each their appointed precedence in Durbar. And when assembled on some special occasion in the hall of the rock-built palace vied with one another in the brightness of their dress and the splendour of their jewels. Hardly a person in the state spoke English. None wore European dress. All was purely Indian.

Such was a really Indian Indian State. Most beautiful to look upon. But stagnant—lifeless. And when famine came upon it the will to resist it was wanting. It was a calamity to which humble submission must be made. I have described the result in the first chapter.

Adjoining this Hindu State of Bundi was the Moslem State of Tonk, to which I was also attached as Political Agent. The founder of this state was, in the estimation of his descendants, a "mighty conqueror." He was, in fact, one of those adventurous spirits who came to the front when the Moghul Empire was breaking up and who had seized patches of rich land in various parts of Rajputana and Central India. The inhabitants were nearly all Hindu and the ruling family was as alien to them as a Highland family would be to Spaniards. But there was a certain masterfulness about these Moslem rulers, and if their administration was not particularly efficient there was no serious discontent.

Again, there was a difference in the next state to which I was appointed. This was no ancient state like Bundi, where all was run on lines of heredity. It was no older than the commencement of British rule in India. Indore, ruled by Maharajas who are always named Holkar, was a Mahratta State. In an earlier chapter we have heard how the Mahrattas fought with the Moghuls and on the break-up of the Moghul Empire aspired to be the dominant power in India. The original Holkar was one of the Mahratta Generals. He had been of a lowly caste and had risen by his own capacity and energy. In course of time he had settled down on the lands his armies had conquered and set himself up, like the other Mahratta Generals—Scindia of Gwalior and the Gaekwar of Baroda—as semi-independent Chieftains owning but nominal allegiance to the hereditary Prime Minister the Peshwa, at Poona. The State of Indore was not a compact state like Bundi, enclosed within a continuous boundary. It was composed, like the other Mahratta States, of numerous scattered parcels of lands often separated from one another by twenty or thirty miles of intervening territory of some other state. And very few of the inhabitants were Mahrattas. But the rule was firm and masterful. The Holkar of my time was a capable ruler—though an erratic one, and subject to fits of ungovernable temper, which eventually necessitated his abdication.

The interest in this state was rather in the Minister and Administration. Nanak Chand was an example of what Indians may become as Ministers. He was born and educated in British territory—at Delhi. But he gained his experience in Indore. And the experience had made him resourceful and adaptable. Affairs in an Indian State are not conducted with the same rigidity and regularity as they are in a British Province. A Minister in an Indian State has to be ready to adapt himself to the more changeable will or whim of an autocratic ruler. He therefore acquires—or anyhow requires—a certain pliancy. And this Nanak Chand had. But he had also great pertinacity of purpose. And though he was naturally of a timid nature he could show fine courage on emergency. On two or three occasions he had had to flee from Indore almost in terror of his life on account of the outbursts of temper of Holkar, yet the two always eventually made up their differences, and Nanak Chand would again courageously face his task.

As President of the Council of Regency, which was established on Holkar's abdication during the minority of his successor, I saw much of Nanak Chand. I never found him anything but beautifully poised, clear-headed, and wise in the transaction of business. As a man of deep religion, and a great admirer of the Swami Vivakenanda, he was most anxious to introduce religious education into the schools. And one would think that in a Hindu State there would, of course, be religious instruction. But there was not; and even Nanak Chand could not carry it through. For in Indore, as in England with Christianity, there was the difficulty of deciding *what* form of Hinduism should be taught. Even as to what was orthodox Hinduism there was grave difference of opinion. Nanak Chand was not successful here. But he held the Administration together, and was a good example of the capacity of Indians to govern.

The other Ministers had not the ability, or the rough experience, or the pliability of Nanak Chand.

But they were keen on everything that affected the welfare of Indore, and with Nanak Chand to lead them, worked with a will. They took a pride in bringing Indore on. If they heard that things were done better in Baroda or Mysore they would try to get Indore up to that standard. The most efficient Minister was a highly trained Revenue Official from the British Government Service. But with all his good points he had not the adaptability of Nanak Chand. He was an excellent wheel in a machine. But he was accustomed to serve in a smoothly running, well-regulated engine rather than to work in the atmosphere of an Indian State. And outside the administration of his particular department he did not count for much.

My experience in Tibet I do not refer to here as it was outside India. I will only say that under that very autocratic form of government the people seemed remarkable happy. After Tibet I was appointed to Kashmir. It is a state with an area seven times the size of Switzerland and with mountains twice as high—the most beautiful country in all the world. The population of three and a half millions is extraordinarily varied. Only a very small proportion is Hindu. The bulk is Moslem. But there are also Buddhists of the Tibetan type. And the people varied in culture as much as in religion and race. At the one end of the scale were the hardy Hunza raiders who had not a glimmering of education. At the other end were the astute and cultured Kashmiri Pandits. Thus in this single state there was more difference than there is among the peoples of the whole of Europe.

The Maharaja of Kashmir in my time was of the

old-fashioned orthodox Hindu type, very strict in his religious observances, and also convinced of the efficacy of consulting Hindu seers at Benares before important interviews with the Viceroy or Resident. He was greatly respected by Indians all over India on account of his good and religious life. Every Englishman who knew him also had a great affection for him, for he was kindly and warm-hearted, and profoundly loyal to the British Crown. No one would call him a progressive ruler. When told that there were large quantities of oil in the state his reply was, "Let it stop there." But he was closely in touch with his people and knew everything that went on in the state and every official in it.

His Chief Minister was his younger brother, Sir Amar Singh—a singularly capable man, and combining much dignity with his capacity. He was not so naturally devoted to religion as the Maharaja. But he was, like his brother, a great gentleman. He was always beautifully dressed—in a semi-European way. He was very fond of sport, and was at his best when arranging for the entertainment of a Viceroy. He spoke English perfectly, and in matters of business was particularly shrewd; his own personal affairs he had managed so well that he had made himself, with what he had inherited, a man of very great wealth. Compared with Nanak Chand of Indore, he had not perhaps quite the same character or capacity. But he had that peculiar power which comes of ancient lineage and which in India is so valued.

It was sad that between the two brothers all through their lives there was perpetual rivalry. The one used to think the other was plotting against him and using occult powers. Deep down each had a great affection for the other. Sir Amnar Singh often spoke to me affectionately of the Maharaja, and on Amar Singh's death the Maharaja was heartbroken. But in state matters the suspicion and rivalry was always there—as I suppose it would be even in England if the Prime Minister was a brother of the Sovereign.

In Kashmir there was no Legislative Council. There were simply Ministers in charge of various departments. And these Ministers were appointed or dismissed by the Maharaja. And one of the difficulties of the Administration was that the Maharaja thought he had the right to appoint or dismiss any official, however small. If he could not put in some favoured person as clerk to an assistant commissioner or dismiss a police constable what was the good of being Maharaja? This was a difficulty Ministers had to contend with. They had not to be responsible to an elected Chamber, but they had their delicate difficulties with an autocratic—though kindly—ruler. They were nearly all men from outside the state, generally from the Punjab. Some were lent from the service of the Government of India. And these Government servants had all the same trait of machine-like rigidity. They were excellent and conscientious workers, but lonely without the machine. There were also several Englishmen in the Maharaja's service—a Commissioner in charge of the Land Revenue Settlement, a Conservator of Forests, and an Accountant-General, and several military officers lent by the Indian Government. There were also English engineers not of the Government Service,

English employés in the state silk factory; and a Frenchman in charge of the vineyards. All these made up the Kashmir Administration. And it quite evidently took its cue from the Punjab Administration, which afforded a standard or pattern to which it would try to adjust itself.

These were the Indian States of which I had personal experience. Their variety in size and importance and degree of civilisation is evident; as also is the variety of the population included in them. And the rest are much like them in their variety. Some, like Mysore and Travancore, are more "advanced." Others are even more backward than Hunza.

Perhaps a few in one or two particulars are in advance of British Provinces. Mysore and Travancore and Baroda have all paid great attention to education. But, taken as a whole, my experience was that the Indian States were behind the British Provinces in education as in all material development. They were less able to cope with famine or with great outbreaks of disease, and their people were less prosperous. The people had distinctly less freedom, for the vilification of the Government in the Press and on platforms which goes on in British territory would not be tolerated for a moment in an Indian State. And certainly in my time, in adjustments of boundaries between an Indian State and a British Province, a village in British territory would object to be taken away and included in an Indian State. And in thus saying that, in general, the Indian States are less efficiently administered than the British Provinces, I do not think I am biassed by my nationality, for I find in a book written by an Indian member of the Legislative Assembly proposals for raising the Indian State to the level of the British Provinces. The men who made British India what she is should be given a chance in the Indian States. Mr. Iyer says: "He would increase the powers of intervention of Residents in Indian State affairs. And he would have the Chief Ministers and the Chief Justices Englishmen."

Yet, though I believe that the British Provinces are more efficiently administered than the Indian States, and that the individual in the former has more freedom and is more certain of justice, I also think there is more colour in Indian State life. The people like the sight of a ruler of their own. And they love the pomp and pageantry of Indian rule. They have to pay for it indeed. And the percentage of the revenue which an Indian ruler arbitrarily appropriates for "Palace Expenditure" is quite scandalous. Still, the people do get something for their money in the way of a Chief decked with gorgeous jewellery seated on a richly caparisoned elephant with a scarcely less brilliantly attired nobleman sitting behind him whisking off flies with a yak tail. So they are not as discontented with the less efficient rule as their kinsmen in British India might expect them to be.

And a noteworthy fact is that in Indian States there are seldom any Hindu-Moslem riots. The Hindu-Moslem tension is there all the time, but it is kept under subjection. If the ruler is a Hindu the whole Administration is predominantly Hindu, and the Moslems think it best to accept the inevitable without rebelling against it. And likewise the Hindu when the Administration is predominantly Moslem.

Viewed as a whole, it may be said that the states are behindhand but not stagnant. They had at one time a tendency to stagnate, but now the force of emulation is beginning to tell. They are getting more out into the world. They are observing where they are behindhand. And they are beginning to emulate one another and imitate what they see to the good in the administration of British Provinces round them. So progress is certainly being made, and the Chiefs are becoming more sensitive to the welfare of the people.

And in their relations with the British the rulers of these states show a remarkable loyalty to the Sovereign. They instantly declared for the Empire on the outbreak of the Great War. They offered their military forces. And many of them personally served in France and other theatres of war. The Indian delegation to the League of Nations always includes one of them—this year it is headed by the Maharaja of Bikanir. And they have a great part to play in the India of the future.

CHAPTER XI

EMASCULATION

ACROSS the path of India's progress there stands, as we have seen, one great obstacle—the incapacity of the Indians to defend India. Until Indians themselves can recruit, organise, and control an Indian National Army drawn from India as a whole and fit to undertake the tasks which armed forces have to discharge, so far as those tasks are the special concern of India itself and not of the Empire as a whole—until Indians themselves can raise an Army adequate in its high command, staff, and organisation, sufficient in numbers, suitable in composition, and efficient in equipment and training, capable of undertaking unaided the task now discharged by the Army in India—until India can defend herself she cannot be fully self-governing. Indians themselves are not at present in the position to discharge this duty. They are still dependent upon British officers and British troops. And this inability to defend India against outside aggression and internal trouble is the block in the way of India's progress towards the declared goal of responsible self-government. Army administration cannot yet be a function of an Indian Government responsible to an Indian Legislature. And without an effective National Army there can be no true self-government.

These are the conclusions of the Simon Commission. But we must not jump to the conclusion that the fault is all the Indians'. The fault is largely our own. A century ago Ranjit Singh, the great ruler of the Punjab, could hold his own against invaders from the North-West. How is it that to-day even the whole of India—much less the Punjab alone—is deemed incapable of doing the same? The reason is that we have unwittingly emasculated the Indians. We have done too much ourselves and left too little to them, till now the result is that their muscles have grown limp and they are not strong enough to defend themselves. Emasculation has set in.

Indians make many silly accusations against us. When Ghandi, for instance, accuses the British of impoverishing India he is talking palpable nonsense. That India has grown richer, not poorer, under the British is shown by the way in which the peasants are now better clothed, have better household utensils, travel more, and enjoy a few simple luxuries. And the immense increase in trade shows the same thing. As we have seen in a previous chapter,* the evidence that India is not being made poorer is incontestable. That we might have done more to diminish the deplorable poverty is possibly the case. But to say that we have increased it is to deny the plain facts of the case.

And, similarly, when Indians say that our rule is *evil* they are again speaking against the evidence. It may have given the impression that we cared more for material than for spiritual development. Its impartiality towards religion may have been mistaken for indifference. And British rule may

* Pp. 94-96.

have been too leisurely in its efforts at education. But it did take up education before Indian States themselves took it up and before it was taken up even in England itself. And impartial as it is towards religion, it did not, like the present Soviet Government, make deliberate *war* upon religion and execute priests and mullas. Nor did it preach atheism. In the very latest speech by His Majesty there is a reference to the Almighty. It has been at least a "good" Government—even if it might have been better. It has established order and set up a system of impartial justice. So when Ghandi accuses the British Government of being "Satanic" he is guilty of a very unsaintly inexactitude. And I know of no Asiatic Government who would have tolerated his accusations as the British Government have. Certainly the Government of no Indian State would.

But while Indians are not justified in condemning our rule as "evil," or in saying that we have impoverished India, they are fully justified in saying we have emasculated India. This has never been our intention. Emasculation has come about through the very sincerity of our desire to maintain order in India and preserve it from outside attack. None the less, it is the fact. Through taking too exclusively upon our own shoulders the burden of defending India and maintaining internal peace we have atrophied the muscles of the Indians. They are soft and flabby.

Lord Sinha was quite right when he said, in his Presidential Address to the Indian National Congress in 1915, that the British nation should think it discreditable to itself that "after nearly two centuries of British rule India has been brought to-day to the same emasculated condition as that of the Britons in the beginning of the fifth century when the Roman legions left the English shores."

We do think it discreditable. And we must reverse the process. Emasculation must be stopped and remasculation must be initiated.

Now, I have had the opportunity of watching the insidious process in its incipient stages. I have seen how emasculation first sets in, and this has helped me to understand what goes on and what must be done to stay the mischief. So may I be excused giving one more personal experience? Forty-one years ago, as I described in the last chapter, I visited the remote mountain state of Hunza, then owing allegiance—though of the most shadowy—to both China and Kashmir, but raiding impartially the subjects of both. Two years later these same raiders put up the stoutest resistance to us. And when a year later, in 1892, I was sent there in the capacity of Political Officer and began turning them into levies, I found the material excellent. They lived on the lightest fare, but they were capable of marching forty miles in the day armed and equipped across the mountain. And they had an extraordinary *élan* and capacity for working rapidly together under their own leaders. In Chitral, Yasin, and other little states on that frontier, I subsequently found the same thing. But twenty years later I could feel some subtle spirit—shall we call it spice, the spice of life?—had begun to vanish. Peace had been established. There was no more raiding. The different Chiefs could not invade one another's territories. Struggles between brothers, cousins, and uncles for the thrones were put down with a high hand. And the occupants could remain on them in perfect security. But this security did not satisfy them. It bored them to extinction. At last one of them could stand it no longer and, giving up his too comfortable throne, set off on his own into independent territory to live more dangerously. We have, it is true, organised levies in these parts, and I have seen photographs of them drawn up in perfect lines and as erect and stiff as the guard at Buckingham Palace. But an elusive something I could see was slowly disappearing. And that something is just what is so very precious. It is the dash and initiative and enterprise which can produce leaders. And leaders are what the frontier needs. Leaders who in their own way can lead their own men, though they may avail themselves of the wider experience of others and be assisted with arms and instructed in the way to use them.

This is only my own small experience. On a much bigger scale was my father's experience. I have in my possession the draft of a memorandum by him with the pencilled title "Commissions to Natives the same as Europeans." It must have been written about fifty years ago, and it referred to events of eighty years ago. As I have mentioned in the first chapter, he was sent by Lord Dalhousie in 1850 to the Punjab frontier with "three regiments of the old Sikh Army to bring under British organisation." He had also to raise another regiment. And he was the only European officer.

One of these Sikh regiments was commanded by a Moslem who had formerly been in the East India

Company's army. The other two were commanded by Sikh gentlemen. And all three commandants had seen a great deal of active service. And as two of the Sikh regiments were at stations a hundred miles away, and my father's time was much taken up at headquarters in raising and disciplining the new regiment, it was obvious that if those regiments maintained their discipline and efficiency the credit was mainly due to their native commandants. And that they did so sustain the reputation was, said my father, "a matter of history." And he added: "I can emphatically say in regard to the officers I have named [the commandants] that in the field I found them brave, resolute men, prompt in action, and fertile in resources; and, whether in the field or in quarters, excellent soldiers in the best sense of the word."

As regards the regiment he was to raise, he was "to draw into the ranks men of the warlike tribes and classes belonging to the Punjab and make the service popular." And in order to carry this out he promised certain Sirdars he would give a native officer's commission to cadets of their houses provided the cadets brought each a company of eighty men of his tribe or class. He thus got two companies of Sikhs, a company of Punjabi Mussalmans, four companies of Pathans, and one of Hill Rajputs, with a young man of good family for each company. And he selected for the commandantship a native gentleman of the Kangra Hills who had seen service in Afghanistan and also under himself in Scinde.

These personal experiences he gave because he had "strong views that it is very essential to extend the sphere of action of the native officers." Besides which there was a type or class of men for which the Army would furnish a suitable career. "The cadets of noble houses" would find in the commissioned ranks of the Army such a position as they might obtain in the Civil Service by passing examinations, but which they did not care by that means to strive for. Under "native Government" such a class would obtain positions of honour. But under our rule they were failing to find a place. To men of this class my father suggested commissions should be given. And he would have these put "in exactly the same position as regards rank as British officers." And a military college should be established. For "if commissions are to be given to young native gentlemen, and they are to rank side by side with British officers, they must be educated and trained to the same degree that British officers are." And in regard to the delicate question of British officers serving under Indians, my father's comment was: "If the officers selected for these regiments are of undoubted social position, good address, and thorough soldiers, they will soon disarm any prejudice against them."

Now my father had served under Sir Charles Napier in Scinde and Sir Henry and Sir John Lawrence in the Punjab, and with such men as John Nicholson, Herbert Edwardes, and Dighton Probyn on the frontier. And during the Mutiny he was able not only to keep his own regiment loyal, but to raise 2,000 additional men. He was speaking, therefore, from a ripe experience. Moreover, he was not the only man who was speaking in these terms. For at least fifty years the same kind of proposal has been made by high officers of Government—notably by Sir George Chesney when military member of the Viceroy's Council. But always till after the Great War the proposal had been turned down. The obstacle that continually stood in the way was the unwillingness of the British officer to serve under an Indian officer in time of war. In time of peace he had no strong objection. On active service, when lives were at stake, it was a different matter. And the result is as disclosed by the Simon Report. There are only thirty-nine Indian officers all told. And there is no military college. On the civil side an Indian may rise to the position of Governor, as Lord Sinha did. And in an Indian State an Indian who was a sowar (trooper) in a Bengal cavalry regiment has risen to the position of Chief Minister. But in the Army no Indian has risen higher than captain. In consequence, the whole advance of India towards full responsible government is held up.

This is not creditable. We could hardly have expected India to have raised Indian officered regiments fit to fight against Germans in France. But it most certainly should have been possible in the last eighty years to have created an Indian Army capable of holding the frontier against an invasion by Afghans and frontier tribes. There are only ten million Afghans and perhaps a million independent tribesmen. And the three hundred and twenty million inhabitants of India ought to be able to cope with these. For an invasion by Russia no doubt India would expect to be backed by the Empire. But against an Afghan invasion the Punjab and the North-West Frontier Province, with their thirty millions of virile population and splendid communications, should alone—putting aside the rest of India—be able to put up an adequate defence.

The Simon Report speaks of "the formation of an Indian National Army drawn from India as a whole." It says that the objective is "to develop an Indian Army organised upon a purely Indian basis and officered by Indians." And it adds that "it is a matter of vital consequence that Britain should prove that it is actively desirous of assisting in those changes in the Army in India which make in the direction of the ultimate goal." But it also adds that "the evolution of an entirely Indian military force capable of undertaking unaided the task now discharged by the Army in India must be a very slow process indeed." And it makes no very definite suggestion how the process might be quickened, except that "we should like to see the constitution of some Committee on Army affairs in which the Central Legislature—and in time, we hope, the Indian States also—would have representatives for the purpose of discussing, and keeping in touch with, military questions."

The Simon Commission may have thought it outside their province to make any further suggestion. But they do refer to what is known as the "Eight Unit Scheme." Lord Rawlinson, when Commander-in-Chief, initiated a scheme of "Indianisation." He realised the many "snags" in the way—especially in its effect on efficiency. But he saw that a start must be made. So he began in an experimental way by working towards making a few cavalry and infantry regiments wholly Indian. And he thought it would be two or three generations before the whole Army could be Indianised. But evidently it is a matter which has to be taken up on a bigger scale than this. And, if the process is to be a long one, the sooner it is taken up on that scale the better. But it may not be so long as might be thought if one great force is brought to bear. If the mighty force of Indian national spirit can be harnessed and then focussed on to the creation of an Indian National Army, the objective may be gained in a surprisingly shorter time. The Simon Commission suggest the formation of a committee for military affairs. Say that on that committee were men of the type of Sir Umar Hayat Khan—men of position and standing in India with some knowledge of military matters and in touch with the military classes. Say that they were commissioned to work out a plan for the formation of an Indian National Army. Say that British and Indians entered whole-heartedly into the scheme, realising the advantage it would be to India and England alike if the most were made of the military material available on the spot in India. Say these measures were carried out with all the zeal that the Indians put into their civil disobedience campaign, might not the "very many years" be reduced to "a few years" and Indians have something better to think of than boycotting what is becoming more and more their own Government?

The Indian officer of the right type is the prime essential—the young man who will put his heart into his profession, submit himself to the necessary discipline and to the arduous study and training that is required. Unless India can produce men of this stamp she must always lag behind in her progress towards self-government. But if Indian nationalists realise this, and have the will, may they not also find the way to produce them?

And while this much might be done by Indians on the military side for maintaining the integrity of India, might not Indians of another type use their energies on the political and diplomatic side to the same end? Bengalis have never made such good soldiers as the Sikhs and Pathans of the north. But they are far more distinguished intellectually. And for their intellects a fine field may be found in politics and diplomacy, where they could make their own special contribution towards ensuring the safety, honour, and tranquillity of India. And this contribution may be as valuable in its way as the contribution of the more martial Punjabis. Lord Sinha was a Bengali and did great service to India in the councils of the Empire. And men like him, with his persuasive power, his reasonableness, his even temper, and his grace of speech, may do like service to India in the councils of the world. At the Assembly of the League of Nations the case for India might be put by some Bengali with a force and distinction which would be a mighty power not only in enlisting the support of the nations in any case of aggression upon India, but in raising his country high in the esteem of the world.

The great variety among the peoples of India has often been noted. In this field of national defence in its broadest aspect is an opportunity for turning this variety to good account. While those of more sturdy frame and more martial spirit are employed in the military defence of India, those of subtler intellect and finer capacity for speech may be used in the council chamber and assemblies for the same main purpose of defending the integrity of India.

But British officers—civil and military—who are to take part in this work of fitting Indians for national defence must either trust the Indians or not touch it. And if they trust the Indians they will need a nerve of the finest temper, inexhaustible patience, and tact the most delicate. We have seen that Lord Ripon, in launching his scheme of local self-government, urged the civil officers not to be over-anxious about efficiency at first but to foster sedulously the small beginning of independent political life, to accept loyally as their own the policy of Government, and to realise that the system really opened to them a fairer field for the exercise of administrative tact and directive energy than the more autocratic system which it superseded. And all this and much more will be required of those British officers who have to handle the really risky and dangerous operation of preparing Indians not for mere local self-government, but for national self-defence. For while for the loss of efficiency in civil administration the civil officer would only have to pay by disappointment at seeing his good work go by the board, in the case of military affairs it would mean for the military officer the loss of his life. Efficiency and discipline cannot be lightly tampered with in matters of national safety. The price to be paid for error is too great.

The British officer must always be keeping the balance true between efficiency on the one hand and Indian self-respect on the other. But on pain of death he cannot afford to reduce the efficiency.

He must therefore increase the Indian self-respect. By not the turn of an eyelid must he detract from an Indian's self-respect. And everything in his power he must do to bring into the scale all the national pride he can gather and then fruitfully employ it in national defence. In that way only can the defence of India by Indians be achieved. And if British officers in the past have drawn satisfaction from having led Indians to victory, British officers of the future should have the yet greater satisfaction of having helped Indians to achieve victory for themselves.

Thus only will the process of emasculation be stayed and the reverse process of remasculation begin.

CHAPTER XII

THE CRUCIAL QUESTION

ONCE upon a time a Minister high in the Government of the day put straight to me this startling question: "What would you do if you were Viceroy and Prime Minister and Government combined?" It was difficult to answer straight off on the spur of the moment. And I replied that I always knew what to do when responsibility was pricking me, but did not find it so easy to decide in cold blood. Also, in India, as much depends upon the manner in which you do a thing as on the thing done. "But," I said, "there is one thing I most certainly would do; I would first remind the Indians that we have set before us and them the goal of responsible self-government for India, that we have already taken great steps in that direction, that we were contemplating more, and, in especial, were going to help them build up a National Army capable of defending India. And then I would tell them that in the end, when they were able to govern and defend themselves, we would leave upon them the responsibility of deciding whether they would remain within the Empire or become completely independent." This, I told the Cabinet Minister, was the vitally important thing to do.

Let me now state fully my reasons for this conclusion. I hold it because to me it seems to be the only worthy course we could take. We have a perfect right to be in dominion over India as long as she is incapable of governing herself. As I have shown, we never sought dominion. We tried our best to avoid it. But world-circumstances forced us into the position of dominion. And when we were there we did in our rough way try to do our best by the Indians. We first established and then preserved order. And we went beyond the policeman stage. We deliberately set about educating the Indians, associating them more and more with us in the government of their country, and finally fitting them to govern themselves. Well, if we are successful in our endeavours, if we find that in due course we are able to create in the British Provinces governments at least as capable of governing as are the present governments in the Indian States, if a firm Central Government can be established at least as capable of holding India together as was Akbar's, and if we can bring into being an Indian National Army as capable of fending off tribesmen and Afghans as was Ranjit Singh's army—if we are successful in all these things, then should we not crown our success by having the grace to say to the Indians: "We did not seek dominion over you. It was forced upon us. And now that you are able to exercise dominion for yourselves we have no desire to remain if you no longer wish us to do so. We will leave the choice to you. But, for ourselves, we would prefer that you and ourselves should always remain associated together. We have fought together on many a field in many parts of the world. We have worked together for the material and intellectual progress of India. We believe that it has been to your advantage that we have been associated together. And we frankly acknowledge that it has been to ours. Our connection with India has greatly contributed to our wealth and prosperity. And we still think that this continued connection would be thoroughly worth while for both. The advantages we ourselves now have would continue. And you would reap the benefit of having the whole Empire in support of you if you were attacked by sea or by a European Power by land, and, in addition, you would have the support of our Diplomatic Service all over the world and the advantage of a higher financial credit than you would have outside the Empire. These advantages we believe that both you and we would have from a continued connection. And we earnestly wish that this connection should always continue. But it must rest with you to decide. We would not have you to remain in the Empire as unwilling members. Only we trust that whether you remain in it, as we wish, or sever yourselves from us, as you may desire, we may always remain good comrades. And we would assure you of this, that the friendship of our country will always be yours."

Now what are the objections to our taking such a course? Perhaps someone will say that it is based on too many "ifs." It is not likely that for many a long year to come India will be able to create a National Army capable of defending India from outside attack and preserving internal order. Nor is it probable that India will for many years be able to evolve a Central Government strong enough to keep in unity together all the Indian States and Provinces. I agree with these. I think it will be a long time before these things can be. But I think it all-important that Indians should know *now* that if and when that time does come, however far it may be, they shall then have the opportunity of deciding their own destiny. The Dominions of Canada and Australia already know this, though they are not yet in a position to defend themselves without Imperial aid from an attack by, for example, Japan, on British Columbia or Queensland. And India should be put in the same position. We owe it to ourselves. And we owe it to the Indians. We ought to be too proud to have it said of us that we are determined to keep India permanently under our dominion whether she like it or not. We would occupy a much better position in the world if we said definitely and at once that we were going to leave to Indians the decision of their own future. And the position of the Indians themselves would be greatly raised if they were able to say to the world that they were remaining in the Empire—if so they chose—of their own free choice and not under any compulsion.

It should be a point of honour with us only to have India—after she is capable of governing herself—in the Empire of her own free will. There will be disputes between us and the Indians as to exactly *when* they may be safely left to govern and defend themselves. And accusations of bad faith will be hurled against us year by year. That we must expect. But we will go steadily on our course. We have pursued it for a century and a half now, and a few years longer or shorter will make very little difference in the whole long history of India. The essential thing is that we should intend in the end to have India voluntarily with us in the Empire or not at all.

Another critic might say that in giving to Indians the chance of separating from us we are surrendering the whole position. We are deliberately throwing away all that generations of Englishmen have achieved. We are letting the whole delicate fabric fall to pieces. And we are letting India slip back into the chaos in which we found it. We are allowing India for years and years to become the scene of civil war such as China presents. And we shall lose the eight hundred million pounds we have invested there, and the best market we have for the sale of our manufactures. Thousands will be put out of employment here in England. And in India peaceful villages will go up in flames, bands of brigands will be raiding over the land, and men, women, and children will be slaughtered as in the days of the Pindaris.

And there is this risk I do not deny. And it would be heartbreaking for us who have worked for India to witness the results of our labours all slithering away into black chaos and rapine. But what I maintain is that if it is a risk for us it is a ten times greater risk for the Indians. England risks losing her money. India risks losing her life. And as the time drew near for India to take the responsibility for a decision which would involve that risk, we may presume that she would become the more vividly conscious of what that responsibility entails.

We cannot say how many years hence it may be before the decision would have to be made. Let us therefore call it *x* years. According to the recommendations of the Simon Report, during those *x* years in each province there would be an Indian Minister in charge of law and order and responsible to the Provincial Legislature for maintaining the peace of the province. These Ministers would therefore be learning by experience what responsibility for these things means. So, also, would those members of the Committee on Military Affairs which the Simon Commission recommend should be formed to keep in touch with military matters. And so, too, would the Council for Greater India on which it is proposed that representatives of Indian States as well as of British India should sit to deal with matters of common concern to all. During the *x* years these men would be realising something of what maintaining order in India and defending it from outside attack meant. They would come to understand that as long as India was included within the Empire they could count on having British officers as adjutants in the regiments of the National Army, as staff officers at Army Headquarters, or in any other military capacity, just as the Australian Navy has officers of the Royal Navy in its service. They would understand, too, that in case of a serious invasion by land or by sea they could count on the British Navy to protect the coasts of India, and upon the whole Empire to assist in defending her frontier by land. Finance Ministers, too, would be alive to the advantage of obtaining loans at a cheaper rate while India was a member of the British Empire.

Then as the zero hour drew near when responsible men would have the responsibility of making the great decision, Indian Ministers, and Indian leaders of the new National Army, would become increasingly sensitive to the risk they would run in foregoing these advantages. Acute controversy would arise, on the one hand, between those with a real stake in the country and those with experience of responsibility for maintaining internal peace and order and keeping India safe from invasion, and, on the other hand, those impetuous patriots who would irresponsibly be clamouring for completest freedom at whatever cost, and regardless of the fact that even freedom is not an end in itself, but only a means to something which could be equally well gained within the Empire as without.

And not only politicians of British India, but the Ruling Princes also would be anxiously considering the position as the end of x years approached. As long as they remain within the British Empire they are entitled to the protection of the British Government. The British cannot withdraw from that engagement without their agreement. But if British protection were withdrawn they would have to fend for themselves. And what that would mean the case of Kashmir shows. It is a great prize, and time and again it has been invaded by Afghans and Sikhs. The present ruler is only there, in fact, as a result of a conquest by the Sikhs. His great-grandfather held the position of Commander-in-Chief of the Sikh army of Ranjit Singh's which invaded Kashmir less than a century ago. So it was with a Sikh army, not his own, that Kashmir was conquered. And it was after we had conquered the successor of Ranjit Singh that, for a consideration, and for our mutual advantage, he was confirmed in possession of Kashmir and recognised as its ruler. But if Imperial protection were withdrawn Kashmir would have to defend itself against all who coveted it—and they might not only be Afghans.

Hyderabad, likewise, would be open, as in old days, to attack from Mahrattas; the fertile plains of the Ganges to attack from the Gurkhas; and Travancore and other states in the south to attack by sea.

Moreover, the Indian Provinces and States would have to bear the responsibility for the proper protection of all foreigners living in India. It was because there was no adequate protection to the lives and property of French, Dutch, and English that intervention in Indian affairs originated. And if, again, proper protection were not available for their subjects, foreign Powers might be compelled to intervene as they have had to in China, the Philippines, Egypt, Morocco, Mexico, and Central American Republics. And of this responsibility, too, Indian Ministers would become more alive as the time for decision approached.

So all these responsible men, as well as industrialists with great factories established, or valuable mining properties, or tea plantations, or railways, would be asking themselves why, if these advantages can be had while remaining within the Empire, they should risk losing them by severing the connection.

If, therefore, we are alive to the risk that would be run in leaving to Indians the choice of remaining or seceding, we may count on Indians being at least as conscious as ourselves of what would be involved.

There does, however, remain one grave consideration. A small but violent and energetic minority might stampede India into giving a decision which might be contrary to the real wishes of the majority. This has sometimes happened in other countries. And against such an eventuality careful provision must be made when, by mutual agreement between the Indians and the British, the conditions are laid down under which the expression of the will of the people should be made. The energetic minority should be given its chance. But so, also, should all minorities. The interests of minorities would have to be most anxiously guarded. And it would have to be the decision of India as a whole—Indian States as well as British Provinces.

And in making the decision we may be sure that sentiment will play a predominant part. There will be not only a cool weighing up of advantages this way and that. There will be the surge of sentiment sweeping through Indians. The deep sentiment of nationality, in especial, will be powerfully swaying their decision. But in this lies the great hope for India. For it may do more than anything else to *unite* India, and particularly to bring Moslems and Hindus together in the common sentiment for India as a nation. The having to make the decision may in itself do more than anything else to unite India and make Hindus and Moslems come together in working for the common cause, so that whether the decision is or is not to remain within the British Empire there would be the better chance of the India of the future being a united India bent on keeping together for a common purpose. And this would be to everyone's advantage.

This sentiment of nationality may, of course,

carry India to separation. The cry may be then, as it is among some now, for a completely independent India. But a further sentiment by no means incompatible with Indian nationality will most certainly also be at work. Nationality is a great force in Canada. "Canada—a Nation" is a cry which penetrates deep into the heart of all Canadians. Yet Canadians are as devoted to the Crown as Englishmen themselves. I saw an instance of this when I was in Canada this year. The King made his speech to the Naval Conference at about eleven in the morning. And this was broadcast all over the world. But to hear this, owing to the difference in time, Canadians had to be up at six. Yet nearly every Canadian I met was up at that hour to hear the King's voice. And in the Montreal Cathedral a service was held specially for the occasion, and loud speakers were used that the congregation might listen to the speech. Moreover, not the least loyal portion of Canada is the French portion. Now this same sentiment of loyalty to the Crown, so powerfully at work in Canada, might equally well combine in India with loyalty to India. The two sentiments are by no means contrary one to the other. And the sentiment of loyalty to the Sovereign is something very real in India. When the King went to Delhi to be crowned Emperor of India, there were the most fervent demonstrations of reverence and attachment by both Princes and people. Apart from the natural craving of a people for some single object upon which all can focus their desire for unity, the Indian people have known by instinct that British Sovereigns have cared for India and had the welfare of India at heart. This was notoriously so in the case of Queen Victoria. And it has been the same with King Edward and King George. And the Sovereigns have been able to voice what is the basic and permanent feeling of the British people towards India as distinguished from the more surface and changing attitude which is necessarily expressed by the Government and Viceroy of the day. Governments and Viceroys have necessarily to be dealing with the practical affairs of the immediate moment. The Sovereign stands for the deep-running sentiment at the foundations of national life. And when he utters expressions of goodwill towards India he is voicing the deepest feelings of the British people.

To this sentiment Indians are quick to respond. And they may come to see a very practical advantage in the continued presence in India of a neutral, impartial Viceroy occupying a position gradually approximating to the position of the Governor-General in Canada or Australia or South Africa. He would be the representative of the Sovereign, and as such would be a steadying influence and a rallying point such as China is so sorely in need of at the present time. With him as a central figure in India, a single direction would be given to national life. And round him all the varying influences and interests might gather. Nor need he invariably be an Englishman. Like the Governors of provinces, he might sometimes be an Indian—one of the Ruling Princes, for example. And occasionally he might be a member of the Royal Family. But in all cases he would be the direct, personal, representative of the Sovereign. And it would be good for India if he came more and more to represent the Sovereign on the social and ceremonial rather than on the political side. Immense benefits result from the interest the British Sovereign takes in the life of all grades of British society from the lowest to the highest. And if his representative had more time to do the same, he might be of untold benefit in welding together the various elements of Indian life into a united whole.

The sentiment of loyalty to the Crown may therefore be a very powerful factor in determining the choice of India. And there may be another sentiment telling in the same direction. Whirling words of hatred are often hurled against the British. And we must expect to have to pay for much arrogance and offensive language and neglect of the niceties of intercourse. Even when we have meant to be friendly we have been rough in our manner, and our rudeness has jarred upon the sensitive Indians. For all that, Indians and British have for a century and a half now fought together on many a field in India, in many other parts of Asia, in Africa, and even in France. And we have worked together in fighting famine and disease, and in building up a healthy and prosperous India. All this has produced a sense of comradeship which may outweigh our roughness. And a sentiment of attachment to British officers, both civil and military, may also have some weight with Indians in making their decision.

So when we sum up the position as it is likely to be; when we remember how whole-heartedly India declared herself on the side of Great Britain immediately on the outbreak of the Great War, and refused to use it as an opportunity for breaking away or causing us trouble; when we see her never-failing attachment to the Sovereign; and when we reflect that responsible Indians themselves must be, at least, as aware as we are of the risks they may run in severing the connection, we may well believe that the chances are that Mr. Sastri was right when he said the other day that Indians had no wish to secede from the Empire. Indians love to have an ideal. Even if they do not live up to it they like to feel it is there in their minds as a guide and as something to be striven after. And, like all human beings, they like to have hope. And as long as they could have hope of fulfilling their ideal while still remaining within the Empire, it is not likely that they would have any strong desire to part from it. They and their fathers for several generations now have grown up within it, and if they can live in it as freely as French Canadians or Dutch South Africans, they would probably find no special cause for seceding.

For the above reasons I do not think that the objections to the proposal to give the Indians the chance of deciding for themselves whether they will remain within the Empire are of sufficient weight to prevent us from adopting the course I suggest. But, as I said to the Cabinet Minister, the *manner* in which we say or do a thing is almost more important than the word or deed itself. And from now onward we ought to be more than ever careful of our manner. All talk of showing who is the top dog must cease. We are not engaged in a dog-fight with the Indians. Nor is India the "enemy." All through the history of our connection with India we have always had a great many more friends than enemies in India. And India as a *whole* has never been the "enemy." At the time of our greatest trouble—during the Mutiny of 1857—the major part of India was friendly. India is not the "enemy." She has been called the partner. But she is something more than that. She is the comrade. Like all comrades, India and England may have their little tiffs. But they pass over and the deeper feeling soon regains possession of both.

And particularly important is it that we should get out of the attitude of mind which looks upon the reforms as "concessions"—as if Indians were wrenching from us what we would only reluctantly and ungraciously give up.

Dominion is not a bone which we have snatched from the Indians, and which with bulldog tenacity we mean to hold on to with all our might and main. Dominion is something which of right belongs to the Indians themselves, and which we are only exercising during their temporary inability. We should therefore avoid giving the impression that we are clutching on to dominion for dominion's sake. And now that we have declared it to be our intention gradually to transfer it to them, we should adopt a more positive attitude and show that we realise the grandeur of the great constructive work upon which we are engaged—the creation of an Indian-governed Indian Empire more populous, more prosperous, more united, than any Indian Empire which has gone before; and that we desire to work loyally with the Indians in the transference of dominion.

Looking back over our history we can see that always in our mind we have had the idea of preparing India for the day when she will be able to govern herself. And the nearer that day draws nigh the clearer ought we to have this purpose in our mind, and the readier ought we to be to help the Indians in the final delicate stage. And if we do this we shall recognise how fatal to our purpose it is to keep repeating that the Indians are unable to govern themselves. The particular *métier* of us Englishmen is to govern. The governing instinct is strong within us. We are experts in the art. And we are apt to judge all others by our own high standard. But here is the fact that a third of India actually is governed by Indians to-day. And in the Indian States at least law and order are maintained. Both they and the British Provinces have had an opportunity now of seeing what "good" government is, and of appreciating its value. There are no good grounds for telling Indians they will never be capable of governing themselves. What they need now is encouragement in the idea that they can.

And on the civil side we have, indeed, already made vast strides in helping India to fit herself for responsible government. On the military side we are still far behind. But we have the matter in hand. And in the immediate future nothing is more urgent than an effort to make India capable of defending herself. For in no other way can we better show Indians the sincerity of our purpose. And when the day at last arrives when India, strong and self-reliant, is able to take over her own government and defence, and to discharge her responsibilities to the nations, we shall have the joy which comes from contemplating a noble work well achieved. And on that proud day we may discover that in losing ourselves we have gained India.

And ever should we remember that, whether in the end India should decide to remain within the Empire or secede, British and Indians in business and in culture will aways be associated together and dependent upon each other. From all points of view it is essential, therefore, that we British should have a care over our manner. I do not think the French have much to teach us in the matter of government. I think in that respect we are on better lines than they are. But in the matter of manner we have much to learn from them. The spirit of *camaraderie* is better developed in them than in us—or, at any rate, better expressed. And it is that spirit that we have most need now to foster.

Our own pride—if nothing else—should teach us to treat the Indians as we would treat ourselves—and with all the more courtesy, as they are not of our own kith and kin. Englishmen in India when exasperated beyond measure at the idleness or slackness or inefficiency of some Indian worker, or when bored past endurance by the importunity of some petitioner, or when stung to the quick by the evil imputation of some irresponsible agitator, must remember the race to which they belong—and the race to which the Indians belong. They must keep a hold on their tongues. They may have to be stern, but they should ever be on their guard not to say one hasty word which would endanger that delicate fabric we have been, and are so patiently, building up.

And Indians also might well be on their guard.

They do themselves no good in imitating our own political manners. In our political life we follow the rough usages of rude ages of the past, when men were accustomed to use still more violent language about one another. And when a politician says of the Government of the day that it is the worst, the most barbarous, and the most unjust Government that the world has ever seen, we know that he means nothing more than that he thinks he could govern the country better himself, and would be highly indignant if anyone else but an Englishman—if even a Canadian—said the same thing. And Indians would much better serve their country by keeping to their own innate courtesy and politeness; and in that respect remember the race to which they belong.

And in all this essential question of manner Government itself might well afford its servants some guidance. If officers were given a clear line, told what was the firm purpose of Government, called upon faithfully to adopt that purpose as their own, and informed that they would be judged not by the amount of work they did for India but by the amount they got Indians to do for themselves, they might safely be left to carry out the work in their own way and so bear themselves towards Indians that Indians would work readily with them. But they need a lead.

Yet when all is said and done the fact remains that we are engaged upon a great adventure. The whole history of our connection with India has been an adventure. And the most risky part of the whole is that on which we have now entered.

And like all adventures our Indian adventure must rest on faith. Faith is the one thing needed. Faith in ourselves, faith in the Indians, and, above all, faith in God.

We must have faith in ourselves—in our capacity for identifying our own interests with those of the people with whom we work and of carrying them along with us in great enterprise.

We must have faith in the Indians—in their capacity for development as conditions are bettered, in their devotion and loyalty to those with whom they are working, in the high intellectual capacity of some, in the martial quality of others, in the innate courtesy and capacity for affection of all.

Finally, we must have faith in God—faith that working through us, through the Indians, and through the whole world, is a Power making for all that is best and noblest in life; and faith that what that Power is working for must in the end come about.

In this faith we can go forward with courage on our great adventure, and be assured that just in so far as we work in with this Power for Good to that extent but no farther will we succeed.

PART II

SPIRITUAL

CHAPTER XIII

INDIAN SPIRITUALITY

The political revival in India has now been sufficiently described. Not, indeed, in detail, but full enough, I trust, to show the main trend of political thought and action, and to show that Indians are more alive and more progressive than they have been for centuries.

The subtler springs of all this activity have now to be sought. We have to probe deeper into the Indian nature and seek the ultimate spirit from which this political activity is derived.

And this is the more necessary in the case of India because the Indians are essentially a spiritual people. The English are mainly interested in politics, the French in art, the Americans in business. But the Indians in religion. India, as the Indians keep proudly saying, is the motherland of religions. From it have sprung both Hinduism and Buddhism. Neither the Chinese nor the Indians have any genius for politics. But as the Chinese have a genius for art so the Indians have a genius for religion.

Against this view, however, it has lately been contended that the Indians are not so spiritual as they claim to be. The young students who issue in thousands from Indian, English, Scottish, and American universities are said to be mainly atheists. Their contact with Western learning and Western customs has turned them into materialists. They are poor, and their main desire is to earn a livelihood. And they are more intent upon material gain than upon spiritual attainment. They have been caught up in the great wave of irreligion and antipathy to the very idea of God which has been sweeping over Asia as well as Europe since the War and the Russian Revolution. And they are losing all faith. So it is contended.

And about those at the other end of the scale—the poor villager—similar doubt has been expressed. They have to face grinding poverty. Half the people of India do not have enough food. The average daily amount they can afford is below the scale of diet for prisoners. The villager is always hungry, always in debt, and always thinking of his crops, of how he can meet the moneylender, and of many another material care. And with his mind so absorbed in the wants of the body, how can he think of his soul? What thought can he give to spiritual matters when he has to think so much of material things? And even when he does get his mind away from providing bare sustenance for himself and his family it may be occupied in some lawsuit against his neighbour or in devising means for defraying the expenses of a marriage ceremony. Again, villagers are bound by blind custom. They dare not call their souls their own. A multitude of fears and superstitions crush their spirits. They think much of propitiating dangerous powers. Their villages are filthy. Their life is sordid and squalid. An air of hopelessness pervades them. In such people how can there be any true spirituality?

About the villagers as about the students these

questions have been asked. And many say that the spirituality of India is a myth. India may have been spiritual in the past. A few Indians may be spiritual to-day. But both the educated classes and the plain villagers are frankly material. This is what some say. Yet I would maintain precisely the opposite. I would say that the educated and the villagers are both in their hearts religious. Gandhi would not have made the appeal he does to both classes if they did not set store by religion. True, his appeal is to the sentiment of nationality. But others have made that appeal. And what has made Gandhi's appeal go home is its being backed by religion. He introduced *religion* into politics, and he won their hearts as no other politician has. The students and educated classes, though they have fallen off in religious practice and may no longer hold the ancient beliefs, may still have their old religious disposition at bottom. Indeed, it could hardly be otherwise. Great natural dispositions are not thrown aside in a moment. And as for the villagers, I cannot efface from my memory the sight of them in the Great Famine of 1900 throwing up their arms to Heaven and praying to God for help. And if they live a life of grinding poverty they have a wonderful capacity for enjoying themselves too. They love festivals and going off on journeys and pilgrimages. And, like all who spend their lives in continuous and close touch with Nature, they are intuitively conscious of a Great Power producing their crops and bringing forth the young, and they believe that Power to be good and kind and merciful. There may be bad powers to be propitiated. But back of all is this kind Power which produces the good and necessary things in life; and they are grateful to it.

And from the very outset of the new movement in Indian life we can see the spiritual impulse. Long before the political revival there had been a spiritual revival. A century ago, in Bengal, Ram Mohun Roy fought to free himself and those about him from the fetters of Hindu orthodoxy and founded the Brahmo Samaj. He was a hero of the truest type—a great, big-minded, big-souled, religious reformer. The society which he formed has not, indeed, made any wide popular appeal. But it has always included among its members the very élite of Bengal's intellectuals. And the most notable of his successors, Keshub Chunder Sen, in the latter half of last century gave a very decidedly spiritual emphasis to the stir in Indian minds.

Sixty years ago—well before the Indian National Congress was founded—he spoke of India rising from the death-like slumber of ages and exerting its best powers to move onward in the path of true enlightenment and reform. Unless the heart of the nation were reformed and purified there could not be anything like true and lasting reformation. He therefore urged Indians to work earnestly and prayerfully for the ultimate regeneration of the country, and to be conscious of the ever-present Divinity that would achieve the salvation of India and all mankind. For not man, but God, had kindled that spirit of reform which like wildfire was spreading from province to province. The Indian nation had been selected by God in modern times that He might convert it and show forth unto the world the riches of His redeeming grace. And God would have His own way and evolve a new scheme of redemption out of India's native resources. This was Keshub Chunder Sen's message—delivered before Gandhi had even gone to school.

His present-day successors—at least some of the most inspired of them—have written and spoken in the same vein. Bepin Chandra Pal, of whom mention has already been made, a most earnest and eloquent preacher in the Brahmo Samaj, was of fine spiritual disposition as well as of high intellectual attainment. Arabindo Ghose based his whole hostility to British rule and Western civilisation on his passionate desire to preserve the life of Hinduism. The old prejudices and superstitions with which it had become encrusted in the course of ages he might denounce. And he might wish Indians to get back to the pure teachings of the Bhagavat Gita. But it was the purified life of Hinduism that he would wish to preserve. And it was religion that was the mainspring of his political activity.

So, too, was it with Barendra Ghose, Arabindo's brother. He had intended to start a religious institution. And his heart was more set on a religious rather than a political revolution. Righteousness was declining in India and unrighteousness was springing up. But Indians were not to lose heart. God would not remain inactive at the sight of such unrighteousness in His kingdom. He would descend in the midst and destroy unrighteousness (especially we may presume he meant the British). Then the independent flag of righteousness would be unfurled, India's virtues would be restored, and the unlimited strength, knowledge, and righteousness of India would be used for the benefit of the whole world.

A man of a very different type from these sensitive, agile, refined, highly emotional, quickly affectionate Bengalis was the more solid, powerful, capable, ambitious Mahratta, Tilak. But he, too, founded his political action upon religion. He founded this action upon the old orthodoxy and appealed to the prejudices of the crowd. But it was the forces of religion that he tried to awake. And it was as destroyers of Hinduism that both the British and Moslems were denounced. He was a patriot standing forth as the champion of his country's rights. But he saw that to gain the support of the people he must base his patriotic efforts upon religion. He must appeal to the religious disposition of the people. His action presupposed, therefore, that the people were at heart religious, and that if you wished to stir them deeply you must reach their souls.

That religion is the basis of the national life—as I contended in my Rede Lecture—is thus proved by the way in which political leaders up to the present day appeal to it. And in the religious field, just as much as in the political field, there has been a great quickening of the national life. The foundation of the Brahmo Samaj I have already referred to. That appeals more to the educated classes, and more especially to the Bengalis. A movement within Hinduism with a more popular appeal is the Arya Samaj founded by Swami Dayanand Saraswati.

He, like Gandhi, but before him, came from Gujerat in Western India. But he was not English educated. His education was wholly in Sanskrit. He was Indian to the core. And his main idea was to get Hindus back to the pure original fountain-springs of their faith. "Back to the Vedas" was his cry. He would not even call them Hindus. That was a word which came in with the Moslems. They should be called Aryas. India had fallen from her ancient high estate. And he would restore it. He would restore it by religion. Religion alone could give a nation life. He would reconvert the Hindus. He would revive the Vedic religion. He had a passionate love of the national ideals and of the old models of the saintly life. He was in constant communion with the ancient types. He would revive the good old days. All the present miseries were due to their having departed from the time-honoured line. He would have men retrace their steps. He would lead them back to the true line. He would root out the evil which was eating into the vitals of the people. The evil of idol-worship, the evil of caste, the evil of child-marriage, he would destroy. And he would establish schools and restore again the sanctity, the purity, and the serenity of the old Hindu way of life.

And we who here and there have met with examples of this ancient type—kindly, courteous, unruffled old Hindu gentlemen, immense in their dignity and self-respect—will sympathise with Dayanand. Over-rigid they might have been and wholly unamenable to new ideas. Yet there was about them a large composure we could not but admire. And they had real justification for their pride when they claimed that, in spite of invasions, and revolutions, and social upheavals, what they stood for had survived when Greek and Roman and Egyptian civilisations had all disappeared. And in studying Dayanand and what he approved and disapproved we shall see illustrations of what real India is like, and what religion means to Indians.

Dayanand was essentially a fighter—and a doughty fighter at that. He loved challenging the strongest in their strongholds. He had a hatred of all that was unholy and impure. He was of great strength of mind and stability of purpose and a master of invective. And in attack he was downright and uncompromising. Nothing daunted him. And he would face the strongest opposition and endure the severest physical hardship to achieve his aim.

His whole appearance was imposing. Over six feet in height, with a full body and broad, expansive forehead, his expression when in repose was contemplative and dreamy, but when roused was like "a storm of thunder and lightning."

His father was a Brahmin of the strictest school. His mother is described as the personification of patience, gentleness, and sweetness, the soul of simplicity, purity, and goodness. He himself was intensely religious by nature. His imagination was fired by stories of the ancient heroes. But he noticed that those about him were not like men of old. And he began to question what he was taught.

Were idols really gods? He saw a mouse come out of its hole, run over the image of Shiva, and eat up the offerings of the worshippers. Could this image who could not hunt away a little mouse really be the Maha deva—the great God? He doubted it. He doubted more and more. And from these doubts sprang his vehement striving against idol-worship.

As a youth he would have gone to holy Benares to study under the most learned in the land. But his parents had other views. They would have him marry and settle down. In horror he fled. He forsook his home for good. He gave up all his possessions. He led the austere life of a Sanyasi, begging his livelihood from kindly villagers and wandering by the sacred rivers of India, through the great forests, and up into the eternal snows of the Himalaya. For days and nights together he would remain in contemplation. And in the coldest weather he would have no other bed but rice husks.

He would seek out holy men, too, and go on pilgrimages and attend fairs up and down India. But his soul sickened at what he saw. So much idolatry, so much fraud! Even the learned Pandits carried on practices and advocated views that both reason and authority condemned. What could he, by himself, do against all this? He must strengthen his soul-force. He must find some real master and study under him. So he sought far and wide, and at last found.

He found a stern old Sanyasi at Muttra and settled down as his disciple. Dayanand had no money for food or for books. And there was a severe famine in the land so that people were not able to give him much, and he had to live on bare fare. But he persevered on and toiled incessantly day and night. And as his reverence for his master grew the more his master beat him. By all the greater humility he would regain the Sanyasi's favour. And when the master struck him so hard with his stick as seriously to injure his hand, Dayanand's only answer was a request to his master not to exert himself so much on his account as his body was hard as iron and could not feel the stick, whereas his master's delicate hands might suffer from the exertion.

After two and a half years' strenuous study under this stern master, Dayanand asked for his blessing and departed. And now his great mission in life began. He went out into the world. And he challenged anyone to come forward and prove that the ancient Aryan religion was not the purest and noblest of all.

Idol-worshippers in particular he attacked. He attended a meeting at which a learned Pandit maintained the orthodox view that the worship of idols was inculcated in the Manu Smriti. Dayanand opposed this contention, and said that what was meant was reverencing learned and virtuous men—not worshipping images. The Pandit thereupon fortified himself with a ruling from learned men at Benares that recitations unite a deity with an idol, and that the chanting of mantras did endow it with life. Worship of images was lawful on the authority of many a verse in the Puranas. And it also was written in the sacred books that idols laugh, weep, sing, and feel pain, and dance, and shine. Deities were summoned into or dismissed from idols. Dayanand, however, would not accept the ruling of the Pandits. Their statement contained no authorities from the Vedas in support of idol-worship. And the Vedas only would he accept as authoritative.

The Bhagavat Gita—the sacred book of the

Hindus to which Ghandi owes his chief inspiration —Dayanand also attacked. It was later than the Vedas and not at all after his heart. Krishna could not be an incarnation of God. The book was an execrable production—an outrage upon the glory of the Supreme, who alone should be worshipped.

And now, in 1869, Dayanand with his challenging views boldly entered Benares itself. For centuries upon centuries this has been the seat of learning and the very centre of Hinduism. And if he was to deliver his blow at idol-worship, it must be here in the very citadel of orthodoxy. He meant to be the aggressor. And to bring things to a crisis he challenged the most famous Pandit to debate. The Pandit sent back the reply: "Let a knife be placed between us before I answer your question. If I can satisfactorily reply I will cut off your nose. If I fail you may cut off mine." As preliminary to the contest, there was an enquiry into what books each believed in as authoritative. And then on what authority they were authoritative. At least ten thousand people were present at the debate, including the most famous Pandits. And the proceedings were presided over by the Maharaja of Benares. The debate lasted from three in the afternoon till dark. But neither side would acknowledge defeat. And, in spite of bad characters throwing stones, old shoes, and dung at him, he remained three months longer at Benares, proclaiming the falseness of idolatry by beat of drum, till the orthodox Pandits threatened to excommunicate those who dared to visit him, and as his following dwindled away he had to betake himself elsewhere.

Against caste also, as well as idolatry, the Swami

waged incessant warfare. Caste was determined by worth alone. If a man behaved as a Brahmin he was a Brahmin whatever his caste might be. And if a Brahmin by caste neglected his duties he was worse than a Sudra—lower than the lowest caste. And there was no justification for the common abhorrence of promiscuous eating. The Vedas lent no countenance to any such repugnance. These were the Swami's views, and his promulgation of such aroused the bitter enmity of the orthodox. But he cared not for their enmity and reiterated his standpoint. Caste was merely a civil institution established by the rulers for civil or political convenience. Certain persons fitted for the purpose were chosen by royalty for conducting worship and for the cultivation of moral science and philosophy, and these were named Brahmins. Others were constituted Kshattryas, to guard the Empire against external danger and to preserve internal order. The Vaisya class was reorganised for trade and commerce and for agriculture. The people that yet remained were put into the Sudra order. Every caste was granted privileges of a distinct nature. And all were made hereditary. This was the Swami's theory of caste. But caste had no religious sanction. God did not create four castes as four distinct kinds of men. And the salvation of men in the world to come did not depend upon caste.

In opposition to the Christians, he contended that neither the Christ of the Christians, nor Krishna of the Hindus, nor any other great man, was an incarnation of the Deity, for God could not be incarnated. Nor could Christ, nor God Himself, forgive sins. Forgiveness of sins was impossible.

If God forgave sins he would be an encourager of sin. But God was absolutely just. He meted out punishments and rewards for all actions according to their deserts.

And he had no belief in a corporal God who would come down to Eden for Adam, or descend on Mount Sinai, or talk with Abraham and Moses. Nor did he believe in a multitude of gods. He believed in one God. And this God was primarily the author of the Vedas and then of the universe. He was distinct from the world though He pervaded and permeated it as the principle of life. God is All-Truth, All-Knowledge, All-Beatitude. He is Formless, Almighty, Infinite, All-pervading, Holy, and the Maker of the universe. To Him alone is worship due.

The four Vedas, according to Dayanand, were the Word of God, and, therefore, absolutely free from error. They were the supreme authority for the conduct of life. And, in his view, an energetic and active life was preferable to passive acquiescence in the decrees of fate, for "destiny is the consequence of acts." Acts being the maker of destiny, virtuous activity is superior to passive resignation. And the most approved behaviour of one man towards his fellow-creatures lies in his treating everyone according to his worth. Everyone is to be treated according to his worth, but the stern Swami does add one note of tenderness. A man is to sympathise with another "from the core of his heart in his joys and sorrows, in his losses and gains." And he had kindly views on the subject of marriage. "Mutual choice and consent are the indispensable conditions of every marriage." "Early marriage is something positively injurious, being destructive of physical, mental, and moral vigour and stamina. It is a bane of the individual and the curse of nations." No male should marry till he is at least twenty-five, and no female before she is sixteen. Of female education he was also an ardent advocate. As long as the Indian women remained ignorant and bound in domestic thraldom he saw no hope of India making any progress.

The destruction of ignorance and prejudice, the diffusion of knowlege, the creation of a national union, and an all-embracing civilisation which would make India a model for the world was the Swami's final aim.

For this purpose he founded Samajes—societies—in many parts of India. These are now known collectively as the Arya Samaj. And after his death in 1883, at the age of fifty-nine, the Anglo-Vedic College was founded at Lahore to carry on his work. The idea was to give an education which was *national* in its tone and character. It was to strengthen the ties which naturally bind individuals into one common nationality. It would meet the demand for the study and culture of national literature. Especially would it "promote the study of the classical period wherein lie deep buried and crystallised the fruits of whole lives spent in secluded meditation on the nature of the soul, of virtue, and, so far as can be vouchsafed to man, of the Creator."

The education imparted by this college was undoubtedly a reaction against excessive English education. At one time Arya Samajists were suspected of being anti-British and "seditious." And Swami Dayanand was, indeed, strongly opposed to

Western influence. Yet he himself said: "If you expel the English, then, no later than to-morrow, you and I and everyone who rises against idol-worship will have our throats cut like mere sheep." And if Arya Samajists have been suspected of "sedition," Moslems are convinced that the Arya Samaj is animated with no less bitter hostility towards Islam than towards British rule.

To us the Arya Samaj seems to place an excessive reliance on the authority of the Vedas. And the whole education of the Arya Samajist seems too exclusively based on authority. Little room is left for the use of the critical faculty and honest doubt. The Vedas, and they alone, are the word of God. What they say must be obeyed unquestioningly. Dayanand inveighed against idolatry. But he himself made an idol of the Vedas. And his followers remain in like bondage. For all that, the Arya Samaj is a very earnest and patriotic endeavour to purify Hinduism and restore the ancient glory of India.

Equally characteristic of Hinduism, though of a more "New Testament" type than Swami Dayanand, was Rama Krishna. Dayanand was of the stern, austere, uncompromising mould. Rama Krishna was gentle, sympathetic, and loving. But both were essentially Hindus. Neither of them was directly influenced by English thought. And both initiated movements from the very heart of Hinduism.

Rama Krishna was born in 1833, in Bengal, and died in 1886. His father was a Brahmin. He himself was of a peculiarly religious and lovable disposition, and from his childhood, through all his life, made religion his supreme interest. He could, indeed, tolerate no other interest. He was sent to school, but finding the sole aim of the teaching seemed to be making a livelihood, he took no interest in it. And when, at the age of twenty, he was appointed priest at a temple to the goddess Kali, at Dakshinesvara, about five miles from Calcutta, he found himself in his true element.

And here at once is apparent how differently different Hindus look upon the same subject. Swami Dayanand, as we have seen, detested idolatry and inveighed against it all his life. And to the poet Tagore idolatry is an abomination. Yet Rama Krishna believed the image of Kali in his temple to be living and breathing and taking food out of his hand. He would sit for hours singing hymns and talking and praying to her as a child to his mother and begging her to reveal herself more fully to him. His whole soul would melt in a flood of tears as he appealed to her. The image was very necessary for his worship. To attain to a higher state of perfection, Rama Krishna for twelve years went through a course of ascetic exercises. He was initiated into the truth of the Vedanta. He attained the highest stage of trance and rose to a state of union with the absolute Brahma. He would become quite unconscious of the body, and his disciples would have to force food down his mouth.

The great idea he conceived was of the *Motherhood* of God. In his early stages, when worshipping the image of Kali, he would look upon it as his mother and the mother of the whole universe. God was not so much our Father as our Mother.

And he would weep for hours when he could not see his Mother as perfectly as he would have wished.

"Why does the God-lover find such pleasure in addressing the Deity as Mother?" he asks. And he answers: "Because the child is more free with its mother, and, consequently, she is dearer to the child than anyone else."

No one could be more humble than Rama Krishna in his ordinary everyday state. He would regard himself as the servant of all men and women and would perform the most menial offices. Yet in his moments of God-consciousness he would regard himself as an actual incarnation of God. He would speak of himself as being able to do anything and to know everything, and of being the soul which had been born before as Rama, as Krishna, as Jesus, or as Buddha.

Again, he was different to Swami Dayanand in having no desire to go forth and promulgate his message and gather a following. "When the rose blooms and sheds its fragrance all round the bees come of themselves. The bees seek the full-blown rose; the rose does not seek the bees." But for those who did come to him he would spare himself nothing. In teaching and in exhortation he would spend hour after hour with them. "I would suffer willingly all sorts of bodily pains, and death also, a hundred thousand times, if by so doing I could bring a single soul to freedom and salvation." Yet, even so, he found it hard to convey what his experience of God had been. "As a little child can have no idea of the love of husband and wife, so a worldly man cannot comprehend the ecstasy of Divine Communion," he would say. But he would try his best to describe it. "God is like a vast shoreless ocean without bounds or limits. He is one, but His aspects are many. Everything that exists is God. God is even in the tiger. God dwells even in the most wicked." God saith: "I am the snake that biteth and the charmer that healeth: I am the judge that condemneth and the executioner that executeth judgment." But God is not *equally* in all; "the manifestation of the Deity must be understood to be in greater degree in those who are honoured by a large following than in those who have gained no such influence." "How doth the Lord dwell in the body? He dwells in the body like the plug in a syringe—*i.e.*, in the body and yet apart from it." "As the rain-water from the roof of a house is discharged through pipes having their mouthpieces shaped either like the head of a tiger, or of a cow, or of a buffalo, although the water does not belong to these pipes, but comes from the heavens above, so are the holy Sadhus, through whose mouths eternal and heavenly truths are discharged into the world by the Almighty." "The sunlight is one and the same wherever it falls: but the bright surfaces like water, mirrors, or polished surfaces can reflect it fully. So is the Light Divine. It falls equally and impartially on all hearts, but the pure and clean hearts of the good and holy Sadhus alone can reflect it." Yet man is not entirely as uninfluenced by the divinity as the rain-water pipe or the mirror. "When the fruit grows out of the flower, the petals drop off of themselves. So when the divinity in thee increases, the weaknesses of thy human nature will vanish of their own accord."

Towards other religions Rama Krishna was very

tolerant. "As the same sugar is made into various figures of birds or beasts, so one sweet Mother Divine is worshipped in various climes and ages under various names and forms. Different creeds are but different paths to the Almighty." He studied Islam and Christianity. Once he saw Jesus in a vision, and for some days could think and speak of nothing but Jesus and His love. But though he thought that all religions were ways to God, he said: "Every man should follow his own religion. A Christian should follow Christianity, a Moslem Islam, and so on. And for the Hindus the ancient path, the path of the Aryan Rishis, is the best." And every man should have religion. "As the lamp does not burn without oil, so man cannot live without God . . . and he alone is really a *man* who is illumined with Spiritual Light."

Rama Krishna, as I have said, made no attempt to start a new religion or found a new sect. But by his intense spirituality, by his combined meekness and unlimited confidence, and by his sweet lovability, he profoundly impressed such men as Keshub Chunder Sen and Vivakenanda. And since his death a Rama Krishna Mission has been founded which teaches a wider conception of spirituality, that sees the value of renunciation and sacrifice for the good of others, and fully recognises each man's responsibility for others. It sees the hostile spirit of materialism abroad in the land. And it strives to "recondition" Hinduism and so win the people back to their ancient allegiance.

"What is that *mantram* that will make the three hundred million hearts beat in unison? The Bolshevik ideal? The lure of material prosperity?

The hatred of the British? We do not hear our 'leaders' speak of anything of this secret of unity. We shall tell them that secret. It is *religion*. . . . Let us warn our 'leaders' that this is the only way to unite the people and make them strong. . . . It is a vain hope to find any other basis of nationality than spirituality."

This is the message which his followers have taken on from Rama Krishna.

Out of Islam in India has also sprung a reformatory movement in recent times. As recently as 1890 was born the Ahmadiyya Movement. It was founded by Ghulam Ahmad under what he considered "an express Divine command." He claimed to be the Mahdi whose advent had been foretold by the Prophet Muhammad and the Messiah whose advent had been foretold in the Bible. And his adherents regard the movement as standing towards Islam in the same relationship that Christianity in its early days occupied towards Judaism. But Ahmadiyyat was not a mere offshoot of Islam : it was Islam itself. And the founder did not pretend to be the bearer of a new law or dispensation. He only claimed to be an exponent of the real teachings of Islam. And he did not ask people to believe that the soul of Jesus was incarnated in him. In claiming to be the Promised Messiah "he merely meant that he had appeared in the power and spirit of Jesus."

True religion exists in the world, but men do not act upon it. True religion is belief in God. And a merciful and loving God will not leave men floundering in error and worldliness. He will take measures for their guidance and direction. For God must be kinder and more merciful than a father or mother. A father and mother are merely means for bearing children. But God is not only the Creator: He is also the end and object of man's existence. And man should so regulate his life in conformity with the doctrines of the Unity of God as to lead him to moral and spiritual perfection. He should love no other thing or being with a love greater than that which he entertains for God. The object for man's existence is unlimited advancement. He is not bound with shackles which he cannot break, and God never shuts on him the gates of liberty. And all men stand in like personal relationship with God. Even the greatest of prophets and reformers are, in their relationship to God, no more than men. The gates of progress that are opened to them are open to all mankind. And God does not permit an intermediary between Himself and His creatures. All prophets occupy the position of guides, but none of them can serve as an intermediary. Every man at all times may attain to the highest pinnacle of spiritual achievement. The gates of Heaven open to all who knock.

This was the gist of Ahmad's teaching. His followers maintain that he cleared every aspect of Islam from the errors which had crept into it. And the proof of his claim was the purity of his life. He served Islam with his time, money, pen, tongue, and personal example. And his whole life was a uniform record of purity and righteousness. He was a believer in personal revelation. He was not merely inspired. He received revelation in definite words from God. And though he lived in the remote little village of Qadian in the Punjab, and from that obscure spot worked for the regeneration of Islam, God revealed to him that "within the space of three hundred years all Western countries shall have accepted Islam, and the followers of other religions will be but few in number."

From the outset he encountered bitter and determined opposition. But the movement he initiated has steadily gone forward. The present elected head of the community is Hazrat Mirza Mahomad Ahmad. His followers are numbered by hundreds of thousands. And there are Ahmadiyya communities in many European as well as Asiatic and African countries.

These examples are enough to show that religion is a real vital force in India, and as powerful to-day as ever in the past. New religious movements are constantly springing out of the old. And the most intellectual men in India, as well as the simplest, are everywhere moved by the appeal of religion.

CHAPTER XIV

TAGORE

DIFFERENT from any of the foregoing—acuter of intellect, more delicately sensitive, infinitely more of an artist, yet fundamentally alike, fundamentally Indian, and fundamentally religious—is Rabindranath Tagore, the finest flower India has produced for many a long century. And, like all truly great artists, he is as universal as he is Indian. His art springs out of Nature. For that reason it rings true. And because it rings true it appeals as much to the Frenchman, the Italian, to the American, or the Englishman, as it does to his brother Bengalis. And the religion by which it is informed is no alien religion. It is as Indian as Walt Whitman's religion was American or Wordsworth's English.

And yet Tagore is not as exclusively Indian as Dayanand or Rama Krishna. He is profoundly versed in English literature—and to some extent in French. He is a product, in part at least, of Europe as well as of India. Perhaps we may say that the British provided the stimulus and the conditions under which his genius could flourish. If Bengal had remained in the state in which Clive found it, Tagore might have felt the conditions about him uncongenial to his poetical development; and even if, in spite of the sordid conditions about him, his genius had yet burst out it could not have obtained the worldwide recognition it now possesses. He might not have been known beyond Bengal. On the other hand, if the French instead of the British had won supremacy in India, if there had been a French Governor-General at Calcutta, if the administration had been manned by Frenchmen, if French culture had been imparted to India with all the Frenchman's conviction that it is the one and only culture worth having, Tagore might now have been a Frenchman instead of an Indian, and the leading French poet of the day.

But widely as he is known on account of his writings in English and in the translations therefrom into French, Italian, German, and Swedish, he has, in the opinion of Mr. E. J. Thompson, greater claims to admiration on account of his writings in his own native Bengali. And Mr. Thompson has lived and taught in Bengal and knows the poet well in his own home. And he not only writes poems; he also writes dramas, novels, and short stories. And he not only writes; he also composes music, he acts in his own dramas, he makes eloquent speeches. And now in the evening of his days he has taken to painting!

To the very foundation he is an artist. And the poet in him comes out in every sentence he utters and every movement he makes. In appearance he is the part to perfection—with his penetrating eyes, his lofty brow, his waving hair, and his long beard, his gentle voice, and his noble bearing. And one cannot hear him speak more than a few sentences without observing his fine sensibility. He gives the impression of an exquisitely delicate instrument responsive to the very subtlest impressions. Agony comes over him at what is the least out of tune with the great rhythm of the universe. Joy untold is his when he has caught the rhythm and expressed it in poem or hymn or music.

Like every other poet, he has had to battle his own way to recognition. But he at least had the advantage of starting amidst congenial surroundings. The Tagores were a wonderful family. Every one was an artist. All—women as well as men—would act or compose music or write plays. All were stimulating one another in artistic production. And living in one of those great Indian family houses, where different generations dwell under the same roof, cultural life flowed along easily and naturally. And in India a poet can live closer to Nature than he can in Europe. Tagore has never shown any desire to get out into the wild places of the earth and wrestle with the great forces of Nature. He is of too gentle a spirit. But he has loved that outdoor life which is so easy in India, when he can feel the soft air circulating about him, and watch the sunsets, and sit out in the moonlight, or drift along the river and note the luscious growth of woodland on the banks. Nature has been much to him. And Nature has been thus very close at hand. So by both man and Nature Tagore has been much favoured.

The flame of a candle is what he strikes us as most resembling. An electric light can be turned this way or that, downward or upward, and it will still throw out its cold, harsh light. A hurricane may blow around it, but it will be unaffected. Not so the candle-flame. It can only burn upward. Deflect it in the least from the vertical and it will work back to it. And it is sensitive to the slightest current of air. The faintest breath will send it quivering. But in its agonies it will always be struggling to regain its position. Only to the highest will its nature ever allow it to point. And yet, sensitive as it is to currents of air about it, it is dependent on that air for its very life. It could not burn in a vacuum. It must have life-giving air to feed on.

Even so is Tagore. He must have the open air about him. A gust may disturb him; he is quiveringly sensitive to every breath. Yet, wounded as he may be for the moment, by his whole nature he is compelled to struggle upward again. He must win back his natural position and point to the zenith of beauty and goodness. And just as men turn from the glare of the blatant electric arc to the mellow light of the candle, so do they turn to this gentle Eastern poet and delight in his charm. In the rough tempests of life they may need a hardier guidance. But in the quiet of the inner chamber the soft beams he sheds from him may be soothing to the soul.

And what does his tender light reveal? What has he to say to us?

Joy in the universe. Love in the heart of the world. This is what he wants most to declare. He himself, in an oft-quoted passage, has described how illumination came to him. One morning he was standing on the verandah of his house in Calcutta. It was years ago, when he was still a young man. And the street up which he looked was sordid and commonplace enough. But there were trees at the end of the street And the sun was just rising through the leafy tops of those trees. As he continued to gaze, all of a sudden a covering seemed to fall from his eyes, and he found the world bathed in a wonderful radiance, with waves of beauty and joy swelling on every side. This radiance pierced in a moment through the folds of sadness and despondency which had accumulated over his heart and flooded it with a universal light. This was what he termed the joy-aspect of the universe. And it came to be so that no person or thing in the world seemed to him trivial or unpleasing.

Many a current would afterwards blow upon this candle-flame of his vision. But always it would struggle back to its true direction and shed forth that radiance which came both from what he had within him and from what he received from without.

He would be acutely sensitive to the wrongs and evils around him. It is natural that he should feel the presence of alien rulers in his country. But even about his own countrymen he would have, and express, the strongest feeling. In his poems and his dramas he would expose the horror of child-marriage. That little girls should be married—and often be widows for the rest of their lives—cut him to the quick. And he would hold up the hideosity of the custom to the eyes of his fellow-Hindus.

The brag of young Bengalis, who boasted as if they equalled the heroes of legend, also wounded the dignity of his essentially noble soul. Outworn traditions and customs roused fierce antagonism in him. Idolatry he detested; he had had, and through his life has continued to have, personal experience of a God working in and through and beyond and above all he saw about him, and the worship of idols was an abomination to him. So, also, was caste.

He is an aristocrat to the marrow of his bones. Yet he has no class-feeling. Every human being is to him in the same fellowship with God, and a fellow-worshipper of God. Why, then, these caste distinctions? In ancient days some distinction of caste may have been necessary. But nowadays it must be removed. It is a retardation—a stumbling-block in the way of progress. His keen and wakeful sense of justice revolted against the degradation that caste involves. And all his powers of expression were used to denounce it.

And if he was thus tormented with thoughts of his own country's wrongdoings, he has naturally felt the degradation of being subjected to an alien rule. His first visit to England, in 1877, made a most unpleasant impression on him. The brusque ways of Englishmen grated on that proud and sensitive soul. And the materialism of Western civilisation in general was repugnant to him. British rule was efficient, no doubt. But it was a cold, impersonal rule. The individual was crushed in the great machine. There was no room for humanity and personality. A dead weight hung upon the land. The Great War added to the poet's agony. The pain to his soul was excruciating. And his dislike for England, and the West in general, was intensified. England and the West had shown their high appreciation of his genius. The King-Emperor had knighted him. English men of letters had brought his work to the world's attention. The Nobel Prize had been conferred upon him. But this did not lessen his dislike of the ways of the West. And, in horror at the manner in which an incipient rising in the Punjab had been suppressed, he sought to return the honour which the Emperor had conferred upon him. Thus sensitive was the flame of a candle to what would have left not the slightest impression upon the more hardy electric light.

But it is when the flame has regained its natural poise that it gives its light. And the poet was usually in most tranquil and beautiful poise. In that spirit he would drink in from the beauty around him and give it forth in loveliest verse. Each poem is penetrated with this profound sense of oneness with the universe. And in the common and particular around him—in a bird, or a flower, or an ordinary human being—the poet would detect the immanence of the universal. Each was in some degree or in some aspect the image and superscription of the whole great universe. And what he himself felt he would convey with that deep earnestness and that lightness and grace which has put him in touch with kindred souls all over the world.

Though he has written a really great poem on a storm at sea, and though he is attracted by the torrential rains and flooded Ganges of the monsoon time, it is in the main the gentler aspects of Nature that most appeal to him. He lives hard by the Himalaya. And the mighty mountains were dear to the heart of his father. And one would have thought that their grandeur, the virgin purity of their snowy summits, and their noble aspiration skywards, would have been the main inspiration of any poet who had the good fortune to behold them. But for Tagore the Himalaya is perhaps too overwhelming. He is a lover of the far-stretching plain rather than of the mountains. He prefers the calm, deep-flowing river rather than the raging torrent. And when he writes of the forest it is rather of the near-by woods than of the far depths of the jungle, where only primitive peoples and the tiger and buffalo dwell.

The Ganges, as it flows placidly through the plains, is his principal love. It runs through all his poems. It is their very life. Looking out on it in the freshness of the morning, drifting on it in the evening, always the great, silent but ever-moving river left its impress on him. It was the symbol of the life that is for ever making towards the great ocean of eternity from which it sprang.

Pure sunsets, too, he would love to watch, drinking in their glory and filling his soul of their calm and peace. And then the silent moonlight, with its stillness and tranquillity speaking only of goodwill—this, too, had a profound influence on him. For eagerly as he entered into the life of the world he had always this urgent need for solitude, and contemplation, amid the gentle, soothing beauties of Nature.

And what he felt of the joy and love in the world he wanted to pass on to others, not only through the medium of poetry, of drama, of music, of story, and of oratory—in every one of which arts he excelled—but also through the medium of a school and of a university of his own fashioning. He would make his impress upon the young as well as upon the mature. And with this purpose in view he first founded his school, and then what he hoped would be a universal university open to teachers and scholars of all nations.

The British system of education in India he abhorred. It was mechanical, hard, uninspiring. He would establish a school in accordance with Indian ideas and Indian traditions. It would be a school not of the confined classroom, but of the free-flowing open air. It would be in touch with Nature. And those who studied would be free and encouraged to dwell on every beauty and aspect of Nature. So, in the quiet of Santiniketan—the Home of Peace—his school was founded in 1901. First as a home for the spirit of India, and later as a home for the spirit of all nations, it has slowly, and in the face of many difficulties, made its influence in India and the world. Tagore himself teaches in it, and he has attracted to it many notable Indian artists and teachers, and such ardent English lovers of India as C. F. Andrews and W. W. Pearson.

And in the system of education here imparted love of God is made one with love of Nature. The shady groves, the great trees, the wide-stretching plains, the flowering shrubs, the sunsets, and the moonlight, are all allowed to have their full influence on the pupils. But one with it, and underlying it, deep religious feeling is imparted. In prayers the boys both begin and end the day, going round the groves chanting the morning prayer:

"Thou art our Father. Do Thou help us to know Thee as Father. We bow down to Thee. Do Thou never afflict us, O Father, by causing a separation between Thee and us. O Thou self-revealing One, O Thou Parent of the Universe, purge away the multitude of our sins, and send unto us whatever is good and noble. To Thee, from whom spring joy and gladness, nay, who art all goodness Thyself, to Thee we bow down now and for ever."

And in the evening they pray:

"The Deity, who is in fire and water, nay, who pervades the Universe through and through, and makes His abode in tiny plants and towering forests—to such a Deity we bow down for ever and ever."

Dramatic performances are one special means for imparting ideas and arousing feeling. Many of Tagore's own plays are acted by the pupils, and the poet himself joins in the acting. Indians have always loved the drama. It has been the means, through thousands of years, by which the ideals the people love have been implanted in the race, generation by generation. And in India, in the open air, with the informality of outdoor production, plays are very easily produced. And as the dramas are performed right in the midst of the audience, the spectators simply squatting on the ground and the actors rising from their midst, there is the closest possible touch between actors and audience. Both alike are taking part in what is meant to have an effect which all desire to have produced upon them. All *want* to be impressed by the impression Tagore wishes to make. Formality and artificiality are reduced to a minimum. The way is clear for the freest possible spontaneity. The dramas, the actors, and the audience have all sprung out of those very surroundings in which the plays are performed.

In the political field Tagore is not so happy as in the sphere of art and education. He seems instinctively to recoil from the rough and sordid part of politics. On the question of the Partition of Bengal he did, indeed, momentarily plunge into the fray, and he was then a most effective speaker and writer. But he as suddenly withdrew to his own proper sphere. And there he has been content to remain. Yet this does not mean that he has no effect upon the politics of India. By the spirit he has been able to impart into the rising India he has aroused India to a sense of the destiny that is in her own hands. He has turned her eyes from the glories of a nebulous past. He has laid the foundations of a new and more glorious national life founded on righteousness, unity, and love. Not "Back to the Vedas" has been his call, but onward to new glories. And this is the vision of India's future which he holds before his countrymen's eyes:

Where the mind is without fear and the head is held high,
Where knowledge is free,
Where the world has not been broken up by narrow domestic walls,
Where words come out from the depths of truth,
Where the clear stream of reason has not lost its way in the dreary desert sand of dead habit,
Where the mind is led forward by Thee into every widening thought and action—
Into that heaven of freedom, my Father, let my country awake.

And devoted admirer as Tagore is of Gandhi, and wholly at one as he is with him in the idea and ideal of relying upon spiritual force for remedying wrongs, Tagore is no believer in non-co-operation. The idea is repugnant to him. He would set up the ideal of perfection over the ideal of power. But he would co-operate. He would not have an India apart by herself from the world. He would have an India out in the world, a part of the world, working with the world. Not independence for India—or any other country—but interdependence for all. That is the only possible line which, in hard fact, any country *can* take. So East and West must work together—each making its own peculiar contribution to the whole.

Such is Tagore. And by him India must be judged. His message to the world is her message. If it had been a mean and degrading message, then India would have been despicable. But it is a lofty and inspiring message, and because of it India is worthy of world-esteem. Just now she is troubled about her status. But no one but herself can give her her status. No Government, however powerful, can confer it upon her. And Tagore has given India a standing among the nations she has never had in the whole of her history. And it is a new status, because Tagore is a transition between the old India which has been slowly dying and the new India which, like the new Italy which has risen out of the old, has now come to birth.

Tagore is perhaps more. Maybe he is another example of what man may become when the tougher, hardier races have done the rough work of the world and cleared the way for the emergence of a gentler, finer, more sensitive race in the future.

CHAPTER XV

GANDHI

ANOTHER famous embodiment of the present spirit of India is Mahatma Gandhi. As a compound of Western influence and Hindu orthodoxy he typifies the result of two centuries of impact of the West upon the East. He remains Indian to the marrow. But the Western impact has stirred him to arouse his country to more vivid life.

Gandhi is renowned as a saint. And because he is a saint it is assumed that whatever he does is good, and whatever he says is both true and wise. But Gandhi has plunged into politics. And in politics not even a saint, with the best intentions in the world, can always be sure he is doing the right thing. And in the opinion of many Gandhi has done much harm where he might, with more political wisdom, have done good. And before I go on to the really heroic and saintly part of Mahatma Gandhi's career I will show where I believe he has been in error. And I feel it necessary to do this because he has spent so much of his time in denouncing the British Government that many are unaware that there is at least another side to the question.

Of Gandhi's love of India there is no question. He has sacrificed his all for India, and has won the devotion and affection of Indians as no other Indian has ever done. But, by some unfortunate inner twist (perhaps due to overmuch fasting), just at the moment when the British were most favourably disposed towards India, when there was in London a Secretary of State whose whole soul was in the cause of India, and who was actually at work developing a scheme of reforms for India, Gandhi proceeds to inflame Indians against the British.

In 1917 the British Government had declared in the most formal way that responsible government in India was the goal of British policy. Mr. Montagu, the Secretary of State for India, had himself gone out to India to consult the Viceroy as to the best means of carrying that policy into effect. He had received deputations, consulted representative men (including Gandhi himself), and tried to ascertain all shades of opinion. He had held meetings with the heads of all the provinces, and with a committee of the Ruling Princes. In the end he and the Viceroy had drawn up a report, published in 1918 while the War was still in progress, in which they had used the following words: "The welfare and happiness of hundreds of millions of people are in issue. . . . Because the work already done has called forth in India a new life, we must found her Government on the co-operation of her people, and make such changes in the existing order as will meet the needs of the more spacious days to come." And they had declared their conception of the eventual future of India as "a sisterhood of states, self-governing in all matters of purely local or provincial interest, but presided over by a Central Government increasingly representative of, and responsible to, the people of all the states, and representing the interests of all India on equal terms with the self-governing units of the British Empire." A new Constitution for India on the basis of this Report was actually being considered by a Joint Committee of both Houses of Parliament. And Gandhi knew all this. Knew of the Report and presumably had read it, for it was published in India; knew of the Committee; knew that India in a few months' time would be granted a Representative Assembly with greatly increased powers; knew that constitutional means were being provided for the fullest possible expression of opinion. And yet at this very moment, when. above all others, it was necessary to keep India calm and composed for the introduction and working of the new great measure of reform, he starts an agitation against the British Government. In his own words, he felt himself "called upon to lead an intensive agitation" against the Rowlatt Act—an agitation which culminated in outbreaks of riots, murders, and incendiarism against the British authority and against all Europeans. Why did he feel called upon to lead this intensive agitation? Again, in his own words—because it was "a law designed to rob the people of all freedom."

But, on the face of it, was it likely that the British Government, when they were in the very act of working out constitutional reforms expressly designed to give Indians greater freedom, would stultify themselves by at the same time bringing in a law *designed* to rob the people of all real freedom? What was the purpose of the Rowlatt Act? It was passed just after the close of the War, and its purpose was to provide Government with the means of punishing those who were attempting by violent means to destroy the Government in India as the Bolshevists had just destroyed the Government in Russia. Such attempts had already actually been made. And Government had to provide themselves with the means of preventing similar attempts again being made. All Governments have to strike the right mean between allowing too great and too little freedom to the members of a community. If certain members by their words and actions would wreck the community, Government, in the interests of the whole, have to check them. The Rowlatt Act was intended to provide Government with the means of checking the wreckers. While the new and far greater and more important Reform Act was intended to give real freedom to Indians. The one was incidental and temporary. The other was of a far-reaching importance and wide-sweeping effect. And when Gandhi ignored the great measure and concentrated on the lesser, when he started an "intensive agitation" against the lesser, though he knew how easily an Indian crowd is inflamed and will go forth killing and burning indiscriminately, and though he knew that India, owing to the high prices consequent on the War and to the failure of the crops and the awful visitation of influenza, which had carried off millions, was in a highly inflammable state—was he acting as a wise man, as a man with a due sense of proportion, as a sane man, as a saint? Or was his ardent patriotism blinding his vision till, instead of the saint in him inspiring the politician, the politician was smothering the saint?

And, apart from the wisdom and the sanity of starting an intensive agitation at that particular moment and that particular measure, was it a *friendly* act? Did it tend towards goodwill between the people of India and the people of Great Britain? He may have had many causes of complaint against the British. But, anyhow, those who had counted most had shown him friendship. Both the Viceroy and the Secretary of State had consulted him and treated him as a friend. And they had not scoffed at his desire for Indian freedom. They were going as far as ever they could to grant it. Was it a friendly act to agitate the people of India against Government at this crucial moment, when the British were starting the very delicate process of gradually handing over the reins of government to Indian hands?

And was it a friendly—let alone a saintly—act to start an agitation in Bombay on the very day the Prince of Wales arrived to convey the thanks of the British Sovereign and the British people to the Princes and people of India for the aid they had given to the Empire during the War? In the words of Gandhi, "the Prince's visit itself, and the circumstances attending the ceremonials arranged and public money wasted for the manufacture of a welcome to His Royal Highness, constituted an unbearable provocation." And, therefore, he organised a public burning of foreign cloth as an "eloquent counter-demonstration to the interested official demonstration." Though he was surprised that this burning of foreign cloth at the moment when the Prince was landing in India led to another wild outbreak of mob passion, to mad rioting, the killing of innocent people, and the burning of liquor-shops, and though he did his best to stop it, and afterwards fasted in atonement, was it the act of a man really intent on creating goodwill?

And, lastly, in December, 1929, when he and other leaders of the National Congress had sought an interview with the Viceroy, and Lord Irwin had granted it; when the Viceroy had just most formally and with the sanction of the British Government declared that Dominion Status for India was the goal of British policy; when he had declared, further, that as soon as the Report of the Simon Commission had been received and considered a Round Table Conference would be held between the British Government and the Princes of India and representatives of British India to consider the Report and determine what further measures of reform might be put before Parliament—was it a wise, or a friendly, or a saintly act of Gandhi to insist that Dominion Status must be granted forthwith, though even the Committee of Indians sitting with the Simon Commission had not asked for immediate but only gradual advancement towards Dominion Status? And when Lord Irwin refused what was not in his power to grant, was it a sane and friendly act to start a campaign of civil disobedience and incite the population to break the law of the land? When he had bitter experience of what "intensive agitation" meant in India, was it a great and a good thing to speak of the Government as "Satanic," to incite the people to disobedience, and to try to bring all government to a standstill?

These are questions we have to ask ourselves, for this matter is of moment to the whole world. If Gandhi had had his way the government of India would have been in the hands of Indians on January 1 of this year. And how three hundred and twenty millions of people are governed is a matter affecting every nation. Some may think that as Gandhi is a saint what he does must be for the best, and that the right thing for the British to have done was to have handed India over to him, as he wanted, on that date. Others, however, think that, saintly as he may be, he is inexperienced in the great affairs of State, and that in starting a campaign of non-co-operation and disobedience just at this particular juncture he was doing no good to India and was alienating a great body of opinion in England from India.

Successive Viceroys had shown Gandhi the greatest consideration. They had consulted him and done their best to fall in with his views. But they had also to consider the interests of others than those whom Gandhi represented, for he does not represent the whole of India, and many Indians are strongly opposed to his words and actions. And Viceroys had at least received him and listened to him and shown themselves willing to meet his wishes as far as they could. And when at last his defiance of the law of the land had brought him before the courts he had received a fair trial; and when he was ill in gaol the kindest treatment from the English surgeon. To an Englishman, at least, it seems, therefore, that if during these critical years since the War, when the British were making a greater effort than they had ever made before to help India along the road to self-government, Gandhi had shown in his political activities a little more patience and forbearance, a little more desire to co-operate instead of "non-co-operate," and had persuaded the people to obey instead of to disobey, there might have been a better feeling now between Indian and British, and self-government for India might have been nearer in sight.

All this, however, is only a part of Gandhi's life, and not the part upon which he will be mainly judged. He had much to engage him besides politics. And if, in our view, he made mistakes in politics, we at least admire his courage in plunging into them instead of sitting fastidiously aloof while others burnt their fingers. He had courage, and we all admire courage. And in spite of these, what appear to me, defects in Gandhi's life, I believe that he has done India four great services. Firstly, he has instilled courage into India and made Indians feel their manhood. Secondly, he has aroused in them a sense of nationhood. Thirdly, he has stressed the importance of religion in the national life, denounced materialism, and emphasised the value of spiritual things. Lastly, he has brought to India the attention of the whole world, till every nation is now interested in what is going on in India. And these immense and permanent benefits far outweigh the temporary harm he has done.

Gandhi was English-educated and for some years studied law in England. And he studied at a time when materialism and atheism were much to the fore. He might very well, therefore, have become, like most young Indian students, a materialist and atheist. What saved him was his mother's influence. "She was," says Mr. C. F. Andrews,

Gandhi's friend and biographer, " a devout Hindu, whose deep religious faith penetrated and inspired his whole personal life and character. She was the main influence which gave his nature its strong religious bent and preserved it predominantly Hindu through all his life.'' But another influence gave it the direction it assumed. Even his mother's influence might have hardly availed if at a critical period he, like so many others in Europe who had tended towards atheism, had not come under the influence of Tolstoi.

The Kingdom of God is Within You profoundly affected Gandhi. Here was the teaching of Jesus so told as to fit in almost exactly with the Hindu teaching as taught by his mother. Here it was, and told with all the force of a great artist. Evil was to be resisted by love, not by force. We were to turn the other cheek—to love our enemies. Gandhi was attracted to the Sermon on the Mount. If to live in accordance with that was to be a Christian he would be a Christian.

Now Tolstoi had one characteristic—a Russian characteristic—which would make special appeal to an Indian. He would concentrate his attention with furious intensity on one part or aspect of the whole. He would be blind to all else and to every qualifying consideration. And he would then with terrific energy enforce that single view. Such a method has certain great advantages. It makes others also think there is only this one possible view. And it makes them hold that view with tremendous tenacity of conviction.

Tolstoi had painted the evil of riches, of capital, of government. He had urged the need of giving up all and leading a life of love and goodwill. And Gandhi had been inspired by his words. He had also written to Tolstoi, and Tolstoi had replied commending him to a life of non-violence.

And here, if I might be permitted, I would like to intrude a personal point. At the very time, 1894, just after Tolstoi's book appeared, I also read it, and I also was impressed by it.

I was then serving in the most distant part of the Indian frontier in North Chitral. I was away from the telegraph. The post took a month to reach me from India. I had only one European companion. I had ample leisure to read and think. And I was naturally drawn to the fundamental things of life. I was working out my basic religious principles for myself and planning my future career in accordance with them. In the course of my studies I had read several "lives" of Jesus. Now I read Tolstoi's *The Kingdom of God is Within You.* And the effect upon me was instantaneous.

Under date August 31, 1894, I make the following entry in my diary: "I have finished Tolstoi's book. It has influenced me profoundly. With the main principles I thoroughly agree, and the whole book has just given that finishing touch to my already half-formed resolution to retire from the Service and lead a freer life, where I can be 'true to myself,' and to that divine spark within me, and in thoroughness and sincerity seek first the Kingdom of God—that is, lead a spiritual life, developing to the utmost the spirit, the portion of God that is within me. . . . I now thoroughly see the truth of Tolstoi's argument that Government, capital, and private property are evils. . . . Tolstoi does not say how society can exist without Government, capital, and private prosperity, but he says that a few great ones—like Columbus—must plunge into the unknown and discover the way."

Thus far had the magic of the great artist worked upon me. For the moment he had caught me in his spell. I applied for furlough, and informed Government that I intended to retire from the Service at the end of it. And it was while I was on furlough—employed by *The Times* as their special correspondent in South Africa—that I met Gandhi, little knowing that he also was under Tolstoi's spell. Gandhi must have been then about twenty-six. He was already engaged in his fight to right the wrongs of the Indians in South Africa, and he invited me to dinner.

He then lived in the European way, and was a very enthusiastic, persuasive young man. I cannot say I recognised in him the grit and determination and courage and qualities of leadership he has since shown. I was too much engaged, as correspondent of *The Times*, in weighing against his argument what the Mayor of Durban had been saying about the British and Dutch having done all the pioneering and dangerous and hazardous work of building up Natal into a prosperous colony—which the Indians might have done centuries before if they had the same enterprising spirit—and not wanting Indians now to pour over in thousands and keep out those British whom Natal wanted for constructive purposes. These arguments of the mayor I was turning over in my mind all the time Gandhi was urging the cause of the Indians. And I could not go as whole-heartedly with him as he wished. Yet

I could not fail to be impressed by his sincerity and his charm. He most assuredly had the good of his fellow-countrymen at heart. And, as I know now, he was even then making up his mind to act on the very principles with which Tolstoi had so impressed me two years before.

And Gandhi really was prepared to go the whole length. He would pursue the principle of non-resistance to evil to the utmost logical extremity. He was quite ready to give his whole life to it. He was quite ready, also, to give the lives of his family, his friends, and his followers. He was prepared to give the life of the whole human race to it—so I once heard that great Indian statesman, Srinivasa Shastri, say. And herein lies the difficulty of following Gandhi—or anyone else who rides a single principle to death. For the world is not governed by logic alone. A certain course may, logically, follow from another. But it may not be wise—it may not be right—to take it. For it may not lead to the highest good on the whole. In following one line we must not lose sight of the whole—or in following a lesser good damage a higher good.

Gandhi throughout his life has had his eye fixed on some "evil." In South Africa the evil was the inferior status accorded to Indians. In India it has been the misconduct of the Satanic British Government. At another time it has been the sufferings of the "Depressed Classes" in India. But whatever the evil may be that he is for the time being fighting, always he refuses to use force or violence to remove it. It must be removed or overcome by non-violent methods. Always he has resorted to non-violence—to passive resistance. This method was in accord with Hindu teaching and, with his own inner disposition, with what he had learned from Tolstoi.

Ahimsa he called it. It was a name long since given to the principle by Hindu sages. And it is to him the heart of all religion. Literally, the term means non-violence. But Mr. Andrews explains that it is not merely a negative virtue, "it involves the positive doing of good quite as much as the negative refusal to do harm. According to the Mahabharata, it is supreme kindness and supreme self-sacrifice."

"In following the doctrine of Ahimsa," says Gandhi, "you may not offend anybody, you may not harbour an uncharitable thought, even in connection with one who may consider himself your enemy. . . . If we return blow for blow we depart from the doctrine of Ahimsa. But I go farther. If we resent a friend's action, or the so-called enemy's action, we still fall short of the doctrine. . . . If you express your love—Ahimsa—in such a manner that it impresses itself indelibly upon your so-called enemy, he must return that love."

And as regards himself, he says: "My soul refuses to be satisfied as long as it is a helpless witness of a single wrong, or a single misery." And this really gives the keynote to Gandhi's life. Being a man of the keenest human sympathies he cannot endure the sight of suffering in others. And suffering there is in abundance everywhere. But seeing all this he does not run away from it. He does not retire into the jungle and live a life of solitude. He plunges into the very thick of things. He goes to any length to remove those sufferings and redress those wrongs. And herein lies his heroism. He fears none. He faces the most powerful. He endures the cruellest sufferings himself that he may save suffering in others. And through all he has the conviction that God is with him; that God will sustain and comfort him.

And it is because of this warm and genuine sympathy, because he will himself make every sacrifice for the good of others, and because he relies on God, that he possesses the hold he has on Indian hearts.

His first activities were in Natal. He was, when I saw him there, enjoying a good practice at the Bar, making two or three thousand pounds a year, though still under thirty. And he was living in a comfortable villa. All this he gave up to redress the wrongs of his fellow-countrymen in Natal. They were treated with disrespect and were under certain disabilities. And he would give his life to champion their cause. But he would not use force for that purpose. There were many thousands of them. He would not marshal them as an armed force and demand satisfaction. He would put in practice his doctrine of Ahimsa. He would make his protest against what he considered the unjust treatment to which he, as an Indian, was subjected. He would get other Indians to join with him in the protest. And if this meant imprisonment he would go to prison. And if it meant the others going to prison, too, he would encourage them also to face imprisonment. There is, of course, a good deal more to be said on the other side than Gandhi in any of his campaigns allows. The "oppressors" are not all as black as they are painted. Nor are Gandhi and his associates as radiantly spotless as their admirers depict them. Nevertheless, the Indians in South Africa had a clear grievance in being termed "coolies," being made to travel third class, and in general treated as inferior people. And Gandhi did heroic service to India in insisting on Indians being treated with respect. And by his character, by his courage, by his readiness to sacrifice all for this cause, he drew attention to this unfair treatment and raised the whole status of India in South Africa. He won for himself the devotion of Indians. And he won the admiration of the British as well.

And if Gandhi required courage in his South African compaign he required a still higher heroism in his next campaign in India itself. In South Africa he had been fighting the British and Dutch Governments. And for such offences as Gandhi might commit the worst punishment was only imprisonment. In India he undertook to fight religious orthodoxy. And religious orthodoxy everywhere has pains for the soul far greater than any Government can inflict on the body.

By long custom, though not with purely religious sanction, certain classes had been treated by Hinduism as outcasts, as "untouchable." For these Gandhi had from his boyhood felt sympathy. Why should *any* human being be treated as "untouchable"? How could the mere touch of any man pollute another? Orthodox Hindus, his own mother included, taught him that if, even by accident, he touched an untouchable he was defiled and would have to purify himself. Gandhi could never believe that this was the Will of God. The custom had its origin at a time when the Aryan invaders of India had to preserve their community intact as opposed to the original inhabitants of the country. These "untouchables" are the remnants of the original inhabitants. And the custom of keeping apart from them had, in the process of time, acquired a kind of religious sanction. The original inhabitants had become "untouchables." They are now the "depressed" classes and have to have their separate wells and live completely apart.

Gandhi's warm human heart rebelled against this custom. He found in the ancient Hindu scriptures no sanction for it. And he started a campaign to clear Hinduism of what he called "the ineffaceable blot." Now Gandhi is a Hindu of the Hindus. As a youth he was very nearly becoming an atheist. For a time he wavered between Christianity and Hinduism. But all the heritage of tradition, all the influences of his childhood, told in the long run. The Bhagavat Gita was more to him than even the Sermon on the Mount. And he always claimed to be "an orthodox conservative Hindu." And thus, being a Hindu, to set himself and set others against a thing so ingrained in Hinduism as "untouchability," was to fly in the face of all social opinion. It meant incurring the deadliest hatred from his own people, the dire pains of social ostracism, and the determined opposition even of his wife.

Yet Gandhi never flinched. He declared that, "so long as Hindus wilfully regard 'untouchability' as part of their religion, Swaraj is impossible of attainment." He met the "untouchables." He prayed that if he had to be reborn he might be born an "untouchable," that he might share their sorrows and sufferings and save them from their miserable condition. He scavengered himself. He encouraged a Brahmin to do scavenger's work in order to teach the regular scavenger to do it cleanly.

All this he had done for the depressed classes. And besides battling to redress their wrongs, Gandhi has fought valiantly—as we shall see in the next chapter—against the evils of child-marriage and child-widowhood, and moral evil in the towns, and against everything which lowers the position of women in India.

So when we view the life of Mahatma Gandhi as a whole we are deeply impressed by the courage with which he has sought to remove the evils and sufferings his country has had to endure, by the fervour with which he has imbued Indians with a sense of nationality, by his nobility in insisting on spiritual values and appealing to the best religious feeling in men, and, finally, by his success in raising India high in the esteem of the world. He is a true national hero. He is revered even by those who oppose him. And his name will be honoured in all Indian history as one of India's greatest saints.

CHAPTER XVI

THE WOMEN

A MOTHER'S influence on her son has been exemplified in the case of Mahatma Gandhi. Devout and gentle, like most Indian women, she inspired him with the deep religious spirit and compassion which are so marked in him. And this is only typical of women's influence in India. It is greater by far than Westerners imagine. We suppose that because they are veiled and live in seclusion, Indian women must be a negligible factor in the national life. The probability is that they have a greater influence than the men themselves—and certainly than the men realise.

Theoretically, the man is the lord and master—a very god. And the woman is his humble and obedient servant and devoted worshipper. This is the Hindu conception of the relation of husband and wife. And for some two or three thousand years Hindu men and women have acted upon it. But the result has been to ennoble the women rather than the men, till now the woman is probably the better "man" of the two. Out of her very humility and meekness has come forth strength. Out of his very pride has issued weakness. And now to-day, as she is coming out into the world, she is displaying a courage and tenacity, a fortitude and love, and a capacity for self-sacrifice, service, and suffering that causes Gandhi to acclaim the female as not the weaker, but the nobler sex.

And here, too, Gandhi has played an heroic part in the building of the new India. With immense courage and spiritual strength he has sternly protested against child-marriage and child-widowhood, and against the purdah system. In the community which he has formed around him he has ruled that none of these things should be. And he has been the champion of free and equal womanhood; of votes for women and an equal legal status.

"I passionately desire the utmost freedom for our women," he says. "I detest child-marriages. I shudder to see a child-widow, and shiver with rage when a husband, just widowed, with brutal indifference contracts another marriage. I deplore the criminal indifference of parents who keep their daughters utterly ignorant and illiterate and bring them up only for the purpose of marrying them off to some young man of means." And as regards the social evil in the great towns, he says: "It is a matter of bitter shame and sorrow, of deep humiliation, that a number of women have to sell their chastity for man's lust. . . . In a self-respecting India is not every woman's virtue as much every man's concern as his own sister's?"

The poet Tagore also has written on the abomination of the child-marriage of girls and of the cruel treatment of wives who were little more than infants. He looks upon woman as different from man and does not, therefore, press her equality. Her sphere is another. And he would have her remain woman and not ape men. But he attacks the injustice which would regard her as unfitted for education. He only thinks that her true field is the home, where she can be the centre of love and inspiration. And he himself, in that wonderful home-circle of the great Tagore family, was greatly encouraged and inspired by the elder brother's wife.

And in the new India it is the women themselves who are now coming forward. Especially since the War there has been a mighty stirring of the women. In India it has been as elsewhere. Women have come out into the world. They have taken up great causes. They have undertaken to fight their own battles. And they, too, claim the right to share in the building of India. Those who thus come forth may be few in comparison with the vast numbers in India. But they are of such a spirit and intelligence that they are a power in the land that must be reckoned on.

Mother India has made known to the world the suffering of Indian women. What needs to be more known is what Indian women themselves have been and are doing to right their wrongs.

Among the pioneers was Pandita Ranabai, the daughter of a Brahmin, and herself an accomplished Sanskrit scholar, who had won the admiration of the highest Pundits in the land. She always remained a true Indian, and would dwell lovingly on the charm and affection of her typical Hindu home. But she was deeply conscious of the sufferings of Indian women. Largely through the influence of the famous Indian Christian, Nehemiah Goreh, she had become a Christian. And she devoted all her courage, all the strong fibre of her character, all her initiative and tenacity of purpose, to bettering the lot of her Indian sisters, and especially of the unhappy widows.

Mrs. Saroj Nalini Dutt was another Indian lady who devoted herself to helping Indian women. She was a Bengali lady, a member of the Brahmo Samaj, of a charming disposition, wide experience of the world, and trained in modern culture. But she had a passionate love of India. She was convinced that India never would come to her own unless the women of India were aroused. She would remove the cruel customs and traditions which now keep them down. And, as a practical contribution, she inaugurated in 1913 some organisations, known as Mahila Samitis, for the promotion of domestic science and hygiene, and maternity child-welfare. And these are now spread to hundreds of villages in Bengal. But while removing the physical suffering and caring for the bodily health of Indian women, she would also restore to them the ancient ideals of service and devotion, the old faith in God, and the intense spirituality of the legendary women saints.

A similar work had also already been done in Western India, in the Mahratta country, by Mrs. Ramabai Ranade, the widow of the great Indian reformer, Mr. Justice Ranade. As far back as 1909 she had helped in forming the Seva Sadan at Poona. This institution gave not only the ordinary education to women and girls, but trained them as teachers, nurses, and midwives. And it has effected such a change that even Brahmin widows are now on the staff of general hospitals, and nurse not only women, but men.

Of present-day Indian women reformers perhaps

the noblest is Dr. Mathulakshmi Reddy, whom the Madras Legislative Council elected as their Deputy President. Her belief is in legislation. Without the help of legislation India will never get rid of the social evils. She sees that the individuality of Indian women is being crushed under the burden of customs and conventions; that early marriage strikes at the root of all development—physical, intellectual, and even spiritual; that the pangs of child-wives and child-mothers, and the unmitigated sorrows of widows and deserted wives demand an immediate remedy; that Hindu society is not justified in conniving at a custom that in the name of religion condemns young girls to a life of degradation and vice. And she demands an immediate remedy for all these social evils, and the liberation of the women from "the servile bondage" to which they are subject, that they may be able to fulfil their "sacred task of training, guiding, and forming the daily habits and character of the future administrators of India."

Besides the work done by these noble Indian women, besides the devoted efforts of Christian missionaries and of British administrators and English ladies, the world as a whole is also having its effect upon Indian women. Even they are affected by the world-movement of the times. Fortunately, it has not yet persuaded them to cut their hair and shorten their skirts or to wear European dress. But it has stirred them as never before. It has produced a deep discontent with things as they are. It has made them stretch out to a fuller freedom. Sometimes it takes the form of violent criticism of British administration and the British system of education.

Sometimes it takes the form of attack on antiquated Hindu or Moslem social customs and traditions. But always it is an effort to break through shackles and to get out into the open.

And among Indian women as among the men, and as among men and women in all countries of recent years, there has sprung up this strong feeling of nationality. They must be Indians. The time for aping Europeans is past. They would be Indian women.

And Indian women are now greedy for education. Young men of education want the companionship of educated wives. So women seek education for the purpose of marriage if for nothing else. But also for a good deal else. They seek culture for culture's sake. And they meet together in conferences to consider educational questions. Annually there is held an All-Indian Women's Conference on Educational Reform. And this is under the patronage of the greatest ladies in India. The old Dowager Begum of Bhopal, a most masterly and capable lady, one year presided over the meeting, though she was herself sufficiently old-fashioned to preserve the strictest purdah and in public always went about veiled. The Maharanis of Baroda and Travancore have also presided. It is attended by the heads of the women's colleges in India, such as Queen Mary's College of Lahore, and Mahboobie Girls' School of Hyderabad, and by the ordinary mothers, widows, girl students, etc. And all are delegates from constituent provincial conferences, which are, in turn, made up of delegates from every town and district, as well as from the Indian States governed by their own Princes. And these women keenly discuss all the educational needs of the time, pass resolutions, and even send deputations to the Viceroy.

Purdah clubs, also, are formed where women can meet each other alternately in various members' houses or in an enclosed garden. Or women build a club-house with library, lecture hall, tennis courts, and so on. They are thus meeting together more, and working together with a common object, exchanging opinions, and forming opinions—and opinions which may affect the whole future of India.

It was in education under the inspiration of that great woman social reformer, Francina Sorabji, that Indian women made the first advance and took university degrees on equal terms with men as far back as 1884. And now there are women inspectors of schools, and professors of colleges, as well as teachers. Then in all connected with the medical profession they have made advance. There are women doctors and women surgeons with a special gift for delicate handling. There are medical researchers. And there are nurses who nurse men as well as women. They serve, too, on hospital committees and Red Cross and baby-welfare centres. In political life women now have the franchise in all provinces of British India and in some Indian States. In Bombay and Madras there are women magistrates, women municipal officers, and women justices of the peace. And in some parts women are proving themselves as capable public speakers. And all this is in great part because the men in the Legislative Assemblies have become keenly conscious of the part women may play in the social life of the country.

In the law women also play their part. They plead in the courts. And Miss Cornelia Sorabji has a worldwide reputation. Lastly, in literature Indian women are beginning to make their mark. The best known is the poetess, Mrs. Naidu, who came into more prominence through the part she played in Gandhi's anti-Salt Tax campaign than through her poetry—but who, nevertheless, had already won esteem in literary circles. Another, who before her had attracted attention in the West, was Toru Dutt, who has written poems of most delicate texture in both French and English.

These are the advance-guard of the one hundred and fifty million women and girls of India, and are only a minute fraction of that vast host. The remainder are for the most part weighted down by custom and saturated with superstition. Yet the light has been seen. The women of India have begun to stir. The advance towards the light has commenced. And the progress already made is amazing.

CHAPTER XVII

RADHAKRISHNAN

As Tagore is the poet so is Radhakrishnan the philosopher of the new India. There is no poet who is not in some measure a philosopher. But, in the main, the poet supplies the insight and the philosopher the reflection on what is seen. And Radhakrishnan is more disposed to systematic thought than Tagore. And while Tagore is versed in English literature, Radhakrishnan has studied English philosophy.

Though a professor of philosophy in a Bengal University, he is a native of Madras. Frail in appearance, he has that acuteness of intellect and delicacy of feeling which is characteristic of India. And in the delivery of his addresses he gives the same impression of grace and finish that "Ranji" gives to cricketers. As "Ranji" had the quickness of eye and suppleness of wrist to play strokes which delighted onlookers by their consummate ease and mastery, so Radhakrishnan will, in perfect English and with great rapidity, give an address on the profoundest problems of existence which will enchant all those who hear it.

Universities, both in the United States and England, have invited him to lecture before them. And he has published a work on Indian philosophy which better than any other has interpreted Hinduism to the Western world. Philosophy is not so popular as poetry. And neither in his own country nor in the West will he be so well known as Tagore. None the less, he deserves well of India, for—especially in his smaller work *The Hindu View of Life*—he has not merely expounded the ancient Hindu philosophy of religion and of life, but transformed it with a new light. He has given Hinduism a fresh outlook.

His presentment of Hinduism is not accepted as orthodox by orthodox Hindus. But, as far as my own experience goes, no one presentment of Hinduism ever is accepted as orthodox. We might go to Benares itself and pick out the most orthodox Pandit to be found there and ask him to expound Hinduism to us. But his exposition of it would not be accepted by his very next door neighbour. There is no orthodox Hinduism. We should find it hard to discover what orthodox Christianity is—even if we went to Rome. We need not, therefore, be surprised at the difficulty of getting a clearly defined statement of what Hinduism is—or at hearing that Radhakrishnan's exposition of it is not everywhere accepted. But his is as clear a one as we are likely to get. And it is so valuable as indicating the direction in which Hinduism is likely to move under the impress of the West that a study of it is imperative if we are to understand the India of to-day.

Polytheism is usually associated with Hinduism. The Hindus are supposed to worship innumerable gods—hundreds of thousands of them. Radhakrishnan shows how this worship arose. The ancient Aryans, with their Vedic culture, had many gods—generally personifications of the forces of Nature. And when the Aryans came in contact with the

Dravidians of India proper they accepted these Dravidian gods and goddesses also. Heroes, ancestors, saints, and tribal gods, were all admitted. Hinduism did not, like Islam, reject these and uncompromisingly proclaim that there was only one God. But Radhakrishnan claims that all these gods, both Vedic and non-Vedic, were subordinated to the one supreme Reality, of which they were regarded as aspects. When Yajnavalkya was called upon to state the number of gods, he started with the popular number 3,306. But he ended by reducing them all to one—Brahman. And Radhakrishnan also insists that the many are merely aspects of the one central reality. The polytheism, he says, was organised in a monistic way. The powerful solvent of philosophy melted them till they coalesced into the one supreme Reality. But the bewildering polytheism of the masses and the uncompromising monotheism of the classes are for the Hindu the expression of one and the same force at different levels. Children in religion may worship images of wood and stone. But the strong in spirit find God everywhere.

And it is this present-day view of the supreme Reality—of God—that is so especially interesting. What is Radhakrishnan's view? In the first place, he acknowledges that our view of God cannot be complete. For God is never ceasing in His revelation of Himself. That revelation is not complete. The nature of God is inexhaustible and the number of its possible manifestations infinite. As our knowledge grows so does our conception of God develop. Moreover, the Hindu thinker admits that different men in different stages of culture will take different views of God. And as they are all the offspring of God their views are entitled to every consideration. But every view of God, from the primitive worship of Nature up to the father-love of a St. Francis and the mother-love of a Rama Krishna, represents some aspect or other of the relation of the human to the Divine spirit. Each gives the truth in part. But none gives the whole truth. For "God is more than the law that commands, the judge that condemns, the love that constrains, the father to whom we owe our being, or the mother with whom is bound up all that we can hope for or aspire to." Yet different as their views may be, and inadequate their descriptions, the reality of the one supreme universal Spirit is never doubted. Self-conscious personality is the highest category we can use. And God is, therefore, regarded at least as perfect Personality—the supreme Knower, the great Lover, and the perfect Will (Brahma, Vishnu, and Shiva) united in one.

Personality at least God must have. If He has produced personality in us He must have personality Himself. But the central reality may go beyond this. There are heights and depths in the being of God which are beyond our comprehension. The supreme cause, and ground, and end of the world—the immanent ground and operative principle in all subjects and objects—may have a supra-personal character. And the supra-personal and the personal representations of the real may be the absolute and relative ways of expressing the one reality.

And Radhakrishnan emphasises both the immanence and the transcendence of God. God is felt as the central reality in the life of man and the world. The Hindu view, he says, rebels against the cold and formal conception of God as external to the world and remote from it. God is immanent in the world. "The natural law of the world is but the working of God's sovereign purpose. The uniformity of Nature, the orderliness of the cosmos, and the steady reaching forward and upward course of evolution, proclaims not the unconscious throbbing of a soulless engine, but the directing mind of an all-knowing spirit."

And this immanence of God is a fact admitting of various degrees. "While there is nothing which is not lit by God, God is more fully revealed in the organic than in the inorganic, more in the conscious than in the unconscious, more in man than in the lower creatures, and more in the good man than in the evil."

But this indwelling of God in the universe does not mean identity of God with the universe. It does not mean that the world is an exhaustive revelation of God—that God lies spread out before us and that outside the world there is nothing of God left. Hindu thought emphasises the transcendent character of the Supreme as well as its immanence. "The world is in God and not God in the world. Whether the Divine spark burns dimly or brightly in the individual, the sparks are distinct from the central fire from which they issue."

Recognising, then, that Hinduism admits a progressive realisation of God, we can the better understand what Hinduism is. It is not a definite, dogmatic creed. It is, in Radhakrishnan's words, "a vast, complex, but subtly unified, mass of spiritual thought and realisation. Its tradition of the godward endeavour of the human spirit has been continuously enlarging through the ages." And it is a growing tradition. The leaders of Hinduism have been busy experimenting with new forms and developing new ideals to suit new conditions, and have always insisted on men working steadily upward and improving their knowledge of God.

Hinduism has not been faithful to its ideals, Radhakrishnan admits. And the task of the uplift of the uncivilised has been sadly neglected. Yet he maintains that there is more unity in Hinduism than appears on the surface. There is an inner cohesion among the Hindus from the Himalaya to Cape Comorin. The spirit of cultural unity has spread through a large part of the land, and racial stocks of varying levels of culture have become steeped in a common atmosphere. And this unity, he quotes Vincent Smith as saying, "transcends the innumerable diversities of blood, colour, language, dress, manners, and sect." While other religions may be marked off from one another by fixed intellectual beliefs, Hinduism sets itself no such limits. Intellect is subordinated to intuition, dogma to experience, outward expression to inward realisation. And religion is for the Hindu not the acceptance of academic abstraction, or the celebration of ceremonies, but a way of life. It is an experience—an experience of reality, an insight into the nature of reality. And this experience is not a mere emotional thrill, but the response of the whole integrate self to the central reality.

And Hinduism moves. There has never been

such a thing as a uniform, stationary, unalterable Hinduism. It is a process. It is a growing tradition, not a fixed revelation. It may have incorporated much that is evil and erroneous, though whatever there may be of that it is endeavouring to throw out. But in its long, slow growth across the centuries its main aim has been to incorporate all that is good and true. And in spite of the fact that it has no common creed and its worship has no fixed form, it has bound together multitudinous sects and devotions into a common scheme. And "the Hindu spirit is that attitude towards life which regards the endless variety of the visible and the temporal world as sustained and supported by the invisible and eternal spirit."

Caste is one of the outstanding features of Hinduism which distinguish it from, for instance, Islam, Christianity, and even Buddhism. And about caste Radhakrishnan has much to say. It has resulted in much evil, he allows. It has degenerated into an instrument of oppression and intolerance. It tends to perpetuate inequality. It develops the spirit of exclusiveness. But he asserts that there are some sound principles underlying it. Hinduism is tolerant. And the system of caste is the outcome of tolerance and trust. The Hindus have faith in the collaboration of races and the co-operation of cultures. And if the progressive thinkers had the power they would transform the institution out of recognition.

Caste is really custom, Radhakrishnan contends. And castes are of many kinds—tribal, racial, sectarian, occupational. But it is clear, from the Sanskrit word *varna*, that caste had originally reference to colour. India has been subjected to one race invasion after another. The aboriginal tribes, and the dark Dravidians, were invaded by Aryans, Persians, Greeks, and Scythians. And great racial problems had to be settled. And, according to Radhakrishnan, the Hindus adopted the only safe course: each racial group was allowed to develop the best in it without impeding the progress of others. The Vedic Aryans started their life in India with a rigid and narrow outlook, and regarded themselves as a sort of chosen people. But they soon became universal in intention and developed an ethical code applicable to the whole of humanity. And when the aboriginal tribes and others accepted the Hindu standpoint they did not surrender their own individuality, but modified it as well as the Hindu spirit which they absorbed. The tribes were admitted into the larger life of Hinduism with the opportunities and responsibilities which that life gave them. They could share in the intellectual and cultural life of the Hindus. And they had the responsibility of contributing to its thoughts, its moral advancement, and its spiritual worth. They were raised above the welter of savagery and imbued with the spirit of gentleness. Bound together by common interests, evolving under the influence of common mental and moral surroundings, the different component tribes not only improved in their level but became adapted to each other—so Radhakrishnan claims.

But while they became adapted to each other indiscriminate racial amalgamation was not encouraged. And the Hindu scriptures recognised the rules about food and marriage which the different communities were practising. Each had its own taboos and customs, laws and beliefs, which they had created for themselves in the course of ages. It was the law of use and wont that distinguished one group from another. And it was a point of social honour for every member to marry within his own caste. Thus caste was the answer of Hinduism to the forces pressing on it from outside. It was the instrument by which Hinduism civilised the different tribes it took in. The Hindu spirit brought about a gradual racial harmony. And Hindu society stands for the ordered complexity, the harmonised multiplicity, the many in one which is the clue to the structure of the universe.

So Hindu society is regarded as an *organic whole.* This is an important point. And Radhakrishnan lays on it strong emphasis. The cultural and the spiritual, the military and the political, the economic classes and the unskilled workers, constitute the fourfold caste organisation. They are known as the Brahmins, the Kshattryas, the Vaisyas, and the Sudras. They all work together for a common end. And they are bound together by a sense of unity and social brotherhood. Each has its own specific social purpose and function, its own code and tradition. Each is a close corporation equipped with a certain traditional and independent organisation. Each observes certain usages regarding food and marriage. And each is free to pursue its own aims, free from interference. But the functions of different castes were regarded as equally important for the well-being of the whole. Each had its own perfection to contribute.

According to this theory, the Brahmins—the

priestly caste—were allowed freedom and leisure to develop spiritual ideals. They were to be free from material cares, and gifts to them were encouraged. They were to be consulted by the State but not bound by it. And as advisers of Government they were to point out the true interests of society. Thus the spiritual was to give the lead. The political and economic life of society was to conform to the spiritual leadership given by the Brahmins. Spirituality was to be the motive-power and the end of Hindu society.

But so long as society has individuals who will break the peace, measures have to be taken to preserve internal order, and to defend the society from outside aggression. A group dedicated to the use of force was therefore necessary. And the Kshattrya caste of rulers and soldiers arose.

The Vaisyas, the economic group, were required to suppress greed and realise the moral responsibilities of wealth. In the great days of Hinduism, says Radhakrishnan, the possessor of property regarded it as a social trust and undertook the education, the medical relief, the water supply, and the amusement of the community. Nowadays, love of wealth is tending to suppress the spiritual side of life. But Hinduism stands for the eternal values and these should be enforced in business as in all other matters.

The fourth of the great main castes consists of unskilled workers and peasants.

These four castes represent men of thought, men of action, men of feeling, and others in whom none of these is highly developed. Each is centred in itself. But all work alongside one another in co-operation as members of one social body. For them the law of life is not cold and cruel competition, but harmony. And a man born in a particular caste is trained to its manner. Each individual is said to have his own specific nature fitting him for his own specific function, and changes of function are not encouraged. As an individual cannot know what his special aptitude may be, heredity and training are used to fix his calling. This is the rule. But in exceptional cases he is allowed to follow his own bent. Members of the lowliest caste have become spiritual leaders. And Brahmins have become warriors.

The perfecting of its specific function is the spiritual aim which each caste sets itself. And the worker fulfils himself through his work. Each kind of service is equally important for the whole. Society is one in purpose, though manifold in its operations. And the system of caste recognises that every soul has in it something transcendent and incapable of gradation. It places all beings on a common level regardless of distinction of rank and status. And it insists that every individual must be afforded the opportunity to manifest the unique in him. Radhakrishnan himself urges the removal of oppressive restrictions. He would dispel the ignorance of the masses, increase their self-respect, and open to them opportunities of the higher life. But he is under no illusion that we can abolish the distinctions of the genius and the fool, the able organiser and the submissive worker. It is not true, he says, that all men are born equal in every way, equally fit to govern the country or till the ground. There will always be men of ability to lead and direct and others who will obey and follow. Brains and character will come to the top, and within the framework of democracy there will be an aristocracy of direction.

In the near future India will have to face the perils of industrialism. In the factory, work is mere labour; it does not satisfy the soul. So the more work tends to become mechanical the more necessary is it that the worker should have larger leisure and a better equipment for the intelligent use of such leisure. And here Radhakrishnan makes the bold suggestion that mechanical work shall be better paid than the work of the artist or of the statesman. His reason is that the work of the artist is its own reward. In ancient India spiritual work was the least paid. The Brahmin who preserved the spiritual treasures had no material wealth. And Radhakrishnan would have it so again to-day. He would not rank men by their material wealth. And he would let those whose work is soul-deadening have at least the advantage of material comfort. He would again emphasise the spiritual value of regarding society as an organic whole, and service of one's fellows as a religious obligation. And he would have the members of the different groups share a certain community of feeling, a sense of belonging together for good or ill. Then they would realise their potentialities to the full. The individual would look beyond his own particular interests and desires. He would not be judged by his economic success and the amount of wealth he amassed. He would be appraised by spiritual values and by his services to the community. And if the system of caste adheres to this organic view of society, Radhakrishnan contends that there is much to be said in its favour. He has put up about as good a case for caste as could be made. Dayanand was by no means so tolerant.

Marriage is closely connected with caste. And about the marriage question Radhakrishnan has much to say. Marriage is regarded by the Hindus as sacred. Men and women are encouraged to enter the married life. Monastic tendencies are discouraged. The very gods are married. And the Hindu does not worship a bachelor or a virgin. The image of Shiva signifies the co-operative interdependent, separately incomplete, but jointly complete masculine and feminine functions of the supreme being. Marriage is not so much a concession to human weakness as a means of spiritual growth. There is nothing unwholesome or guilty about the sex life. Marriage is made the basis of intellectual and moral intimacies. It is prescribed for the development of personality as well as for the continuance of the family ideal. Sexual love is sublimated into self-forgetful devotion. And both man and woman are servants of a higher ideal to which their individual inclinations have to be subordinated. So neither is man a tyrant nor woman a slave.

Some choice there is with regard to mates. But in the best of marriages there is a large element of chance. And that marriage is successful which transforms a chance mate into a life companion. Service of a common ideal binds together the most unlike individuals.

It is commonly supposed that Hindus are polygamists. It is believed that a Hindu may have as many wives as he likes. But Radhakrishnan states that the perfectly ethical marriage is the monogamous one. The relation of Rama and Sita, or Savitri and Satyavan, when the two stand by each other against the whole world, is idealised in the Hindu scriptures. But insistence on the interests of the family led to a compromise of the monogamous ideal and polygamy was tolerated.

He allows that a system which looks upon marriage as compulsory has its own weaknesses. It has to discountenance the remarriage of widows. And it unconsciously tends to lower the marriageable age of girls. But he holds that the Hindus have an exalted view of woman. They believe that she has a special contribution to make to the world. While man is expected to pursue worldly objects, woman should attain heights of self-control and self-denial. This is the Hindu view. And, the spiritual ideal of marriage being recognised, the marriage relation is regarded as indissoluble. The perfect relation between the partners may not be found at first. It has to be created. The existence of incompatibility is a challenge to more vigorous effort.

Holding these views, Radhakrishnan protests against the modern irresponsibility. Exaggerated claims are set up on behalf of the individual will. Discipline is scorned. A life of passion and instinct is confused with self-expression and self-development. Men look upon themselves as healthy animals rather than spiritual beings. Sin is worshipped. The Hindus may have had their share in degrading women. But they regard the woman as the helpmate of man in all his work. And Radhakrishnan would have the old ideal maintained.

The doctrine of Karma is another distinguishing feature of Hinduism. It has, unfortunately, says Radhakrishnan, become confused with fatalism in India. When man had grown feeble and disinclined to do his best he made it an excuse for not exerting himself. And it became a message of despair instead of hope. The sinner came to think that he was pre-ordained a sinner from the beginning of time. And Radhakrishnan says it is true, indeed, that we carry with us the whole of our past, and that it is "an ineffaceable record which time cannot blur nor death erase. . . . There is the march of necessity everywhere. The universe is lawful to the core." Yet Karma, though it says we must suffer for our bad deeds and benefit by our good deeds—reap as we sow—is not a mechanical principle. It is, in Radhakrishnan's view, a spiritual necessity. It is the embodiment of the mind and will of God. And his interpretation of this characteristic doctrine of Hinduism is of peculiar interest.

When rightly viewed, he says, it does not conflict with the reality of freedom. Man is not gripped in the vice of iron necessity. We are every moment making our own characters and shaping our own destinies. The past may be determined, but the future is only conditioned. "The spiritual element in man allows him freedom within the limits of his nature." He can control the uniformity in nature, his own mind, and the society to which he belongs. There is thus scope for genuine rational freedom.

And the world in which we find ourselves is not one in which every act and movement is determined from the first. The world-process is not a mere unfolding of a pre-conceived plan. God is in us.

The real is an active, developing life and not a mechanical routine. And the divine in us can, if utilised, bring about even sudden conversions.

And belief in Karma does not make religious life, prayer, and worship impossible. "If we sow to the flesh we shall of the flesh reap corruption. The punishment for a desecrated body is an enfeebled understanding and a darkened soul. . . . A just God cannot refuse to any man that which he has earned. The past guilt cannot be wiped away by the atoning suffering of an outward substitute. Guilt cannot be transferred. It must be atoned for through the sorrow entailed by self-conquest." But we are fellow-workers with God. We have God in us. Not chance or caprice, but choice governs our actions. God has given us the power of choice. The spirit in man can triumph over the automatic forces which try to enslave him. He can raise the self by the self. He can use the material with which he is endowed to promote his ideals.

And Hinduism insists on a moral life—on right action. Men must act in accord with the law of their being. The Hindu code of practice links up the realm of desires with the eternal values. It binds together the kingdom of earth and the kingdom of heaven. Wealth and happiness may be got only by way of righteousness. That is, if they are to lead ultimately to the spiritual freedom of men. And spiritual freedom (Moksha) can be obtained only through discipline and the surrender of personal inclinations. Therefore, in the interests of spiritual freedom, Hindu society regulated the most intimate details of daily life. Man, it recognised, if he is really to live, must live by the life of the spirit. The fulfilment in the heart of the eternal of the spirit in us—this is what alone gives ultimate satisfaction. And all other activities must be directed to the realisation of this end. And Hinduism observes three ways by which spiritual freedom may be obtained—through jnana, or wisdom; through bhakti, or devotion; and through karma, or service. And in the highest flights devotion coincides with wisdom, and both issue in the virtuous life.

So much as regards Hinduism itself in its main features. In its attitude towards other religions it is tolerant. Its main note is one of respect and goodwill for other creeds. The Hindu, says Radhakrishnan, readily admits other points of view than his own. All men are the children of God. All, therefore, are being "trained by His wisdom and supported by His love to reach within the limits of their powers a knowledge of the Supreme." And in Hinduism "every tradition which helps man to lift his soul to God is held up as worthy of adherence." So it has developed "an attitude of comprehensive charity instead of a fanatic faith in an inflexible creed." It does not contend that the acceptance of a particular religious metaphysic is necessary for salvation. "It is not fair to God or man," says Radhakrishnan, "to assume that one people are the chosen of God, that their religion occupies a central place in the religious development of mankind, and that all others should borrow from them or suffer spiritual destitution." After all, he continues, what counts is not creed but conduct. Religion is not correct belief, but righteous conduct. The truly religious never worry about other people's beliefs. Look, he says, at the great saying of Jesus:

"Other sheep I have which are not of this fold." Jesus was born a Jew and died a Jew. He did not tell the Jewish people, among whom he found himself, "It is wicked to be Jews. Become Christians." He did his best to rid the Jewish religion of its impurities He would have done the same with Hinduism had he been born a Hindu.

Radhakrishnan holds that the Hindu theory that every human being, every group, and every nation, has an individuality worthy of reverence is slowly gaining ground. We are realising that the world is a single co-operative group. Human society is an organic whole, Radhakrishnan insists, the parts of which are naturally dependent in such a way that each part in fulfilling its distinctive function conditions the fulfilment of function by the rest, and is in turn conditioned by the fulfilment of this function by the rest. Other religions have become forces, he says, with which we have to reckon, and we are seeking for ways and means by which we can live together in harmony. We cannot have religious unity and peace so long as we assert that we are in possession of the light and all others are groping in darkness. He therefore favours the Hindu solution, which seeks the unity of religion, not in a common creed, but in a common quest. "Each thing in its place and all associated in the divine concert, making with their various voices, and even dissonances, the most exquisite harmony, should be our ideal." We must look upon different religions "not as incompatibles but as complementaries, and so indispensable to each other for the realisation of the common end."

This is Radhakrishnan's account of the Hindu

view of life. Indians love the ideal. And this may be termed an ideal view of the Hindu view of life rather than one which has actually been realised. But it undoubtedly represents the direction in which Hinduism is moving. And Radhakrishnan himself is profoundly influencing the movement.

CHAPTER XVIII

SADHU SUNDAR SINGH

ANOTHER Indian who has gained a European reputation is the Christian mystic, Sundar Singh. And he is of interest, not only because he is a Christian, but also because he became a Christian against his will. He had deliberately fought against Christianity. Yet, literally, in a night he became so convinced of the value of Christ's message that ever after he spent his life in testifying to it. And his Christianity impressed even Christian Europe. In every European country he was received with honour; crowded audiences listened to his addresses; biographies of him have been written in English, German, French, and Swedish; and the distinguished theologian, Friederich Heiler, has written a combined biography and critical appreciation of his message, which has passed through four German editions and been translated into English.

The determining factor in Sundar Singh's life was the vision—or, as he emphatically puts it, the appearance—of Christ to him when a young man. Till that appearance he had been violently opposed to Christianity and had even burnt the Bible. By natural disposition he was religious, and this disposition was greatly fostered by his mother, another of those saintly Indian women about whom we are now beginning to know so much more than we did in former times. She used to train him in daily devotional habits and take him with her to the temple. And he used to have to read portions of the Hindu scriptures and of the Sikh holy book, the Granth, every day before he had any meal. When he was seven he knew the whole of the Bhagavat Gita by heart. And his mother kept impressing him with the idea of becoming a holy Sadhu. The example and the prayers of his mother were, he said, of decisive significance for his future development.

Yet his family were Sikhs, and it was of no Christian saint that his mother was dreaming in her ambitions for him. And what turned him was solely this vision, or appearance, of Christ. She had died when he was only fourteen, and on her death he had set himself more zealously than ever to study the Granth, the Upanishads, and the Koran. He also learnt the practice of Yoga. But in the American Presbyterian mission school which he attended he came to know the New Testament, as it was daily read there. And he was angry at having to read it, as it was supposed to be against his Sikh religion. So opposed to this reading was he that he became the leader of a group which declared themselves the enemies of Christianity, and he declaimed violently against the missionaries. Finally, he burnt the Bible and said to his father: "The religion of the West is false; we must annihilate it." This was in December, 1904, when he was only fifteen years old.

Yet all the time, in spite of his hostility to the Bible, he was being attracted to it. Some secret power was fascinating his soul. And only three days after he had burnt the Bible came this vision which turned him into a follower of Christ. "I woke up about three o'clock in the morning," he says in one of his addresses, quoted by Canon Streeter in his *Life of the Sadhu*, "had my bath, and prayed, 'O God, if there is a God, wilt Thou show me the right way or I will kill myself.' My intention was that, if I got no satisfaction, I would place my head upon the railway line and kill myself. If I got no satisfaction in this life, I thought I would get it in the next. I was praying and praying, but got no answer. . . . At 4.30 a.m. I saw something of which I had no idea at all previously. In the room where I was praying I saw a great light. I thought the place was on fire. I looked round, but could find nothing. Then the thought came to me that this might be an answer that God had sent me. Then, as I prayed and looked into the light, I saw the form of the Lord Jesus Christ. It had such an appearance of glory and love. If it had been some Hindu incarnation I would have prostrated myself before it. But it was the Lord Jesus Christ whom I had been insulting a few days before. I felt that a vision like this could not come out of my own imagination. I heard a voice saying in Hindustani, 'How long will you persecute Me? I have come to save you; you were praying to know the right way. Why do you not take it?' The thought then came to me, 'Jesus Christ is not dead, but living, and it must be He Himself.' So I fell at His feet and got this wonderful peace which I could not get anywhere else. This is the joy I was wishing to get. When I got up the vision had all disappeared; but, although disappeared, the peace and joy have remained with me ever since. I went off and told my father that I had become a Christian. He told me, 'Go and lie down and sleep; why, only the day before yesterday you burnt the Bible, and now you say you are a Christian.' I said, 'Well, I have discovered now that Jesus Christ is alive and have determined to be His follower. To-day I am His disciple and I am going to serve Him.'"

This was the turning point of Sundar Singh's life. He regarded the vision as a direct revelation. And Dr. Heiler quotes him as saying: "What I saw was no imagination of my own. Up to that moment I hated Jesus Christ and did not worship Him. . . . It was no dream. When you have just had a cold bath you don't dream! It was a reality, the Living Christ! He *can* turn an enemy of Christ into a preacher of the Gospel. He has given me His peace, not for a few hours merely, but throughout sixteen years—a peace so wonderful that I cannot describe it, but I can testify to its reality. That which other religions could not do for many years Jesus did in a few seconds."

Dr. Heiler suggests a natural and psychological explanation of this conversion. Sundar Singh's tension of effort to find peace in religion had been followed by a state of despair and complete cessation from struggle, but the whole effort had culminated in this sudden flow of assurance. And his inward struggles and their solution had been inevitably coloured by the story of St. Paul's conversion, which he must have heard at the mission school. Such experiences of conversion are not at all rare in India, for the Indian mind is much more prone to visionary experience than the European. But

Dr. Heiler adds that this is no complete explanation. And psychology cannot account for the real significance of these experiences. "The religious intuition of the convert alone is able to perceive the Divine reality and the working of Divine grace behind all the historical and psychological processes through which it is revealed. Sundar Singh had had direct spiritual contact with Divine reality."

And whatever the explanation of the phenomenon, the important point, so far as Sundar Singh was concerned, was that he was so convinced of the reality and the goodness of his experience that from that time onward he gave up everything else in life in order to bear witness to the great thing that had happened to him, and to communicate to others the peace and joy that he had known. He broke with his family, he broke with all the tradition of his race, he gave up wealth, and he deliberately sought danger and hardships—in order to spread the good tidings, and make others followers of Christ. And, as a result, it is now acknowledged that he has brought a new message to both Europe and India; he has put new warmth into the old message, and he has spoken it in a way that India can understand.

On communicating his conversion to his family, he had to endure many painful scenes. And we who have lived in India and know what authority a father exercises over his son, and how terrible a shock to a parent the conversion of a son to Christianity is, can realise a little of what pain both father and son must have suffered. Then outside his family he had to endure scorn, mockery, and persecution. Almost hardest of all was his discovery that the pupils in the mission school were mostly nominal Christians only, and did not live according to the teaching of Christ. Yet in spite of all these persecutions and discouragements he bravely made his way.

He broke with the Sikh community by cutting off his long hair. His father disinherited him and drove him from home. And he spent that first night under a tree. But "that was my first night in Heaven," he wrote afterwards. "The world could not give me such peace. Christ, the Living Lord, breathed into me a glorious peace. The cold pierced me through and through, I was a hungry outcast, but I had the sense of being enfolded in the power of the Living Christ. The presence of my Redeemer turned suffering into joy." And when his father afterwards tried to persuade him to return he replied that he had attained such a wonderful peace in Christ that he would not exchange it for any earthly happiness whatsoever.

The Presbyterian missionaries, Dr. Wherry and Dr. Fife, now cared for him very tenderly. He was sent to a mission school near Simla, and in September, 1905, on his sixteenth birthday, he was baptised in the Simla Church by Mr. Redman according to the rite of the Anglican Church. Then, influenced by his mother's hope of his one day becoming a Sadhu, he conceived the idea of appealing to his fellow-countrymen, wearing the sacred garb of the holy men of India in all ages. In the yellow garment of the Sadhu he would go forth and tell India of the peace he had found. By leading the homeless, poor, and celibate life of a Sadhu he would reach all hearts in India. So a month after his baptism he made the vow to be a Sadhu his whole life long. And when only sixteen years of age he set out barefooted and with no possessions but his Sadhu garment, a blanket, and a New Testament. For food he would have to beg, like the Hindu Sadhus. And for shelter he would sleep under a tree, or in a cave, or in some inn.

In this way he wandered through many parts of Central and Northern India, till after four years he was persuaded by his Christian friends to enter a divinity college at Lahore. But he was rather repelled than attracted by the instruction given there. He conceived a deep distaste of theological intellectualism. He also disliked the limitations of a licensed preacher. He had no desire to hold the office of a priest, or to be bound to one communion. This would narrow his field. He wished to be free to follow his Sadhu vocation wherever it led him. And he set forth again untrammelled by ecclesiastical ties.

And soon he determined to fast for forty days. He made the attempt, but for how long he actually fasted is not known, for he lost consciousness till rescued by a wood-cutter. This much, however, he was able to say, that while his physical strength declined his spiritual life became more vivid. In a state of ecstatic concentration he beheld Christ crucified, and His countenance full of love. And while his body was helpless, his soul experienced the deepest peace. The fast had strengthened him inwardly. He was freed from the temptation to give up the calling of a Sadhu and return to his father's house. And he was now sure that the wonderful peace he enjoyed came from God—was the result of the Divine presence within him.

He set out on more travels, and this time he undertook a dangerous journey into Tibet and, afterwards, into Nepal. His fame grew and spread all over India. In 1918 he went to Madras. Morning and evening he preached to adoring audiences. And he could have done with them as he liked.

And now he was assailed by a great temptation. Why should he not found a new religion? Why not weld together Hinduism and Christianity and perhaps Islam? Why not range himself beside Buddha and Jesus and Muhammad? But he resisted the temptation. For him Christ was everything. Christ had made the call to him and brought him peace. And to Christ he would be faithful.

He went on to Ceylon, to Burma, to Malaya, to Japan, and to China. Everywhere he bore witness of the blessedness of peace in Christ. And in Japan and China he was struck by the absence of the caste system—that impediment which is so much in the way of Hindus embracing Christianity.

On his return to India he was reconciled to his father, who wished to be baptised at his hands; but he refused, as he had refused all others, because he said his mission was to preach and not to baptise. As the result of this reconciliation he was, however, able to undertake what his heart had been much set on—a visit to the West. His father paid his expenses, and he travelled to England in 1920. Hindus had often said that European Christianity had had its day and lost its influence over the life of Western nations. He wanted to see for himself.

He preached in churches and chapels to congregations of all denominations—except Roman Catholic. And at the Church House, Westminster, he addressed a meeting of seven hundred Anglican clergymen, including the Archbishop of Canterbury and several bishops. Then he went to Paris, and to Ireland and Scotland, and afterwards to America and Australia. And everywhere he was welcomed, and everywhere he made a deep impression.

He returned to India in September, 1920. But he paid a second visit to Europe in 1922. And this time he went to Palestine on the way. At every step, says Dr. Heiler, from whose work this description of the Sadhu's life is taken, the sense of Christ's immediate personal Presence filled his consciousness. His soul overflowed with joy; and tears of thankfulness were often in his eyes. When he knelt and prayed on the Mount of Olives it seemed as though Jesus were standing by him and saying: "Peace be with you. As My Father hath sent Me even so send I you."

Switzerland he afterwards visited, and, speaking in the hall in which the League of Nations meets, he said: "The League of Nations has made great efforts, but it will achieve nothing until there is a league of human hearts, and such a league is only possible when men give their hearts to Him who is the Master of all hearts. In Him alone is true peace."

From Switzerland he went to Germany, and from thence to Sweden, where he spoke to very sympathetic audiences. Then on to Norway, Denmark, and Holland, and finally to England, where he arrived in July, completely exhausted, for everywhere he had been speaking to huge audiences.

Now the results of these visits to Europe are remarkable and worth careful consideration. He had gone to see if the Hindus were right when they said that Christianity was a waning force in European countries and he came back convinced that they were. His visit to Western lands, says Heiler, brought him bitter disappointment. He used to think that the inhabitants of Europe were all wonderful people. But when he travelled in Western lands he found things otherwise than he had thought. "I began to realise" he says, "that no European country can be called really Christian, though there are individual Christians." Materialism and intellectualism had made men's hearts hard. He was disappointed to find an unchristian spirit, and religious indifference, and greed of money, and love of pleasure. The people of the West put their trust in outward things—comfort, luxury, money, and the things of this world. They allowed themselves to be led astray by unbelievers and intellectual men who denied the divinity of Christ. And he was not surprised that many people did not understand what Christianity really was.

But if the impression which the West made upon the Sadhu was one of bitter disappointment, the impression he made on the West was the precise reverse. "Men and women of the most varied professions, classes, and countries," says Heiler, "agreed in testifying to the deep impression made upon them, both by his appearance and by his words." His dress and his whole aspect and demeanour made the world of the New Testament more living and real to Europeans. The power of his personality changed even learned men who were disposed to be hostile or indifferent to Christianity. The professor of an English university said to the Sadhu : " It is not your preaching which has converted me, it is yourself; you, an Indian, are so like Christ in spirit and in bearing; you are a living witness to the Gospel and to the Person of Jesus Christ." And his unobtrusive modesty and genuine humility remained unscathed through all the adulation that was lavished on him. " He remained the same humble religious soul, whose only desire was to come nearer and nearer to the Lord and . . . to wear himself out in His service."

These are the main facts about the Sadhu, and the significance of his life lies in this, that it gives us an indication as to how Christianity can best be presented to India, and perhaps Europe too. The Sadhu from his youth had caught the true inward spirit of Christ. He had been seeking God and seeking true spiritual peace with his whole heart. And the vision or appearance of Jesus to him as a young man had actually given him that peace. And quite simply he had borne witness all over the world to the joy and peace which he had found. The spirit of Christ had entered deeply into him and filled his whole being. And it was thoroughly congenial to his Indian soul. He could well understand it. But he was right when he followed his own deep-felt conviction and decided to go forth, not as a Europeanised Indian, but in the true Indian rôle of a Sadhu. The Christian message had to be given to India in an Indian way. He could thus testify in a way that Indians could understand—and in a way that European Christians, too, could understand.

And his manner of preaching, or, as he preferred to call it, bearing witness, was also like Christ's, and also most fitted to his Indian audiences. He spoke in metaphors and parables. And he drew his illustrations from his own experiences or from the life about him.

When, for example, he wished to emphasise the value of prayer he resorted to metaphor. Prayer, he maintained, was the greatest necessity of our spiritual life. And he himself was in continual communion, through prayer, with God. Every morning he spent several hours in Bible-study, meditation, and prayer. And in the Himalaya he would dedicate whole days and nights to solitary prayer. To him prayer was the heart of religion. We cannot live a single day, nor indeed a single hour, without God. "In Him we live and move and have our being. Our spiritual dependence upon God is like our dependence on the air we breathe." "The breath of the soul is prayer, through which fresh currents of air sweep into our being bringing with them fresh supplies of vital force from the love of God, on whom our whole life depends." "God has created both the mother's milk and the child's desire to drink it. But the milk does not flow of itself into the child's mouth. No, the child must lie in its mother's bosom and suck the milk diligently. God has created the spiritual food which we need. He has filled the soul of man with desire for this food, with an impulse to cry out for it and to drink it in. The spiritual milk, the nourishment of our souls, we receive through prayer. By means of fervent prayer we must receive it into our souls. As we do this we become stronger day by day, just like the infant at the breast. Prayer is both the air we breathe and the mother's milk of the soul. It is only as we are immersed in the spiritual world that we can understand spiritual things. And the essence of prayer does not consist in asking God for something, but in opening our hearts to God, in speaking with Him, and living with Him in perpetual communion. It is not a begging of favours; it is rather breathing and living in God. . . . There are people who pray as though we could alter God's purpose. . . . We cannot alter God's plan, but in prayer we can learn to understand His will for us. . . . And when we begin to understand His purposes we do not even wish to alter them; we only want to co-operate with them . . . and He gives us strength to live in harmony with His will." These are the Sadhu's views on prayer.

And he believes in a Heaven here and now. "There are unhappy Christians," he says, "who rejoice in the thought of entering Heaven after death, but they do not realise that Heaven must begin here on earth." When a man has received this peace which passeth all understanding he does not remain inactive; he is driven to proclaim the good news. "To him who has received this peace and happiness it is not necessary to say: 'Go and tell others.' He cannot keep it to himself. . . . If we have really received the love of Christ, and been gripped by it, we cannot possibly sit still. We must go out and pass it on to others. . . . Once God has become a living reality to us we simply have to love our fellow-men; we cannot help it. If His life has vitalised us we begin to live in love, quite naturally, and it is a joy to be loving to others."

God is for him "a vast ocean of love." God longs for the happiness of the beings He has created. "God Himself is pleased when we pray. He rejoices in our worship. . . . God needs our prayer, just as a mother does not feel well if her baby does not lie on her bosom and drink."

And God "imparts life, because it is of the very essence of His nature to create. To give men real joy through His creative Presence is of the very essence of His love." And the Sadhu saw evidence of the creativity of God in all nature, though most of all in man. "One day I found a flower, and I began to reflect on its fragrance and its beauty. As I brooded over this I saw the hidden mystery of the Creator behind His creation. This filled me with joy. But my joy was still greater when I found Him at work within my own soul." But God can be seen only through His manifestations. "When I entered Heaven for the first time I looked all round me, and then I asked: 'Where is God?' and they answered and said unto me: 'God is seen here as little as on earth, for God is infinite. But Christ is here, He is the image of the Invisible God, and only in Him can anyone see God, either here or upon earth.'"

The Sadhu was a passionate believer in the divinity of Christ. "I believe that if we receive Christ's outward person only and reject His innermost being—His Deity—our Christianity will be no better than Hinduism." And "Christ came, not only to forgive sin, but to make us free from sin. We receive from Christ a new vital power which releases us from sin. . . . To be saved by Christ is to receive a new life from Him, to become a new creature. . . . To be born again means receiving the living power of Christ into one's soul."

Like most Indians, he was repelled by organisation. "I value order and principle, but not too much organisation. I do not believe in the organisation which you have in the West. . . . Churchianity is not Christianity. God is a God of order, but the order must agree with the leading of the Holy Spirit; otherwise it will be useless."

Certainly, he himself was most effective by reason of his individuality. And it was by his bearing and behaviour that he was best able to bear witness. "He radiated peace and joy," said one. He was "the embodiment of peace, gentleness, and loving kindness," said another. "That which is so surprising about the Sadhu is the quite extraordinary joy which one can see upon his face—no picture can give an idea of the beauty of his smile," said a third.

The Sadhu's great desire had always been to carry his message into Tibet. On a former visit he had been imprisoned there and endured great sufferings. But, undeterred, he set off again, and no one yet knows what has become of him. Possibly he may have died of cold on the way. Possibly he may have suffered imprisonment. But whether he is dead or now survives, he had already lived a life of the purest beauty. He had spread a great joy wherever he went. And he had shown that Christianity can be made a living thing in India, and in Indian hands can revive the West.

CHAPTER XIX

THE ULTIMATE DESTINY

THE work of these four present-day Indians, the first from the East of India, the second from the West, the third from the South, and the fourth from the North, and all well-known in Europe and America, has done more than any Act of Parliament could ever do to raise the status of India in the world. They have not been able to show that India is a pushing, energetic country, keen upon developing its natural resources and rapidly raising its material standard of living. But they have shown most clearly that India has a soul. Each of the four has set the things of the spirit above all else. They have devoted their whole energies to attaining the highest. And they have spent themselves in trying to impart to others the joy which they had found. And the West, no less than the East, has gladly welcomed them and appreciated their message.

To this I should like to have added, not a chapter, but a whole volume, to show what the nations of the West also have done to stir and enrich the spiritual life of India. The Western impact has not been all of a mercantile, a military, and a political nature. A tremendous output of spiritual energy has gone forth upon India through the agency of British, French, Belgian, German, and American Missions—Roman Catholic and Protestant. And missionaries have devoted their lives and made heroic sacrifices with no desire or prospect of material gain, but with the sole desire to carry to India glad tidings of the great joy they had themselves known.

And so as we bring this study of the connection of England with India to a close; as we see how it became linked up with the connection of Portugal, Holland, and France, and then of the whole world with India, we cannot help feeling that we are contemplating the development of one vast world-movement, and that, much as statesmen, and even whole nations, may try to direct it, they are carried almost impotently along in its mighty sweep. The efforts made by English statesmen and the directors of the old East India Company are an illustration. No doubt, if they had represented a less enterprising and more gentle people than the vigorous, adventurous, and combative English, they might have succeeded in avoiding dominion. Yet it is the fact that they did try and did consider it against their interest to mix politics and war with the business of a trading company. They would have preferred to remain what in fact the firm of Ralli is to-day—a company doing an exceedingly lucrative business in India without any responsibilities in politics or war to diminish their trading profits. But against what appeared to be their better judgment, they were carried along in the world-movement, and because of the disorder in India and the pressure of rivals were constrained into assuming dominion.

And now, in our dealings with India, we are realising very distinctly that we cannot carry on our work in terms of ourselves alone, or of only ourselves and India. Both we and the Indians are affected by world-opinion. The present movement in India is largely the result of the impact of Western ideas upon India, of the rise of Japan, of the World War, of the struggle, everywhere apparent, of peoples for greater independence and freedom. And, for our part, we are conscious that in whatever we do or leave undone we must not go too violently against world-opinion and must if possible carry it with us.

We feel ourselves, in fact, as part of a great world-process. The Viceroy of India is put in a position of great power and responsibility. He has been especially chosen for the post on account of his exceptional abilities and good judgment, and he exercises them to his best. But even he, with all his power, can only direct events to a limited extent. The Secretary of State controls, directs, and supervises the Viceroy, all the best advice is available for him, and at need he has the full resources of Great Britain behind him. Yet no Secretary of State would say that he felt himself capable of anything but a very limited control over events. His decisions are subject to many considerations over which he feels he has no control. A sudden activity of some irresponsible agitator in India may upset all his plans. And often he is in the position of the man who took the horse to water but could not make it drink.

And so, also, is it with the Indians. A man like Gandhi may have immense influence over millions, but he cannot control the whole, and always he feels himself fenced in by the British.

All, in fact, are involved in some wider process.

And while each may honestly strive to carry out his own part to the very full of his ability, he feels himself caught up and carried along in a wider and mightier process than he with all the power that may be in his hands is able to control.

Now, if this be so, it is of urgent importance to know what is the nature of this process, by whom or what it is directed, and in what direction it is making. Clearly, the great movements of men and nations that we have been contemplating in the preceding pages are not the result of pure chance. Each movement is the result of purpose. Clive did not win the Battle of Plassey by chance. It was not by a fluke that Gandhi decided whether he would co-operate or non-co-operate. Everywhere there is purpose of some kind. Sometimes it is feeble and infirm. At other times it is strong and insistent. But everywhere there is purpose—not mere flopping about on the stream of time.

The question then arises whether all the individual and national purposes are or are not part of one great world-purpose. Is there any indication that they are tending in the same direction? I think there is. Take the English trading company. It went out to India for its own profit, certainly. It did not go out for the good of India. On the other hand, it did not go out for the harm of India. And trade in itself was good for both India and England. And from the purely material business point of view it was desirable that India should be prosperous and orderly. A rich India was a better market than a poor India. An India in which order was maintained was better than an India distraught by civil war. There was, then, an impetus towards establishing order and making India more prosperous materially. But from England, and from Great Britain, there did go forth a desire to better the intellectual and moral condition. And we can detect a desire in Europe, and America, that we should govern India to the welfare and contentment of the people. I have described the efforts which Government, driven by the force of public opinion in Great Britain, made to bring justice to the people of India, to educate them, and to improve their lot in every way. And, besides these Government endeavours, there have been the immense missionary efforts which the peoples of the West have been called upon to make. We have clearly been working under some mighty spiritual impulse.

And in India herself we can observe an uprising of a desire to enhance her material and spiritual welfare. In the work of those Indians—women as well as men—that I have described we can see the most passionate desire to create a better India. They are all driven by some inner impulse to sacrifice their own comfort and leisure in order that their countrymen may rise to better things.

So if we look carefully we can discern running through the world-process a strong impetus towards, first, the establishment and maintenance of order, and then towards the material and spiritual improvement of peoples. Europeans and Indians alike are striving after the highest spiritual things. The ultimate object seems to be the finer spiritualisation of India.

Now, if we join up the study of India with the philosopher's study of the universe as a whole, we find that India affords a remarkably apt illustration of their theoretic conclusions. Philosophers see everywhere in the universe the operation of two main impulses—the impulse to order and the impulse to change. Order must be maintained or there would be no universe at all. There could not be a universe in which order did not reign. Yet within the order there is unceasing change. But the change is not the chance change of the kaleidoscope. It is change in a certain direction. What direction?

According to modern views, the universe is an organic whole. Its parts are affected by and affect the whole. Each part bears upon it the impress of the whole—some in small measure, others in large. And the whole is a process—a becoming, as well as a being. That being so the direction must be inferred from the most perfect product of the process. That will be the signpost. Man is the most perfect product of which we on this planet are aware—though more perfect products may exist elsewhere in the universe. There is room there, and there has been time enough, to produce beings high beyond all our conception. And man must bear upon him the impress of the whole. And the Highest Man must be in the most perfect image of that Power which is actuating the whole process. What, then, the Highest Man had in mind as the object men should aim at would be the best indication we have of the goal towards which we should direct our efforts. What is that object?

We were told to seek first the Kingdom of God. This, then, must be the ideal which is all the time controlling and directing the manifold changes of the entire world-process. And it must be held in that mind and urged by that will which must be working behind, and in, and through, the whole universe, and, therefore, in all that we feel in ourselves and see around us. The Kingdom of God is the ideal and the will of God is the motive-power of that whole world-movement in which England and India and all nations and men find themselves involved. In so mighty a process the efforts of a whole Empire over many centuries may seem puny and insignificant. Yet, for the harmony of the whole, the efforts of every single man are required. The humblest singer in the chorus, nay, even the lowliest listener in the audience, is needed for the full perfection of the whole. The Kingdom of God wants each one. All it requires is that each should play his part to the full.

Now, many Englishmen have believed that the British Empire is a mighty instrument designed of God for the carrying out of His purposes, and this belief has been the main actuating force of their life's work. They have been convinced that England's mission in the world was to use this instrument for God's ends. But the Indians also think that India has a mission in the world—to pour out over the world great streams of spirituality from the fountain-source of two of the great world-religions. England and India both think that they have a mission from God. But this does not mean that either one or the other must be wrong. Both may be right. They may clash at times, but the clash will only result in a purification of motive and a higher aspiration. Both may have a mission from God. And they may unite. British purpose in

India may combine with Indian purpose in India. And both may be harmonised with that Divine purpose which is actuating the universe. Both may be making towards the Kingdom of God.

And what is the Kingdom of God? May we describe it as a world in which reigns not only that order which is the necessary condition of every perfection, but also the loveliest beauty the poet Tagore ever dreamed of, the highest truth the philosopher Radhakrishnan ever aspired after, the divinest love the Sadhu Sundar Singh ever experienced, the tenderest compassion the Mahatma Gandhi ever felt for the afflicted, and the most yearning love the gentlest mother of these great Indians ever poured out on her son—all these summed up, purified, and surpassed in the holy hush of a Himalayan dawn?

This, or whatever higher we can conceive, must be the ultimate goal towards which the whole creation is being impelled. And it is in that direction that all must bend their efforts on pain of disaster if they attempt otherwise. And, in working towards it, all that the British have to give of experience in the art of government, of scientific skill and knowledge, of organising capacity, and of culture and religion, may be combined with all that India has to offer of refinement and religious genius. Then India with more vigorous intent will carry on her agelong pursuit of a higher perfection and a completer harmony. And she will afford a concrete example to the world of how races of every variety and of all religions may meet and harmonise their different ways of life and modes of thought. This may or may not be a Christian India. But it will be a Christ-like India and a God-like India. To her the whole world will look for spiritual blessings. And from her may arise the great religious leader of the future—another Christ—who will remain an Indian of the Indians, with all the Eastern's alternating fire and serenity, and yet appeal to every nation.

At the conclusion of my Rede Lecture in 1905 I said of the Indians that we had sought them merely for trade, we had found them immersed in strife, and if ever we left them, might it be in that attitude most natural to them, with their arms stretched up to the Divine. But I meant to refer only to leaving them politically. Socially and spiritually we can never leave them.

Whatever be the upshot of the present political discussion, and whether India in the end remain within the Empire like Canada or entirely sever her connection and become as independent of the Empire as Japan, this much is certain, that she can never be wholly and entirely disconnected from England. She cannot go off, like her holy men, into the jungles by herself. She would still have to remain in the great community of nations. Even if the political connection with England ceased altogether there would still be diplomatic relations, and relations on the League of Nations, and trade relations. And beyond these, and deeper far—deeper, too, than the old political connection—there would always remain that social, and cultural, and spiritual connection with England which has in fact been the mighty originating cause of her present revival.

As in the past, and as in the present, so in the future, whether India remains within the Empire or not, men and women will be going out to India from Great Britain and Indians will be coming to England. Then, as now, Englishmen will be serving in Indian States and in Indian Provinces in every kind of capacity. In Indian States even now there are Englishmen serving as Ministers, as engineers, as forest officers, as medical officers. And in the self-governing provinces of the future they will continue to serve in like capacities. As doctors, artists, journalists, politicians, missionaries, lecturers, they will continue to go to India. The flow of men of culture from Great Britain to India will never cease. Rather will it increase as time goes on and communications improve, whatever the form of government may be.

Those who then go in the service of India will serve under some Indians and over others. They will work with Indians for Indian ideas of perfection. Those ideas may be different from their own, but in the service of India Englishmen will freely give of their expert knowledge, or their wider experience, or their resourcefulness, energy, and organising ability. And perhaps a later generation may have a more sympathetic understanding of Indian customs and ideals, and a finer appreciation of the beauties of Hinduism and Islam. They may have an altogether more friendly attitude to Indians, and work as equals with them, each supplementing and complementing the other.

Reciprocally, Indians will be coming to Great Britain, both to study and to tell the West of the cultural development of India. And men of distinction will be received as the Royal Society received Sir Jagadis Bose, the India Society Tagore, the Universities Radhakrishnan, the Churches Sadhu Sundar Singh, and the cricketing clubs Ranjit Sinhji. The best from India will always be welcomed, and there will always be associations composed of men and women who are capable of appreciating that best, and anxious to have it more widely known. Not only men who have served or traded in India, but also men of art and science and religion living in Great Britain, will serve on these associations. And they will not mind what Indians say about the excessive materiality of the West. All they will be concerned with will be to get from their Indian guests the freest and richest flow of spirituality they are good enough to give. They would welcome Indians as comrades in seeking first the Kingdom of God, and draw inspiration from them.

And this deeper, cultural, spiritual connection which will underlie and survive all changes in the political connection we, especially, who have served in India will always desire to draw closer. For both we and the Indians have as much to gain as we have to give. We would like to keep up those personal friendships we have formed and which Indians themselves have shown how anxious they are to preserve. And often our hearts will go back to India. In the weary hot weather days, when we have felt our very life-blood being sapped from us, we have longed for the invigorating air of England. When all around was scorched and brown we have pined for the greenery of our lovely island. When the rains have been pelting down in sheets day and night, week after week, we have sighed for the soft sunshine and occasional showers of our homeland. But when we are actually back in England, when we are shivering in the cold and damp of a December fog, and all is grey and dripping, we have forgotten the heat and dust or torrential rains of India and have thought only of her beauties.

At such times we think of the calm beauty of an early morn when camping in the plains, of the intense blue of the Himalayan sky against the deodars at Simla, of the scent of the pine trees, of the fresh verdure after the monsoon, of the enchanting violet haze in which the lower hills are shrouded, of the glory of Kanchenjunga as seen from Darjiling or Nanga Parbat from Kashmir, and of the majestic passing of great Indian rivers. We remember, too, the peerless Taj Mahal at Agra, the lake at Udaipur with its white palace and surrounding purple hills. We remember, also, our devoted servants and the splendid manhood of frontier peoples, and the courtly Rajputs, and the supple, quick, affectionate Bengalis, and the grace of Indian women. All these things we remember. And our hearts pine for India.

And as I close this book I have one personal remembrance. At the end of a journey I once made from the great plains of Central Asia across the Himalaya to India I rose while it was still dark to make the last day's march which would bring me to the broad plains of India. For twelve miles I climbed through pine woods. Above the tree-tops I could see the stars glittering in the clear sapphire sky. There was no real darkness, but all was still and calm and peaceful. At the end of the march I arrived at Murree, where I was born twenty-four years before. And from there I looked out over the great plains of India. Dawn was just breaking. Over the plains there was the murky red of a dust haze. But above and over the mountains all was clear, the light was spreading over the sky, and with it the beautiful blue of hope.

And so it seems to be with India to-day. Amid all the murkiness and strife of life it is unto the hills that men lift their eyes. And it is to the Himalaya that Indians have ever turned for inspiration. And there as they cast their eyes to-day they see the dawn which is now awakening. The beautiful starlit night is passing. The first rays are just touching the pure mountain summits. Breaking over India is the dawn of a great Hope. And Indians now behold it.

INDEX